THE DUAL PROGRESS PLAN

BOOKS BY THE SAME AUTHOR

Tests and Measurements in High School Instruction (with G. M. Ruch). Chicago: World Book Company, 1927

Child Psychology (with B. L. Wellman). New York: The Macmillan Company, 1934

The Meaning of Intelligence. New York: The Macmillan Company, 1943 (tenth printing, 1959)

Tertiary Education. Cambridge: Harvard University Press, 1944

Frontiers in Education. Stanford: Stanford University Press, 1945

On the Education of Women. New York: The Macmillan Company, 1950

THE DUAL
PROGRESS PLAN

*A New Philosophy and Program
in Elementary Education*

GEORGE D. STODDARD

Chancellor and Executive Vice President
New York University

HARPER & BROTHERS
NEW YORK

372
S 867

ACKNOWLEDGMENTS

During the summer of 1956, the School of Education at Syracuse University celebrated the 50th anniversary of its founding by inviting educators to deliver a series of lectures under the general title "Perspective in Elementary Education." My lecture in this series, which was given August 1, 1956, was entitled "New Ways to Reach the Mind of the Child." That portion of the address which referred to a reorganization of the elementary school is embedded in Chapter 1.

It would be fitting to mention perhaps thirty persons who have taken an active part in the discussions and events leading to the development of the Dual Progress Plan. Of course, the role played by some is referred to in the text. The program could not have reached its present stage without the assistance from the beginning of Glen Heathers, David G. Salten, Charles M. Northrup, and David W. Bishop. The report of the working party (Chapter 5) owes much to Mr. Heathers, who drafted it, and to Walter A. Anderson, Alonzo G. Grace, and E. Frederic Knauth. The school boards of Long Beach, New York, and Ossining, New York, deserve commendation for their acceptance on a trial basis of a plan that seemed visionary to many community leaders.

The financial support of the Ford Foundation, concurrently with the willingness of the two school systems to remodel four grades of their elementary schools, was a crucial factor in moving the plan from words on paper to schoolroom reality. Beyond this financial aid, which totals $1,190,000, the author has enjoyed a steady helpfulness from the Ford Foundation through the probing questions of Alvin C. Eurich and Henry T. Heald.

Sheldon C. Ackley and Margaret T. Stoddard have attended to almost every page of the manuscript. Margaret Hefferon and Helen Thek have assisted at all points.

CONTENTS

THE DUAL PROGRESS PLAN

I

ORIGIN OF THE DUAL PROGRESS PLAN

Over the past few decades the elementary grade system in the United States has been exceptionally free from those massive experiments and demonstrations that are designed to effect radical changes in curriculum, methodology, or school organization. Elementary education is, indeed, a conspicuous example of the unexamined life on the American scene. Criticism is chiefly external, but it is mounting and can no longer be dismissed as the chronic condition of unhappy persons. Neoprogressive schools, having failed John Dewey, have not as yet achieved solid virtues of their own or convinced the American public that education is truly on the right track.

The classrooms are filled with talking and talking about, but they are short on thought-into-action. Outside the school there is a great deal of doing, but for the child it is rarely purposive in terms of the reach of our culture; it lacks form. Casual learning is stultifying if one fact is made equal to another, with only a faint glimpse of any intellectual structure. Schools at their best select and evaluate content, placing it in a framework of reference that is free from guile. Education, to deserve the name, must be the straight goods.

It is not enough for child or youth to be placed in a situation where knowledge is being displayed. The learner, perhaps covertly, must accept a place in a field of force. There must be a tension to which he responds, so that his state will be improved once he has achieved insight. This does not call for the application of irrational or harsh stimuli, but rather for a careful setting that culminates in the desire of the pupil to learn. Frequently the motivation is social,

1

for in the group there is opportunity for a division of labor and there is a sense of belonging. Since children learn to be sympathetic toward—and to help—the child who is on their side, every good teacher attempts to develop a full camaraderie.

Today everybody is trying to reach the mind of the child in order to see if it might become the mind of a mathematician, physicist, chemist, or engineer. These are the disciplines stressed in the Russian ten-year schools, although lately there has been some easing of the pressure there. All we know about children's abilities points to a lack of talent for such subjects at the higher levels on the part of at least half the boys and of a larger fraction of the girls. In spite of notable exceptions, there appears to be a genuine sex difference in technical aptitude and interest. We may predict, therefore, that the Russians, regardless of accumulated shortages, will back away from the idea of advanced technical training for everybody; otherwise, they will turn out a large batch of neurotic technologists. In either case, as Lee DuBridge advises, let us solve our own problems, not theirs.

Since it will take a long time to make up for the shortage of mathematicians and scientists, we had best start soon and far down in the school grades. The whole business of getting beyond the "lick-and-promise" stage calls for enormous expenditures of public funds at local, state, and national levels. It demands a new dedication on a national scale to the principle of *life adjustment through learning*.

There are new and somewhat radical ways to reach the mind of the child. Thus we should consider seriously the extension downward through the first grade of a modified form of the junior high school plan.

A *home teacher* is placed in charge of *two rooms*, on a half-day basis for each. She is responsible for registration and counseling; she teaches reading and the social studies. The other half-day is assigned to special teachers who teach mathematics and science, music, arts and crafts, recreation and health, and—beginning with grade five—an optional sequence in a foreign language. The special teachers in each subject or cluster of subjects offer the work on a longitudinal basis straight through the elementary grades, and in a combined school throughout the twelve grades. Thus the special teachers, as a team, are in a good position to judge the quality of special aptitudes and their course of growth throughout the child's school life. Test scores, profiles, ratings, and sample items furnish a continuous comprehensive record. All special teachers are to encourage pupils to form social clubs based on content interest that cut across the grades.

Generally a pupil's grade standing will be determined by his home teacher, but he will be free to pursue avidly a specialty according to his aptitude. A fifth-grade pupil may play in the high school band or orchestra, and a pupil gifted in mathematics or science may be brigaded with like-minded students in more advanced grades.

The home teacher (usually a woman) is in charge of both sections of her grade. Since one of her functions is to be concerned with pupil orientation, she concentrates on knowing the pupils, the families, and the neighborhoods, linking this knowledge to the work in social studies. The pupils gifted in writing are discovered and encouraged by the home teacher as a part of her work in reading, writing, and speech.

The specialists offer their work as (a) basic education for all, and (b) as an opportunity for the gifted.

At this point we come squarely upon a demand for truth and sincerity in the educational process. Between television shows, there is much worry on the part of adults over the failure of high school and college students to grasp the fundamentals of mathematics and science. Many American parents regard skill in mathematics, science, or a foreign language as something fine for the children—something they themselves missed and never plan to make up. There is a halo effect. Many teachers, too, want these experiences for the child, not for showcase purposes, but in order to prepare him and to deepen his awareness of our culture. They realize that this will not come about through any casual contacts. Hard work is involved, and a serious intention. For example, there will be pupils of low aptitude in mathematics. What mathematical future is in store for them?

Slowly the answers to these and similar questions are appearing on the American scene. Divide and conquer! On the basis of really good tests—new ones are called for—rate carefully, subject to change, the learning potential *of each child* in all the identifiable ability clusters. Discover the slow, the average, and the fast learners, and adjust their programs accordingly. In short, put an end to the concept of average ability for a class, calling for average performance under average teaching effectiveness. This means a playing up of the spread of talent as a means of reducing, on the one hand, the nagging of the dull and, on the other, the indefensible neglect of the gifted.

It may be predicted with confidence that the redesigning of textbooks, methods, and testing procedures in all fields will yield dramatic results. To achieve them, there must be a convergence of three great streams of knowledge: (1) a knowledge of the discipline through to its advanced levels; (2) a knowledge of the psychology of learning; (3) a knowledge of new methods of teaching.

The net effect for special subjects will be a continuity which is lacking in our layer-cake grade system. The principles of mathematics, science, or art engendered in the early years should serve the pupil well. As the special teachers also make use of devices, they will accustom the children to a further degree of self-learning.

The system should reduce lost motion and aimless drill. The time saved should go to a tracking through of the child's concepts and understandings, the teacher acting as a kindly but firm guide who possesses the invaluable trait of expecting each child to do his best. This "best" is not simply the first attempt, the first recitation or report; it consists rather of better and better achievement through the mutual efforts of teacher and pupil.

It may be asked, what will the bright child do under this plan? Presumably if he is bright in most respects, he will be moved ahead somewhat, grade by grade, but only through accomplishments that are truly *at the top* of any particular grade. If he has a special talent, as in music, he may move fast up through the simulated grades, while staying in his particular home room which is based on all-round maturity. This is more easily accomplished under a longitudinal scheme of teaching, counseling, and advancement than under the standard grade system.

It may be asked also, what will become of the dull child? Again, if he is teachable in a particular grade, he will move along at a slow pace with simpler materials, but this does not mean a complete abandonment of the concept of mastery with respect to whatever he studies. The chief concession will be in the substitution of *description* for *analysis,* and in the spreading out at a given level of difficulty. With respect to the mental hygiene of slow-learning pupils, it is important to discover counterpart skills and firmly to equate these children with all others in terms of respect for their character and personality.

THE TWO HALVES OF THE DUAL PROGRESS PLAN

By way of a "preview," it may be helpful to recapitulate the main differences and similarities that obtain between the graded (core) segment and the ungraded (vertical) segment under the Dual Progress Plan.

Segment A *The School Grade*	Segment B *Ungraded*
1. The *cultural imperatives* English (speech, vocabulary, spelling, penmanship, grammar, reading, writing, literature) and social studies (geography, history, government, current affairs) offered in grade units, with sectioning on the basis of ability in each grade; health and physical education.	1. The *cultural electives* (mathematics, science, art, music, foreign language)—organized in systematic subject-matter sequences, on the basis of ability and interest of the pupils, who are grouped accordingly.
2. Each pupil is expected to achieve up to his limit; he may skip a grade if his performance remains superior at the higher level.	2. Except for the rudimentary levels (as in computation or general information), each pupil is expected to achieve in accordance with measured aptitudes and interests; he may, with dignity, avoid the abstract levels; he may, on the other hand, rapidly reach the higher levels.

3. This learning begins at about the age of one, and continues throughout life; it is the standard equipment of the educated adult. The line of learning is relatively steady, massive, broadly based; there is time. (In future, more of the expanding world of science will penetrate this core segment, but a full acceptance of scientific *methodology* will disturb some solidly entrenched beliefs, practices, and superstitions. It is easier to believe than to know.)

4. At one extreme, a lack of learning is called illiteracy; it shades into the designation "feeble-mindedness," if the opportunity to learn is present. Early disadvantages can, and should (it is felt), be overcome, as in the speech habits of the foreign-born. However, imaginative and scholarly writing (poetry, novel, drama) is specialized and not required; with later elementary grades it should form the main content of the curriculum for the gifted.

5. At the other extreme, this learning is a source of personal and cultural maturity

3. Beyond a few useful skills and some information *about*, this learning, for many persons, scarcely begins at all; only a few carry it far. These specialized abilities are not necessarily developed in the "educated" adult. Early discovery and training are crucial, if mastery is the goal.

4. The future is highly differentiated as between the talented and the less gifted. Unlike speech (every one speaks), *performance* in music, art, or science tends to be restricted to those who are able and willing to achieve a measure of excellence; all others are content to *enjoy and appreciate.*

5. This learning is the basis of specialized vocations and professions, or it may be a

for all. Its "top" is the all-round person—the reader, the conversationalist, the man of affairs, the writer.

hobby, a means of recreation and personal enrichment. Its "top" is the person who gives us the masterpiece, the thrilling performance, the original work.

6. This learning penetrates all subject matter; its relation to general mental ability is high.

6. Each specialization is relatively independent of the others. The common factor of reading comprehension, however, is of high importance in many aspects of science.

7. The teacher is a specialist in the culture pattern. (In a large school system English and the social studies may be separately assigned.) The teacher may be unversed in science, art, or music.

7. The teacher is trained in depth with respect to mathematics, science (or both), graphic and plastic art, music, or a foreign language.

8. Teacher education comprises
a. A base in the liberal arts and humanities.
b. Educational foundations in philosophy, psychology, and sociology.
c. A specialization (English and/or social studies) or physical education.
d. Practice teaching and field experience; methods.

8. Teacher education is the same as for the grade teacher, except that the specialization is in mathematics, science, art, or music.

9. The teacher studies child and educational psychology; he is expected to understand and to like children.

9. The same as for the grade teacher.

10. Year by year, the pupils move up to another teacher; their contact with a teacher is limited to one year, although "team teaching" may modify this somewhat.

10. The pupils may again be assigned to the same specialists, for the latter are not restricted to grades.

11. The grade teachers presently are women; this preference based on sex may continue.

11. Many specialists in the ungraded segment will be men; they will be able to avoid a designation such as "fourth-grade teacher," which has become sex-linked.

12. Through counseling, special programs, festivals and the like, a cross-fertilization between the pupil's graded and ungraded classes is maintained.

12. The same as for the grade teacher.

As we shall see, the basic plan as presented at Syracuse University in 1956 has been modified somewhat through criticism in a working party and through the actual inauguration of the plan in two co-operating school systems. However, the theoretical base remains intact. This base consists of four principal elements: (1) the concept of cultural imperatives versus cultural electives; (2) the dual progress of pupils (advancement up through the grades being based on the language arts and social studies); (3) a reorganization of the curriculum; and (4) a new design for teacher preparation.

In Chapter 2, I shall expand somewhat the theoretical basis of this plan of elementary school organization to which the name "The Dual Progress Plan" is attached.

In Chapter 3, a certain ideological kinship with John Dewey will be revealed.

In Chapter 4, a critique of the common scheme of elementary school organization will be presented; this is the concept of the *self-contained classroom* which might better be called the *unitary grade plan*. Over 30 million pupils in the American schools, public and private, experience a unitary grade plan as a standard school environment prior to the programs in junior or senior high school.

Chapter 5 will take up the thread of events that lead to the present study demonstration of the plan in co-operating school systems.

2

NEW APPROACHES
TO SUBJECT MATTER

For the United States in the 1960's, what can be said to be the culture pattern? What is every school child expected to know? Along what lines is he expected to achieve a maturity commensurate with his talent? On the other hand, what forms of learning or proficiency are expected to vary widely with the individual—to be a matter of no special concern if little learning takes place, but of particular gratification if mastery is achieved? It is recognized, of course, that values will change from decade to decade, at times suddenly as in the difference between pre-Sputnik and post-Sputnik thinking on the part of some American educators. Also there are national differences. Common musical understanding diminishes as we go from Italy or Germany to the United States. The Italian child, even in a poor family, is likely to be acquainted with operatic works; the melodies are so much a part of his daily life that he likes to follow every note, appreciating the difference between the good performance and the bad. The American child, on the other hand, generally can do this only for jazz. The Japanese child develops comparable sensibilities with respect to musical forms and instruments that seem primitive to the Occidental. These sensitivities change radically as we go from one art form to another. Japanese pupils in the elementary grades demonstrate remarkable skill in calligraphy, drawing, and water colors. The interest is maintained inside or outside the school, but the school insists upon supervised practice, thus raising the standards of performance.

In American schools it is difficult to find a comparable deep-set interest or proficiency. True, some teachers and school systems place an emphasis on music and the graphic arts, but for the most part our schools treat such achievement as mere exercise, perhaps useful in mental hygiene, but of no great consequence in cultural growth. There is evidence, however, that music, drama, and the dance in the United States are undergoing a true renaissance; there is a fresh artistic spirit in hundreds of American high schools and colleges.

THE LANGUAGE ARTS

What, then, is at the central core of the cultural imperatives for the American school child? For the American adult? The essence consists of only two massive ingredients: language and the social studies. Language in this context refers to speech, reading comprehension, and writing. The child who is deficient in this language complex is regarded as deficient in all-round intelligence. In fact, the common factors as between measures of reading comprehension and intelligence are so significant that tests of general intelligence depend almost entirely upon vocabulary, the understanding of sentences, general information, and the solving of problems whose abstract differentials are found in the English language. In our tests of general intelligence there is nothing of importance with respect to mathematical or scientific insight and nothing worthy of the name in the arts. General intelligence is often defined as the ability to do abstract thinking, with the silent provision that the English language —devoid of mathematical symbols—will carry the weight of measurement. Consequently, a child who cannot learn to read, after a reasonable amount of effort on his part and formal instruction in school, is downgraded in intelligence; he runs the risk of being labeled mentally defective and a candidate for a mental institution. He runs no such risk by being unable to solve technical problems, compose music, play a musical instrument, or paint a picture.

Practically all communication between persons of any age in our culture is carried on in the English language. We speak, listen, read, and write, but above all we talk. Any physiological, psychological, or social blocking of this process is regarded by one and all, in school or out, as a serious matter. It may be called to the attention of the family physician, teacher, counselor, or welfare worker. Is the child deaf? Is his eyesight defective? Does he stutter beyond the wide acceptable limits for speech defects? Is he fearful and withdrawn, leading such an inward imagined life that he lacks interest in communication? Does he have a mirror imagery that interferes with the detailed observation of letters and words? Is there a basic mental defect, ascribable to gene-controlled patterns, to birth injury, to the ingestion of poisons, to disease, or to a combination of bad environmental factors? Whatever the cause, the outcome is unfortunate and in a compassionate society not easily taken as irremediable. We devote an enormous amount of effort to medical and educational programs designed somehow to lift these defectives to a higher level of reasoning and accomplishment. Parents intuitively support this work, while teachers and other experts do so advisedly. Failure in communication through language, while it may be compensated for by special talents, is likely to indicate or induce a general inferiority in the person. In short, a severe deterioration in the language arts results in a person who is progressively incapable of meeting scholastic or occupational standards. Frequently a mounting sense of frustration and failure will alienate the child from his school and family associates, leading him into causally related problems in behavior and personal adjustment. As he moves up through the adolescent years, the poor learner is a poor risk in personal stability and social growth.

It follows that parents, teachers, and citizens cannot afford to be indifferent to a child's progress in the language arts. In the unitary grade plan these arts are not intentionally neglected, although there may be great gaps between the goal and the efficacy of teaching methods. Actually all teachers are teachers of English, for English carries a tremendous load even in specialized activities.

In theory most teachers are well prepared to teach the language arts. They represent for every teacher his earliest intellectual contact with others. A college graduate has had sixteen years of instruction in the language arts, and he had five years of practice before entering school; at the age of twenty-two he has had twenty-one years of "instruction" in English! Of course, his most intensive period of learning occurred prior to kindergarten or first grade. This early period of oral learning is presided over by parents, siblings, and associates who know little about the art of teaching and generally have little access to books, materials, or measures of progress. Each normal child himself supplies the energy and the curiosity that may make such learning effective. What he gets from the home is encouragement and affection, and these virtues obviously are great storehouses of teaching power. The better the home in terms of cultural criteria, the faster such learning takes place. A community of good homes leads to a good school in a good school district, for the circumstances are mutually reinforcing. A home enriched through conversation, journals, books, travel, and a sincere attention to the needs of growing children inculcates habits that are conducive to gratifying progress in the language arts.

THE SOCIAL STUDIES

With modification the foregoing discussion also applies to the social studies. These may be defined as a unified complex of learning elements in behavior, history, government, and current events, spreading out naturally from the self to the larger community. The curious child, hearing talk about such events, about problems that range from a toothache to travel in Russia or the exploration of outer space, will not ignore these matters as long as they are presented at an appropriate level of simplicity. When Sputnik burst upon the scene, it did more than make the headlines of newspapers, journals, and quarterlies for the elite; it promptly appeared in the primary grades across the land, at times with a startling attention to relevant mechanical aspects. Does one adult person in a hundred really know more about the chemistry and mechanics of rockets than the alert pupil in the sixth grade? It is doubtful. The informed adult proceeds not to a greater scientific maturity, but to some understanding of the economic, military, and social implications of rockets. He is expected to do this and he does so, which is one way of defining a cultural imperative. Anybody who has looked at the mechanism of a submarine, a jet airplane, or a computing machine senses that the

American adult gets along well without much technical learning. Rather, his mind is entangled with the implications for industry, business, transportation, communication, and military security. He knows, or soon learns, that governments may rise or fall in relation to their ability to achieve along these technological lines. This knowledge is not in science and not in engineering; it is in the social studies. Like the language arts, they, too, constitute a cultural imperative—a common vehicle of conversation and decision, a touchstone to apply to every mature adult.

What happens chemically in the atmosphere is of immediate concern to all who consider the question of human health and survival. What the chemists, physicists, and engineers produce along technical lines soon becomes a matter for great debate in medicine, education, and politics. Everybody has views on public health, schooling, and national affairs. Any person devoid of interest or a modicum of insight into these matters is brigaded with those to whom the language arts are beyond comprehension.

Are there any other massive cultural imperatives for the school children of the United States in the mid-twentieth century? Yes, there is one further complex. It may be designated *health and hygiene*. Many states legislate minimum standards of physical education, health, and hygiene, following the Greek maxim of a sound mind in a sound body. Because it is an imperative, and also for practical reasons, physical education in the Dual Progress Plan is attached to the graded segment; it is not, however, a factor in pupil promotion.

States also legislate minimum standards in the teaching of English and history. In the state of New York the common branches must be taught in English, although teaching in a foreign language is permissible after school hours. Generally the required history has to do with the state concerned and with the United States; it does not extend to teaching about the United Nations and certainly not to teaching about the nations within the Communist circle. In fact, the curve of public compulsion at this point turns in a negative direction. At times school boards and administrators must defend a teacher who extends the range of the social studies to include a full knowledge of hostile nations or other political systems. To this day teaching about the United Nations or UNESCO is in some quarters suspect!

MUSIC AND THE ARTS

The situation is much different with respect to subject matter which is labeled *special* under the Dual Progress Plan. There is nothing radical about putting music in this category, for nobody seems to expect every adult to read music, sing, play an instrument, or compose. Generally the discovery of such abilities and their furtherance in the school is looked upon with pleasure, and it may precipitate correlative tutorial teaching outside of school. In some circles piano lessons are indeed a part of the social mores, frequently resented by the children themselves and generally not carried far. Schools increasingly offer music through singing groups, bands, and orchestras, but few pupils progress to the point of real proficiency. Left to himself the average adolescent will enjoy singing in a group and playing the simpler band instruments, but he will rarely get far with voice, piano, or stringed instrument, and will almost never set his mind to musical composition. Similarly in the graphic and plastic arts: beyond the therapeutic level of the kindergarten, they tend to become sterile in the direction of unimaginative vocational skill and shopwork. In school we rarely find studios or workshops that give expert and sympathetic attention to the child who is creating new forms and designs. The pupil is much on his own in any attempt to develop a disciplined style that would permit him to communicate in such media. We are pleasantly astonished when children show remarkable talent in drawing or color, but we do not insist upon fostering it. Few teachers would think of withholding promotion from a pupil because of his difficulties in any artistic medium; in the culture pattern of today this is as it should be.

Accordingly, it cannot be said that the Dual Progress Plan is unique in regarding music and the other arts as specialized. We shall see later that, paradoxically, their designation as specialties permits an enormous amount of attention to the talented pupil. At the same time it eases the pressure upon the tone-deficient or nonvisual child of small potential in the arts. For the latter it will suffice to ask only that he achieve a conversational and appreciative grasp of the productions of others in agreeable forms of art. Similarly for music: no matter how unmusical *as composer or performer* a child may be, he can usually learn to enjoy music and enrich his life through it.

Unhappily the curriculum in these specialties, as found in most schools, is designed for children of low aptitude. The fact is that pupils need little talent, interest, or skill in the arts to move up the shaky rungs of the educational ladder; there is no clean-cut ascent. Today's classroom teacher knows little about the arts and is glad to turn the children over *en masse* to a specialist supervisor.

THE SATELLITE FOREIGN LANGUAGE PROGRAM

While it is feasible for a normal child to learn two languages simultaneously, it may not be educationally desirable. He simply will not be as good in either language as he would have been in one of them, given equal time, instruction, and encouragement. In this respect bilingualism is no more desirable than ambidexterity. The experience in France some years ago bears this out: it was discovered that teaching English and French with equal vigor in the first school years was not conducive to rapid advancement in French; it was, in fact, associated with symptoms of insecurity—nervousness, obstinacy, stuttering, and the like. The mind of the young child seems to need a taproot and a solid trunk before branching out; this stability is to be found in one's native tongue. A second language is, and should be in part, a grafting upon the first. If attempted too soon, the process weakens the parent structure; if too late, it meets resistance and may fail altogether.

The inherent value in mastering a single tongue is indisputable. We need language for the social fulfillment of our biological structure. Language makes us human. It is as central as the nervous system itself and, as shown by the remarkable Helen Keller, it can develop with small aid from ordinary sensory cues.

It is, however, unrealistic to argue that a second language also satisfies a deep need. It depends. Greek, Latin (as modified by the Romance languages), and Old English are "good" to the extent that they contribute to a command of English. They contain generic terms and grammatical forms that aid generalization. If studied as rigid systems, they may interfere with contemporary style and spontaneity. That the burden of proof for a foreign language as a desirable academic accomplishment of the American student must be established is seen as soon as practical questions are asked. What language? For what levels of talent? With what degree of proficiency? By what methods? With what opportunity for practice? Toward what ends? There are no complete answers. We might require French, less as a second language than as an integral part of the structure of English. It would be threaded in, as would elements of Latin and Greek. We have twelve precollege years in which to accomplish this fusion. Some words and phrases would be recognized as outgrowths of Oriental dialects. Children usually enjoy word games. It is a fair hypothesis that young pupils would enjoy the alphabet more if they were encouraged to unravel the origin of its characters. Older students could follow the growth of words in various pre-English and non-English forms.

For some pupils French would soon be spun off as a language in its own right. Who should study French? To be categorical (not without overlapping), I suggest:

1. Pupils with a French background.
2. Pupils who show unusual facility in English and desire acceleration in its study; this group includes the talented ones in imaginative writing.
3. Pupils pointing toward the performing arts.
4. Pupils gifted in science.
5. Pupils who manifestly enjoy the study of French.

Analogous statements can be made with respect to the study of German, Spanish, Italian, or Russian. Does the study of Russian merit a special place? If we place in the curriculum what is needed from Greek, Latin, early English, and French—thus insuring a unified structure of English—we can afford to answer the question on the basis of contemporary affairs. The answer, then, is: eventually the *majority* of American students. The English-speaking and Russian-speaking worlds have become part of each other's future. Coexistence, unilateral conquest, or mutual destruction all lead us down the same linguistic road: we should be able to communicate with a people we are going to live with or die with.

A recent report of a conference jointly sponsored by the National Education Association and the Modern Language Association of America presents the combined judgment of foreign language specialists on the *when, what,* and *wherefore* of foreign language instruction.[1] The gist of its recommendations follows:

1. A beginning in Grade III is recommended, although Grade IV is also "satisfactory."
2. Pupils should have about one hundred hours of "completely audio-lingual" instruction before contact with printed or written words.
3. Pupils in Grades III, IV, and V need instruction fifteen minutes per day by "a teacher who speaks the language fluently and correctly and who follows a planned program." Emphasis is on drill, dialogue; grammar comes later. In Grade VI, the pupils start reading what they have already learned to hear and say. The program calls for fifteen minutes every school day. At the end of Grade VI, the teacher should provide guidance "in selecting the pupils for whom further study will be profitable."
4. The selected pupils carry on through Grade VII, and a few may now add a second foreign language. Instruction for a full class period, three days a week, is required. Emphasis on dialogue continues, but more reading is introduced. Writing is introduced and laboratory facilities are utilized.
5. In Grade VIII, classes are again held for a full period three days a week; there is oral reading and more homework.

For those who do well in a foreign language the sixth-grade plan briefly outlined above is carried on, with instructional shifts of emphasis, through the twelfth grade, or senior year in high school. It is a massive curricular assignment that few schools are prepared to meet. As a transitional stage, the conference recommends a four-year or a six-year sequence to replace the common (and utterly inadequate) two-year program.

[1] Wilmarth H. Starr, Mary P. Thompson, and Donald D. Walsh (eds.), *Modern Foreign Languages and the Academically Talented Student.* (Washington, D.C.: National Education Association, 1960.)

I had proposed to Dr. Alvin C. Eurich in April, 1959, the running of a so-called "satellite" study to accompany the Dual Progress Plan:

A further matter on the horizon is the way in which contemporary methods of teaching a foreign language as early as the 4th or 5th grade might be included in the Dual Progress Plan. Since such teaching is special in nature, it does not call for a new philosophy, but it does call for new methods, materials, and programs in teacher training. If the (Ford) Foundation is interested in such a development as a rider to the Dual Progress Plan, we would undertake to set up a collateral research project beginning this fall. . . . In essence, we would utilize recordings, cubicles, and self-teaching materials for basic practice, bringing the pupils together for social group instruction, preferably with the aid of films and TV programs. Our experience has already shown that a period of careful preparation in the teaching of a "special" subject can produce dividends in greater speed and assurance later on.

Three kinds of activity are presently under the aegis of the Experimental Teaching Center:

a. a survey of the present status of foreign language instruction in American public schools, with particular reference to the New York metropolitan area;

b. the development of a theoretical framework for foreign language instruction: objectives, the learning process, materials, teacher training;

c. studies in methods, optimal pupil age of beginners, and the like.

MATHEMATICS AND SCIENCE

The radical part of the Dual Progress Plan, as far as the organization of the classroom is concerned, lies in the placing of mathematics and science in the ungraded, longitudinal portion of the program. This is done advisedly. The self-contained classroom contains little mathematics or science, and its teachers will remain hopelessly in arrears if they now attempt to catch up. To put it baldly, the self-contained classroom (to be described in Chapter 3) is a pre-science invention; the accelerated pace of science in recent decades has only brought out its inherent defects. Since the designation of mathematics and science as *ungraded* is a controversial point invariably raised by teachers, administrators, and parents, it may be well to devote some space to it.

While it is easy to maintain that mathematics, or at least arithmetic, is as much a part of our cultural inheritance as the English language, the analogy will not bear up under inspection. If arithmetic were taught as number theory, it would perhaps lead smoothly to genuine mathematical structures. But there is a mountain of evidence to show that arithmetic is taught as a series of concrete, overlapping skills. There, for millions of American children and adults, the story ends. In high school they get some plane geometry, which they may like as a game but are rarely called upon to use afterwards. Perhaps they get some algebra, which they almost never use and generally dislike from the beginning. I do not imply that there is something inherently disagreeable about elementary mathematics; rather, I hold that if repeated exercises are related neither to external applications nor to a growing sense of intellectual structure, they become wearisome. Often the "felt need" of children is confined to a rote learning of the common arithmetical *operations;* no one doubts their usefulness, but no one can transmute them into the basic units of scientific thought. Such schools *build in* a resistance to scientific growth in mathematics, and they fail to prepare the minds of students for applying mathematics in closely related disciplines. There is, of course, an enormous mathematical area in the physical, biological, and social sciences, but textbooks in these fields, in order to be acceptable, play down the mathematical ingredients.

In the words of John R. Dunning,[2] dean of the School of Engineering of Columbia University:

. . . If we are to wipe out scientific illiteracy and mathematical illiteracy, we must start in our elementary schools. For just as the child who does not want to read is more incurably illiterate than the child who does not know how to read, so the child who misses the point of science is more ignorant than the child who lacks information about science; and it is in the first few years of school that we are now almost systematically crushing that lovely combination of wonderment and shrewd inquiry which is the real point of science.

There is no such creature as a child too young for science. In fact,

[2] *New York Times Magazine,* November 29, 1959, p. 80.

since toddlers are more interested in discovering the world outside themselves than in probing their own psyches or their interpersonal relations (unless they are pretty sick toddlers), the beginning of all rational intellectual activity lies in the realm of elementary science and mathematics.

Nor should we be lulled into thinking that "scientific" activities will suffice to reduce illiteracy. Professor Duane H. D. Roller of the University of Oklahoma has this to say:[3]

First let us look specifically at what our distinction between science and technology can tell us about elementary school science education. To begin with, science is the search for explanation of natural phenomena. To interest children in science one must interest them in explanation of phenomena. It is important to note that science is not phenomena, but *explanation* of phenomena. For example, rocks are not science nor are the characteristics of rocks science. Only when one turns to explanations of those rocks and their characteristics has one begun to talk about science. Thus a child collecting rocks is not engaging in science nor is he engaging in science when he describes those rocks. If he reads or is told about explanations of those characteristics, he is beginning to come into contact with science. If, for example, he learns that rocks can be classified according to such-and-such a scheme, the child has been brought into contact with the results of the work of a scientist. But not into contact with science. For science is what scientists do, not what a scientist did; that is history. . . .

. . . If one wants to teach children rock collecting, then send them rock collecting. But if one wants to teach them science, then it is necessary to teach them creative thinking; and the best way to do that, as far as I know, is to try to tell them what creative thinking is and try to get them to do some of it. . . .

In the elementary school, children should learn a great deal: they should learn to read and write, they should learn something about the world around them, that is, something about the phenomena and something about current scientific theories. But at the same time they need to learn that science is an intellectual activity and to learn what that means; in brief, they need to learn some science. To teach science one needs teachers who know what science is and conditions under which it is possible for them to teach.

[3] In *Science and Mathematics: Countdown for Elementary Schools,* Frontiers of Science (Foundation of Oklahoma, Inc., 1960), pp. 20–21.

Having taught statistical method to university students, I can testify to their substantial unreadiness to perform simple operations involving equations, graphs, and algebraic manipulations. Frequently mathematics as an intellectual tool had no meaning for these students. Even after such concepts as *population, sampling, central tendency, deviation,* and *correlation* are accepted as descriptive terms, there is a hesitancy to undergird them by the utilization of the necessary formulas. Students not majoring in science or technology see little relation between what they studied in the elementary school years and anything academic to follow. They display an amazing facility for sloughing off anything that has to do with "figuring."

Apparently my experience with these students—and of course there were gratifying exceptions—is widespread among teachers of statistics or other technical subjects at the college level. There is, further, a feeling that the blight, if we may call it such, extends downward into the elementary grades. Thus the distinguished Marshall H. Stone,[4] professor of mathematics at the University of Chicago, states:

What is involved is not only the recasting of the traditional high school subjects (algebra, geometry, and trigonometry) but the introduction of entirely new subjects (such as symbolic logic, probability and statistics, and mechanical computation) and the incorporation of traditional college subjects (such as analytic geometry and elementary calculus). . . . In the current discussions, not enough attention is being paid, I feel, to the reform of courses in general mathematics or to the revision of the mathematics curriculum in the elementary schools. I am convinced that we shall have to give very careful thought to both these matters. . . .

. . . the discussion of high school mathematics, whether general or special, cannot be separated from a consideration of what is done with mathematics in the elementary school. My own educational interests are directed especially to the problems of elementary instruction because I am convinced that they are the most difficult and the most important educational problems of all and that they will eventually lead us into the most profound and challenging aspects of pedagogy and educational psychology. It is clear that until we achieve much greater success in

[4] In Francis S. Chase and Harold A. Anderson (eds.), *The High School in a New Era* (Chicago: University of Chicago Press, 1958), pp. 401–402.

teaching mathematics in the elementary schools, we shall be seriously hampered in our effort to make high school mathematics what we believe it should be.

Beyond school, what is left of "mathematics" in nonscientific, everyday life rarely goes beyond a slight facility in arithmetic. If the figures to be added exceed a dozen, it is a rare person who can complete the task rapidly and perfectly on the first try; there is a quick turning to the handy little adding machine. The point is that none of these operations is mathematics in any dynamic sense of the term; it is memoriter learning, undertaken as such and dropped as soon as the minimum skills have been achieved. In general conversation there are only code references to quantity, cost, temperature, time, distance, and the like. There is, for example, an appreciation of how difficult it is to run a mile in four minutes because of the number of years it took to achieve such a record and because of the few living men who can perform this feat. In discussions of this and other athletic records there is a nascent recognition of the concept of limits and of the scarcity of items several standard deviations out from an arithmetic mean, but the conversation is sure to rest at the level of descriptive language. Similarly for games of skill and chance: expert players, without benefit of mathematics, have mastered certain rules of probability in card playing, dice throwing, or roulette. But it has taken a most sophisticated mathematical approach really to play the games out, as it were, and to show their significance in genetics, economics, and military science.

There is in the orthodox textbook small mental preparation for useful outcomes, and we need not expect them as long as arithmetic is paramount and is taught by teachers who know little about mathematics, and may even find it repulsive. Running short of materials at the lowest levels of mathematical insight, they spread out into foolish computational repetition. They fail to observe that, after a certain point, repetition is monotonous and stultifying; in their endeavors to amuse children they sell them short.

It would be edifying to answer this question: Why has mathematics degenerated as an intellectual tool within the structure of general education? Why has mathematics, unlike literature, social studies, current events, music and art *appreciation*, become so alien to our conversational moods? Perhaps a few hypotheses will serve. The simplest explanation is that beyond the uses of arithmetic in counting, measuring, and recording, all that is needed along mathematical lines can be safely delegated to the scientist, the technologist, and the teacher of technical subjects. The calculation of the interest to be paid on an installment loan is left to the "expert," or perhaps printed in a table; no original computation is called for. None of the operations required in buying or operating an automobile demands more than simple arithmetic. If he is curious about mechanics, the driver of the car may occasionally look under the hood, but he need not. If he does look under the hood to adjust the carburetor or change a spark plug, he is likely to remain oblivious to the mathematical formulations that underlie the principles of the heat engine. He sees only completed objects, unless some interfering condition is introduced. He may look for this blockage and remedy it, or at least know it to be beyond his mechanical resources. Today, even this level of mechanical proficiency characterizes only a small proportion of car owners. It calls for neither mathematics nor science.

In our civilization we are confronted with completed objects. While automobiles, airplanes, and television sets are indeed complicated, most of the men who manufacture them—like their counterparts, the salesmen, credit men, and service men—have only an incidental knowledge of mathematics or science. Needless to say, scientific knowledge is available; it has been put to work in the design and construction of such machines, but this knowledge is confined to an elite group—to a handful of mathematicians, physicists, chemists, and engineers. A little mathematics stretched into mechanics goes a long way. A little theory in electronics or radiation will yield vast amounts of consumers' goods. In auxiliary specializations, such as metallurgy, ceramics, or rocketry, there are similar yields almost in geometric proportion to the basic scientific principles involved.

THE ARTS

The same can be said for developments in art. A beautiful car body may be the creative work of a few people or perhaps of one person; it does not arise out of opinion surveys, committee meetings, or executive orders. What the consumer brings to the total picture is, above all, *a response*—hopefully a response on his best artistic side. The creations of the good designer first evoke appreciation and acceptance on the part of persons whose general education has embraced the fine arts, and subsequently of millions of others who follow the leader. Some horrible designs for buildings, bridges, and devices that plagued whole generations of engineers sprang from the alienation of mechanics and creative art. Now the gap is being closed, so much so that it is doubtless easier to sell a beautiful car with a mediocre engine than a fine engine encased in an ugly body. Increasingly we witness a happy merger of the efficient and the beautiful. Success is assured only when there is an informed, devoted, and creative group of persons—albeit small in number—who, as scientists, engineers, and artists, work together. Theirs is the specialization. What is general about it could be called *consumer education*—a topic the schools barely touch upon as a proper subject either for curriculum development or teacher education.

DIFFERENCES IN THE APPROACH TO SUBJECT MATTER

There are other social phenomena that illustrate the difference between our approach to mathematics-science and our approach to the language arts. Recently at a private school, 95 per cent of whose pupils were pointing toward college, I inquired of the teachers about their habits with respect to the English language, literature, and drama. Living in or near New York and teaching in Manhattan, these teachers were notably well informed in language and literature. They were familiar with the leading English and American authors of the nineteenth and twentieth centuries, and they had read translations from the French, Russian, and Scandinavian. They were at home in the theater, having seen within the year plays by Shakespeare, Shaw, O'Neill, Arthur Miller, and Tennessee Williams. They read and enjoyed "the greats" in literature down to the contemporary winners of the Nobel prize; they were discovering Camus. But these same alert teachers, carrying their work up through eight grades of the elementary school and thus into levels where the scientific interests of bright pupils would clearly emerge, knew practically nothing about the mathematical and scientific discoveries of our time, or of any other time. To a man (they were mostly women), they had failed to attend a free, well-advertised lecture especially designed for the nonmathematician given in a nearby hall by one of the greatest living scientists, Niels Bohr.

This would mean nothing as an isolated example, but it was characteristic of their attitude toward any lecture in mathematics or science, however "popular" its presentation. They were unacquainted with scientific magazines; they knew about only the most dramatic scientific demonstrations that were found in literary collections—not the Newton of the laws and formulas, but the young man watching the apple fall; not Darwin correcting the errors of his predecessors and contemporaries in biological science, but Darwin in his effect upon the pious and the superstitious. In short, their approach to every subject, intrinsically technical though it might be, was literary, social, and personal. No one should discount these concentric rings of influence that spread out from scientific theories or discoveries, but for a teacher to fail to place the *scientific* aspects of a theory in a scientific framework of reference is to miss its chief significance.

Of course, we have illustrations that are more contemporary. Since there may be a causal relationship between even small amounts of irradiated elements in the atmosphere and deleterious physical and genetic effects in persons, we have a social and political crisis of the first order. Is it not futile endlessly to extend this speculation without intensifying the needed scientific research? Once research has established, as indeed it has, the bad effects of certain forms of strontium or carbon on biological structures, the next question bears upon the amount of such materials in the atmosphere and on the ways in which what is there enters into living organisms. It is understandable that few persons are prepared to make such studies, but it is less defensible that so few persons are willing to demand that such studies be made, and made in a thoroughly objective, nonpolitical manner. Here is crucial knowledge which only the scientist can give us, but there is less call for its acquisition and dissemination than there is for the results of yesterday's ball game or horse race. Similarly for the relation between cigarette smoking and lung cancer or heart disease: there is a curious reluctance on the part of a supposedly science-minded population to demand clean-cut, objective reports on this important problem. This indifference is overdone; it contains strong elements of fear and personal defense.

In general there is an inability to lay out any criteria of objectivity by which even college graduates may sort out valid results in a confusing mixture of scientific report, rumor, and propaganda. What we have is another illustration of the resistance of the unscientific mind to scientific endeavors, or perhaps we should say the resistance of departmentalized segments of the mind to scientific results. Many a physician who knows better indulges in unhygienic actions as far as his own personal health is concerned; many a scientist displays innocence and prejudice in fields other than his own. He will be taken in less often than other persons, but he is not immune to quackery in such fringe areas as magic, miracle, and mental telepathy.

I predict that science, when it breaks over the barrier and becomes at least an incipient cultural imperative, will achieve a huge success in the area of statistics—statistics viewed not as a static collection of data but as a dynamic intellectual pattern within which some of our most difficult economic and political decisions must be made. It is clear that no advancing *skills* in arithmetic, geometry, algebra, trigonometry, and analysis, useful as they are along prosaic lines, can be used directly to solve such broad-gauge problems. The engineers will build whatever structures we need. The more difficult decisions have to do with: *What structures? In what places? For what purposes? For what people? In what order of priority?* It is not held that statistical analysis could be decisive with respect to the question of air bases in Spain versus slum clearance in New York. Rather, we need an objective approach to both problems in which the segments amenable to scientific study are given the benefit of such study. This applies to many major decisions involving the military, public health, public finance, education, and the growth of whole systems of transportation, communication, and industrial production. We should know the price to be paid in all such decisions and then extend our knowledge and wisdom to include measures of beneficence and beauty. This analytic approach would light up some dark places now given over to unexamined propaganda, habit pattern, and dogmatic assumption.

A NEW AGE OF REASON?

We are in, or close to, a new age of reason which hopefully can avoid the excesses and corrupting influences of its European predecessors. For one thing, it need not make the mistake of laying claim to infallibility. It does not have to postulate "progress" as a sure by-product of hard work and good will; it will leave room for indeterminism. Never again will we believe that all problems are to be solved simply by delineating the rights of man or man's slow ascent from ape-like creatures. These insights were themselves the fruit of philosophical and scientific inquiry on the part of a whole succession of great men. Every age that has accepted its Newtons, Galileos, Darwins, Pasteurs, and Einsteins, is the better for having done so. In fact, a deep and wide-scale acceptance of scientific learning is itself an indicator of intellectual health. In each instance, Einstein perhaps excepted, there has been a massive, organized attempt to vilify the man, to discredit his findings, and to downgrade the whole apparatus of the scientific search for truth.

A new age of reason, if it arrives in the United States, will not rest its claim as a cultural imperative on giving the complete answer to any problem in personal life or social organization. It simply will stake out the claim within which science, and only science, is truly competent to find the answers. Science will be recognized as a way of thinking, a tool of thought, a means of understanding and controlling nature. As such, the scientific approach cannot safely be excluded from any complex human endeavor. But the scientist, *as scientist,* cannot assume responsibility for decisions that go beyond his area of competence. Science itself is neutral in regard to political, moral, or esthetic decisions; in effect, it states if *a,* then *b.* As I have said elsewhere:[5]

The frontier in the education of the scientist lies in both the foundation and the crowning tower. We need his skepticism, his urge to be shown,

[5] George D. Stoddard, *Frontiers in Education* (Stanford: Stanford University Press, 1945), pp. 33, 34–35.

his way of testing the strength of materials and ideas. We need his ethics. The good scientist is good in all matters that affect his procedures; he establishes a special world of fellowship and exchange. Within it, he is inherently moral and reliable. When a bridge falls down, it is front-page news, so rarely does it happen. Given this objectivity, this intellectual freedom, the scientist should be able to move serenely in other areas that involve the exercise of judgment. Frequently, however, he relies on common stereotypes, staying within airtight compartments. . . .

Does not the burden of complaint against physical science pile up against its outcomes? The method is feared only when it seeks admission to new places. There is, too, a vague resentment against noise, heat, dust, smoke, and the factory profile. Science even gets blamed for the ugliness of cities, cheap advertising, and radio claptrap, every one of which falls within the purview of the fine arts.

Except in methodology, physical science (not the individual scientist, of course) cannot be said to have any preference as between beauty and ugliness, noise or silence, sin or virtue. It undergirds homely or handsome buildings but never the poor design. It is the greatest noise producer in the world and the greatest silencer. If your good health is a virtue, science will contribute to it with amazing effectiveness; if your enemy's ill health is an equal virtue, science is quick to burn him, poison him, or blow him to bits. In a gentler mood, as it were, science will discover strange things in a cup of water, leaving for the humanist, the moralist, or the educator the delightful task of making cleanliness a virtue. Is it reasonable for any one to get angry at so obedient a servant?

In short, science is supreme in its own realm, but it does not represent the whole man nor the full circle of civilization. To observe, analyze, and predict in the realm of nature, is to give one's thought to abstract formulations that may be sustained by, or corrected by, physical operations.

In the realm of art we frequently seek to arrive at truth or excitement by other means. We introduce distortion and illusion; we seek to produce in small objects or short series of events the essence of great generalizations. The physical beauty of Michelangelo's "David" may exceed that of any man who ever lived, but beyond physique the great work must show the rarer virtues of thought and deed. The perfect sculpture used to need a heroic or godlike designation in order to live in terms of human aspiration. Nowadays, *man* will do. Imagined characters are often more real than the real men we have known, and living men are made more real by the myth-makers. Up to recent years scientific psychology had little to offer the artist, but all has changed. Since Freud, psychology has delved into realms which had hitherto been the domain of the artist, philosopher, or saint. The classic Greek dramatists many centuries before Freud had learned a great deal about the human mind and the aberrations of human behavior. From early times artists and physicians shared an extraordinarily accurate knowledge of animal and human anatomy, but such observations alone do not make a scientist or an artist.

We cannot expect that the freedom demanded by both scientist and artist is something easily transferable to large sectors of a population. Unscientific men with no feeling for art have fought and died for personal liberty and civic virtue. The right to think is more precious than the habit. Doubtless most of us would prefer to have the free, all-round man as a leader in public affairs. It is no accident that a Benjamin Franklin, a Thomas Jefferson, or a Joseph Priestley should be at once imaginative along scientific lines and fully endowed with human virtues. There is a strong element of pragmatism in all science; to the extent that in the person or the group this element is carried over into other facets, we have a basis for progress. The freezing in of a scientific formulation without constant attempts to test it or revise it is not good for science, especially if the freezing process is imposed from without. I can think of no edict of church or state that has ever advanced the cause of science, except that noble cluster of edicts which proclaimed the right to deviate. We would have been spared the flat, sinister, soul-centered world of the theologian if the astronomy, mathematics, and biology of the early Egyptians, Arabs, and Greeks had been more widely accepted. The darkest part of the Dark Ages is found in the terrifying belittlement of the intellect of man. Soviet Russia, with no Renaissance to guide it, has not yet fully learned this lesson: thus its government insists upon the validity of Lysenkoism in genetics beyond any objective confirmation of its theories or support from scientists who are themselves free. In many forms today, the world over, this disparagement of science is still with us; it is a by-product of imputed supernatural power in human affairs.

Now it would be folly to assert that the development of a school plan that places mathematics and science higher than heretofore would, in itself, move these great branches of learning over to the status of a cultural imperative. Only if the Dual Progress Plan, permitting a new freedom in these subjects and encouraging bright children to go far and fast (and the dull charitably to remain behind), is itself an indicator of a change in our cultural pattern, may we expect significant results. After Sputnik there was some indication that the country was at last about to move in this direction.

Still, this impulse did not result in any extensive change in adult education, nor did it lead to a sudden influx of students in engineering and science. The impact was vicarious. More adults—parents, teachers, editors, and school board members—were willing to consider an educational emphasis which would yield more mathematics and science for the next generation. They were willing, they said, to have their children move into scientific and technical fields. Of course, this is only a straw in the wind. Many curriculum planners, bolstered by local, state, and national measures, have indeed given more attention to the teaching of technical subjects, but few have got beyond regarding such subjects as similar to what is already offered in the schools. It is not enough to say that science is good, and good for everybody, without asking the professional questions: *What stages of sciences? What branches? With what groupings of children? Under what conditions?*

There has been little attention to the waste of talent among scientifically trained persons who find themselves in the backwashes of industrial enterprises. There has been small support for the view that eventually everybody will need some mathematics and science in order to avoid a functional mental deficiency; that substantial numbers need to become expert in the technological application of scientific processes and discoveries; that a far smaller, but important, group of young persons should be encouraged to move rapidly toward teaching and research in the various scientific branches.

INTERNATIONAL CONSIDERATIONS

The talented group especially will need to be brigaded with other scientists around the world to form teams that push against frontiers. The International Geophysical Year furnished a good example of this

massive endeavor. Not only scientists but technologists and prac-
titioners also—for example in agriculture, medicine, industry, and
business—have much to gain from a free exchange of ideas and
products. They are perhaps the forerunners of a political exchange
and a new diplomacy that should unite nations, not only in form but
in fact, and not merely on the basis of mutual fear. In the long run
it may turn out that the chief contribution of the United Nations
Educational, Scientific and Cultural Organization (UNESCO) will
lie in the success of its efforts to bring together diverse national
groups on the basis of a common need for technical, economic, and
cultural development. The chief proclivity for war that seems to be
left to us in the twentieth century is found in the irresponsible actions of the leaders of nations: it is the nature of dictators to regard
all science, language, and art as useful tools for power and for self-
glorification.

3

BACK ON THE TRAIL
WITH JOHN DEWEY

What may seem to be a diversionary section of this book is an attempt to answer the question as to why the language arts and social studies are accepted as cultural imperatives of the United States—and of other countries, too—while mathematics, science, and performance in music and the arts, are not so regarded. I had long supposed it was an accidental choice or perhaps a case of harmless negligence. Actually it is much more than that: by and large, people fear science as they do not fear the English language, or history, or economics. Language has been given over to a bolstering of communication among ourselves; most Americans speak English or they do not speak at all. In this provincial image, the United States *is* the free world, the Western world, with other nations crowding around us for support. The American Revolution thrust this role upon us and it has been handsomely sustained through a combination of vast natural resources and a genius for technology and organization. From the beginning we drew upon, and are still drawing upon, the wisdom and courage of a group of leaders unmatched in modern times. Under stress, these men of the American Revolution produced the documents needed to clarify their philosophy and to justify their dangerous actions to the whole world. These doctrines have served us well ever since. In fact, the few that have been added in the eloquence of a Lincoln, a Wilson, or a Roosevelt, stem from the same political heritage. Our greatest struggle has been to apply such doctrines to all persons regardless of race, religion, or place of origin; this struggle, beyond its bloody stages, is still with us. No wealth of science, music, and art—we cannot forget Germany —will combine to solve such problems; it is the other way around. Once we solve more fully the problem of individual and group freedom, we shall witness a tremendous upsurge in the creative aspects of science and art. A submerged people may send up a few geniuses now and then, like Roman candles. Can these few be expected to reform their detractors? Freedom, not science, is sovereign. The true liberal joins with the conservative against a common enemy: the enemy is enslavement in any form under any circumstances whatever.

As we sense the need for freedom that impinges on every one of us, we should be able to accept the full consequences of a scientific approach. The blocking, as we know from the bitter struggle against cosmology and biology, is not in the inherent nature of the subject matter but in the fear of consequences. When men are free to think in *all* areas, they will think differently from the constituted authorities. The young free student will question the pronouncement of his elders, whether they be parents, professors, priests, or politicians. He will have achieved new ways to judge the validity and character of their acts. He will also have tested means of recognizing leaders whose thinking is straight and whose decisions are in the public interest. Not only is the examined life the only life worth living, as Socrates put it, but it should be the only aim worth defending on the part of those who would lead us in cultural, political, or religious affairs. As we embrace the idea of a program of every child and every adult a thinker up to the top level of his talents and every association of men a structure designed to surpass private wisdom, we do not disturb the true leaders; we endanger only those who keep their positions of power through the nurtured ignorance of those they seek to influence.

Such observations are not comfortable to false leaders. They frighten the demagogue and alienate those whose security rests upon a lack of thought or responsibility on the part of individuals. Democracy is difficult because of its demands on the informed and freely deciding person. Any subject matter is hard that requires the learner to learn beyond bounds. In these considerations we find the essence of the attack upon John Dewey and his followers.

The trouble was not that Dewey would settle for small content in any curriculum (indeed he would not), but that he demanded subject matter and self-reliance as against intellectual spoon-feeding. Throughout his long life, Dewey held that ideas should be tested in action and, further, that they should be subjected to scientific probing to see whether affirmations said to be true for all time were not really a protective device for men or ideas in power.

It may be that, from the considerations above, the success of the Dual Progress Plan is more to be feared than its failure. When learning is viewed as a dynamic *process*, and is unconfined, new vistas open up—alarming or wonderful, depending upon one's theory of values.

To designate certain scholastic content as a "cultural imperative" is no guarantee that it will be well taught, but only that it will be offered as a common element in the schools. Teachers of these "core" offerings will be less esoteric than their colleagues in the specializations: after school hours the core subjects are still marketable goods. Not so mathematics or science: the world of the spoken word, the printed page, and the TV image largely ignores these branches of learning. Music, art, and recreation fare better. One can always listen and look and enjoy; it is only *creation* or *performance* that remain special in the sense that there is a free choice. If, however, one does desire to become proficient in drawing, painting, composing, or performing, a price must be paid. Such learning requires a sustained, tedious, meticulous approach. Mainly the children of selected parents are asked outside of school hours to indulge in these learning patterns; even so, the pressure for proficiency in piano, voice, dance, or creative writing, is usually kept within genteel limits. Nowadays the talented ones in good comprehensive schools are able to get much of their instruction there and to fortify it by tutorial work outside or, on occasion, to transfer to a specialized public or private school.

THE BRIGHT AND THE DULL

The bright pupil of specialized talent has long been the nemesis of the grade school teacher, but this need not be so from now on.

The ungraded portion of the Dual Progress Plan is not just an opportunity to escape from an all-day teacher who is weak in some subjects. It permits the child to come early within the instructional field of teachers who are themselves talented.

For all pupils, the organization of subject matter is at once logical and psychological. On the logical side it demands a step-by-step development of a single discipline from first essentials through to rather advanced levels. Theoretically there is no ceiling on any one of the columnar structures. The first hour of systematic instruction in mathematics *is* mathematics. It may be a small step cheerfully taken by most of the pupils, but it is not a pussyfoot approach to a substitutive activity. It is no mindless doing of sums or filling of slots. It will soon permit the child to check his mother's grocery bill, as the *least* of its alluring possibilities. The *logic* is in a structure of knowledge, at once ascending and spreading out as a network.

The psychological validity, that is, the *method,* lies in closely following a learning sequence agreeable to most children, the slopes being interspersed with plateaus for resting and for consolidating one's position on a learning curve. The essential psychological factors are only four in number: (1) the child's general mental maturity; (2) the degree of the child's special ability in a subject; (3) the child's complex pattern of motivation (this is hard to disentangle from the first and second factors); and (4) the child's present knowledge. Success feeds upon itself and it gets external rewards. Failure in classroom situations can be so devastating as to push the child at all costs away from further encounters.

Unfortunately, in the present mélange of talent, method, and material to be found in the classroom, these variables are scarcely distinguishable from one another. Consider the pupil who is said to be "failing in fourth-grade arithmetic." Is he:

1. Mentally defective?
2. Particularly inept in this subject matter?
3. Emotionally disturbed?
4. Resistant to a particular teacher?
5. Protecting himself against ridicule by not responding?
6. Bored with the repetitive nature of the work?
7. Unable to see any "reason" for the assignments?

The teacher of twenty-five or thirty pupils in a self-contained classroom will be unable to sort out these factors in a half-dozen content areas and, more importantly, to knit them together so as to get an organismic view of Johnnie's troubles. Little of value is passed up to her from the preceding grade teachers. She herself may have no real insight into the "reasons" for a thorough, continuous study of arithmetic. What *does* it lead to, beyond a few humble skills? To fifth-grade arithmetic, yes. To a few more skills added just a bit faster than counterpart forgetting, until finally, and not without mystery, the novel approaches of geometry and algebra are introduced. These, in turn, at the high school level, may be carried through to vague, monotonous, dead-end stopping places.

The ability to count precedes mathematical meaning and does not necessarily lead to further understanding; after all, birds can count. Further, the drive for speed in the common practices of addition, subtraction, multiplication, division, fractions, decimals, and roots, may absorb an inordinate amount of time in the school day. The remedy calls for the adoption of tested teaching procedures at an acceptable level of proficiency, combined with tutorial devices and self-study. From the start, a facility with large numbers may be regarded as relatively unimportant, but this cannot be said of concepts, conventional usages, and the knitting of small manipulations into larger patterns of mathematical operation. A pitfall for the teacher consists in moving the child from one mechanical performance to another "higher" one equally devoid of abstract references and perhaps less useful in daily life.

THE REWARDS OF TEACHING

The standard course of such scholastic events, for England at least, was eloquently described by A. N. Whitehead in a lecture given nearly fifty years ago and published some years later:[1]

The main ideas which lie at the base of mathematics are not at all recondite. They are abstract. But one of the main objects of the inclusion of mathematics in a liberal education is to train the pupils to

[1] A. N. Whitehead, *The Aims of Education* (New York: The Macmillan Company, 1929), pp. 121–122.

handle abstract ideas. The science constitutes the first large group of abstract ideas which naturally occur to the mind in any precise form. For the purpose of education, mathematics consists of the relations of number, the relations of quantity, and the relations of space. This is not a general definition of mathematics, which, in my opinion, is a much more general science. But we are now discussing the use of mathematics in education. These three groups of relations, concerning number, quantity, and space, are interconnected.

Now, in education, we proceed from the particular to the general. Accordingly, children should be taught the use of these ideas by practice among simple examples. My point is this: the goal should be, not an aimless accumulation of special mathematical theorems, but the final recognition that the preceding years of work have illustrated those relations of number, and of quantity, and of space, which are of fundamental importance. Such a training should lie at the base of all philosophical thought. In fact elementary mathematics rightly conceived would give just that philosophical discipline of which the ordinary mind is capable. But what at all costs we ought to avoid, is the pointless accumulation of details. As many examples as you like; let the children work at them for terms, or for years. But these examples should be direct illustrations of the main ideas. In this way, and this only, can the fatal reconditeness be avoided.

It is not my purpose, and not within my competence, to lay out the natural stairsteps of mathematics viewed as a structural unity, to show which portions deserve the greatest attention, and to correlate advancing subject matter with the growing maturity of children. At long last, experts in the teaching of mathematics are busily engaged in these tasks, and some examples of their work will be found in Chapter 7. Nobody seems to be happy with the state of mathematics in our schools. Teachers, supervisors, scientists, and the heads of educational foundations have taken alarm. There is ferment in a dozen academic institutions and interest everywhere—everywhere, that is, except among some thousands of classroom teachers who teach arithmetic in old, fragmented ways and do not care to be disturbed. Well, they are going to be disturbed! The upset will not be caused by the requirements of the Dual Progress Plan or of other plans that have for their aim a closer relation between teacher competence and teacher assignment. In fact, I predict that the Dual

Progress Plan eventually will be viewed with relief. Teachers who "hate" mathematics will not be called upon to teach it; those who like it will live with it, following their pupils' frustrations and successes, perhaps up through high school and community college. Pupils will be, and will have been, *their* pupils in particular disciplines. They can be as proud of their "product" as any music school, art studio, or technical institute.

In this new concept of teacher-pupil rapport, the "core" teachers of English and social studies and the teachers of physical education will also find a rewarding place. The range from speech correction to grammar, rhetoric, imaginative writing, and literature, enhanced by work in the social studies where sheer reading comprehension counts for so much, is exciting enough to permit a new pupil loyalty —a loyalty to teachers who know and love these great segments of human endeavor and delight in bringing them to the unfolding minds of children and youth. They can teach at various scholastic levels, being already prepared by our cultural system to do so, but the paramount task is to appraise and encourage the *massive* growth of the child in the vast area of communication. Here the failures are more poignant than in any cultural option. Here the successes imply a totality of mature advancement that will saturate every form of adult life, for no one can escape the impact of the linguistic-social continuum. To be effective and happy one must read, write, and converse some of the time, even if one's deepest love is for nature study, music, or the graphic arts. Similarly, to be happy, the nonartist must enjoy the works and the performances of artists. In this reciprocal pattern of general culture, the role of language is never minor. The highest convergence is found in the theater arts, deeply set in all mature cultures.

In the Dual Progress Plan, mathematics and science appear as twin columns in the ungraded or vertical section of the program to be taught every day. Clearly there will be opportunities for cross-fertilization between these two developing areas. From the beginning the natural interdependence of mathematics and physics can be illustrated. Thus demonstrations of the principles that apply to a ball rolling down an inclined plane lead to more than visual imagery or a vague sense of generalization; they lead to mathematical formulas. A spreading out then takes place as physical happenings demand a formula, and, concurrently, as formulas accurately describe or predict events otherwise regarded as disparate. Such considerations are acute for the upper elementary grades and the junior high school. The mathematical component of chemistry, biology, or sociology need not preside at the very beginning of these disciplines but should be eased into them, permitting the mathematical stem to be well set up before too much weight is put upon it. The child himself will reveal his readiness, if given a chance.

Throughout, the aim is to establish channels, easements, and stirrings *in the brain of the child,* and to do so not by a neglect of content, but through a subtle integration of a structure of knowledge and a theory of learning. When a notable advance in the former is demonstrably inconsistent with the learning ability or zeal of the child, the silly compromise of petering out the business by rote and repetition should not be attempted. This common practice is indefensible; it adds nothing but boredom to the child's experience and it adds nothing of use to him in later life.

Under the Dual Progress Plan, it will be better, after full testing, *to allow the mentally backward child to abandon mathematics beyond the commonest skills,* in order that he may concentrate on what surely will be demanded of him, namely, an optimum proficiency in the language arts and social studies. He can improve, however slowly, in reading comprehension and general information; through such means, as far as subject matter can help, he will best be able to achieve personal satisfaction and vocational fitness. After all, his need of science will be no more than a modicum, thus placing him, if we were to be cynical about it, near the average rating of adults in the mid-twentieth century. Any special talents may help to take up the mathematics-science slack; they can be emphasized, in school and out. There is more "low-level" reading, performing (in sports or art), and deciding (in family affairs) than "high-level." It is no part of scholastic virtue to force upon a pupil standards which he is truly unable to meet. It is better to have a child's resources fully mobilized toward a modest success than to have them continually serve receding, impossible goals.

In short, when necessary it is all right to "take the heat off," especially for content outside the cultural imperatives, provided we know what we are doing. This is different from "relaxing standards"; it is, rather, a reaffirmation of the basic principle of individual differences in ability. In the Dual Progress Plan standards of achievement should rise, for each pupil is expected to perform at his highest potential level. It should be possible to proceed without inconsistency through attention to four factors: (1) a more orderly presentation of subject matter; (2) a distinction between cultural imperatives and cultural electives; (3) a better understanding of the ability and motivation of each pupil; and (4) a higher teacher concentration in areas of interest and special preparation.

Now, we may *partially* agree with the critics of education that the chief function of the schools is to "train the mind"; at the same time, we must know that the mind is not a muscle, and it does not behave like one. This failure to recognize the essential difference between nervous tissue and muscle tissue led to the fallacy of "mental discipline" or "transfer of training." The proponents of the liberal arts are mistaken if they hold that professional educators admire memorization. It was James, Hall, Dewey, and Judd, most of all, who urged professors in the humanities to get beyond details and fragments. What we all seek is the combining and creating power that moves through the analysis of facts into the territory beyond. Beyond the musical notation lies music.

Perhaps it would clear the air were we to admit at once that victories gained in education at the cost of the intellectual component are not victories at all. We do not seek an enrichment of personality through ignorance. We have no confidence in character if it is to be built on sentimentality. We do not cherish a love built upon false pretensions. In my opinion, educators are right in seeking to extend knowledge beyond memory and wisdom beyond knowledge. Also they do well to emphasize character and personality.

One day a group of teachers will confound their critics by doing what their critics ask them to do: in every field of human endeavor they will teach their students to think. They will not be satisfied with the lessons of the past but will try them out in the "dust and heat" of the day. They will confront not only the gentle critic but the mindless fringe in American life. One thing that a rabble-rousing group hates and fears is the art of thinking. Has any one ever heard of a teacher or professor who got into difficulties by being prosaic? Dull orthodoxy is never suspect; its adherents arouse about as much controversy as a breakfast of pablum. Imagine what will happen, and in fact does happen, when students ask serious questions and have the "arrogance" to criticize! By all means let us dedicate ourselves to thinking in the classroom. Let us extract from literature, science, and art, not only a shrewd assessment of man and nature, but also a guide for action today and tomorrow. The aim never was to recite Caesar, but, through Caesar, better to understand ourselves.

OUR DEBT TO JOHN DEWEY

Believing that the underlying theory of the Dual Progress Plan and (what is infinitely more important) the emerging design of contemporary education in the United States are consistent with the main facets of John Dewey's thought, I am now adding a few observations along this line. They should be assessed in relation to the numerous experiments and demonstrations that characterize the elementary and secondary systems of today. Particularly since Sputnik, numerous editorial writers in the "pulps" and the "slicks" have set up Dewey as if they had discovered a new, easy target to shoot at. Actually it is an old, sorry, rear-guard game they are playing. This little piece by William James (from a lecture at the Lowell Institute in Boston in 1906) tells of the early days:[2]

You will probably be surprised to learn, then, that Messrs. Schiller's and Dewey's theories have suffered a hailstorm of contempt and ridicule. All rationalism has risen against them. In influential quarters Mr. Schiller, in particular, has been treated like an impudent schoolboy who deserves a spanking. I should not mention this, but for the fact that it throws so much sidelight upon that rationalistic temper to which I have opposed the temper of pragmatism. Pragmatism is uncomfortable away from facts. Rationalism is comfortable only in the presence of abstractions. . . . [The rationalist] accuses us of *denying* truth; whereas we have only sought to trace exactly why people follow it and always ought to follow it. Your typical ultra-abstractionist fairly shudders at concrete-

[2] William James, *Pragmatism* (New York: Longmans, Green & Co., 1907), pp. 66–68.

ness; other things equal, he positively prefers the pale and spectral. If the two universes were offered, he would always choose the skinny outline rather than the rich thicket of reality. It is so much purer, clearer, nobler.

We already have some inkling as to the reason for the persistence of the opposition. Nobody would claim that either William James or John Dewey can be set up as fully reliable guides for our time. James's world was enamored of the wonders of technology. Natural resources were not thought to be "plundered," but utilized. Farmers were lucky to have markets, and laborers, jobs. The authority of business, largely unchecked by law or labor unions, was at its peak. For America, the rest of the world was a matter of trade and worker supply. Travel eastward was confined to the elite; its cultural rewards were reserved for spectators and collectors. The great heroes were men of business and finance. Inventions that led to greater ease and comfort were the new hope.

Dewey outlived this age and saw what he had feared—a cynical old-world fear of democracy in action. This rush to get in ahead of the people led to an attempt, once more, through two world wars utilizing modern implements and techniques of organization, to keep all power in the hands of a self-chosen few. (The same drive persists in Communist Russia, but it may take a different course. A new development, not planned by its leaders, may arise from the smuggling in of liberal ideas that are subversive to dictatorship.)

Now that the older free democracies have established some balance among the forces of government, agriculture, labor, management, and ownership, a complete *preoccupation* with such issues is less justified than ever. They never did mark the whole of life. The most favored and protected elements in our society display a hunger long dormant; it is for freedom, beauty, creativeness, and love in human affairs—for personal fulfillment. Dewey sensed this and many schools following his early patterns have stressed it. But what slow progress for the richest great nation in the world! Only in very recent years, and sporadically, has real attention been paid to the beauty of design of bridges, buildings, cars, or homes. A new part of our culture, expertly and enthusiastically represented in our schools, may now fill this gap.

To furnish the *opportunity* for a better life, now that the need is acutely apparent, is the business of those who work for peace between nations. The same peace will assure human rights; they go together. For the first time, these basic legal and economic structures may yield something beyond themselves on a world-wide basis. Having set a pace, below art, it would be reassuring if the American culture could now exercise this new leadership. As an unreconstructed optimist I believe it can, and if I were to seek the forward elements in such a march, I would look to the performing arts.

The high plane of Dewey's thinking and writing is apparent from the briefest excerpts, but single paragraphs serve to rouse the fury of those who feel attacked: they almost never respond in kind, but resort to satire and mass disdain. Consider the import of these three paragraphs from Dewey's later writings:

Thinking includes all of these steps—the sense of a problem, the observation of conditions, the formation and rational elaboration of a suggested conclusion, and the active experimental testing. While all thinking results in knowledge, ultimately the value of knowledge is subordinate to its use in thinking. For we live not in a settled and finished world, but in one which is going on, and where our main task is prospective, and where retrospect—and all knowledge as distinct from thought is retrospect—is of value in the solidity, security, and fertility it affords our dealings with the future.[3]

Knowledge, as an abstract term, is a name for the product of competent inquiries. Apart from this relation its meaning is so empty that any content or filling may be arbitrarily poured in. The general conception of knowledge, when formulated in terms of the outcome of inquiry, has something important to say regarding the meaning of inquiry itself. For it indicates that inquiry is a continuing process in every field with which it is engaged.[4]

Intellectual operations are foreshadowed in behavior of the biological kind, and the latter prepares the way for the former. But to foreshadow is not to exemplify and to prepare is not to fulfill. Any theory that rests upon a naturalistic postulate must face the problem of the extraordinary

---

[3] John Dewey, *Democracy and Education* (New York: The Macmillan Company, 1916), pp. 177–178.

[4] John Dewey, *Logic: The Theory of Inquiry* (New York: Henry Holt and Company, 1938), p. 8.

differences that mark off the activities and achievements of human beings from those of other biological forms. It is these differences that have led to the idea that man is completely separated from other animals by properties that come from a nonnatural source. The conception to be developed in the present chapter is that the development of language (in its widest sense) out of prior biological activities is, in its connection with wider cultural forces, the key to this transformation. The problem, so viewed, is not the problem of the transition of organic behavior into something wholly discontinuous with it—as is the case when, for example, Reason, Intuition and the A priori are appealed to for explanation of the difference. It is a special form of the general problem of continuity of change and the emergence of new modes of activity—the problem of development at any level.[5]

Progressive education, antedating John Dewey but owing a priceless debt to him for his lifelong devotion to its true principles, having served us well, is now in process of transformation. Teachers of good intent who commit excesses in its name still engage the flogging attention of persons who dearly love a scapegoat. *We know, now, what Dewey helped to chase out of American schools,* not to return unless we lose our senses: mass education with almost no attention to individual differences; "book" learning as the exclusive aim of the school; intellectual orthodoxy; the teacher as autocrat; a lack of reality in content; the neglect of social behavior and inspiration; the divorce between the past and the present; the sanctity of memory; primitive tests and measures; absurd art; a neglect of meaning; a lack of problem solving; a reliance on "mental discipline"; the view that higher education was for the socially elite; the low status of teachers; a lack of interest in world affairs; the disdain of teaching facilities; the rattletrap, firetrap, dark schoolhouses; the capture of ardent children for four or six years in a single schoolroom; the hostility toward play, teamwork, and projects. This catalogue admittedly emphasizes the dark side, but it is not much below the central tendency of schools in the 1890's; and that was when Dewey's theory, work, and example were at their best. He was busily practicing in the experimental schools of the University of Chicago what, for an additional half century, he was to preach!

[5] *Op. cit.,* pp. 43–44.

It is often said that there were *good* things about the one-room school—a sense of discipline and orderliness, the opening of new vistas through illustrated readers in the days of few journals and no motion pictures, radio, or TV. Surely we recognize this; there is always good in people, and almost any school is better than none. Also, even when the school influence was "bad," it was rarely malicious; there was no lack of love, even in the sadistic ritual of whipping. Such punishments were considered good for body and soul—anyway for the soul—and the souls of little children were very much on the minds of the pioneers who labored to establish schools and colleges.

Neither Dewey nor any other one person ever claimed credit for the gradual reforms that took place. Many persons and many forces were involved. Our population kept moving toward the city, augmented by enormous floods of immigration. Industrialization and the mercantile life took hold. The new virtues inevitably were more verbal, more technical than the old. Mobility increased. And there were the voices of Rousseau, Pestalozzi, Herbart, Froebel, and William James for those who found Dewey too painfully on the target of American educational deficiency.

I believe we are approaching the end of a dismal cycle. We can forget the adjectives and turn our attention to *education;* that is something we all believe in. As General Marshall used to say, "Stop fighting the question. Answer it." If things are wrong in education we can study, get ready, and demonstrate what we have in mind; we can carry reasoned reforms up through the elementary, secondary, and college years. Above all, we can begin the reforms in our own classrooms and communities, do what, in short, Dewey would have us do—not follow him as a master, but follow our own tested hypotheses.

John Dewey set education upon a reasoned basis that notably affected the progress of American preschool, kindergarten, and elementary education. In stressing the excitement of learning—its immediacy for the child in a social setting (the classroom, laboratory, or community)—he brought out the essential ingredients of interest and allurement which for centuries had been disregarded. The child-centered school became a reality and then, unhappily, for many a follower, a sticky slogan. The child's center, after all, is in his brain.

Conceptualization follows fast upon sensation and perception—indeed, there is no gap—and everything is tinged with meaning; life soon revolves about symbols, images, and values.

The search for new directions still has Dewey for its guide and mentor, for he clearly saw in the child and the school the true measure of the well-being of society. We do well to get back on the trail with John Dewey. In a fearful world of scientific power and social backwardness, we have come full circle to a new structure of learning. Not thing-mindedness, not skills, and not "the pale cast of thought." We are no longer afraid of books, but few persons in our society are likely to be unwholesomely bookish. Things, as usual, are all about us and in the driver's seat; above all we *consume*. All psychologists know that *to be, is to be in relation;* this is a healthy state as long as we are deeply in relation to *people*. We get off balance by casting our lot with possessions—a caretaker relationship that becomes irksome. To avoid this dull outcome elementary schools properly set up within each child some growing clusters of skills and achievements along physical, mental, and artistic lines. Unless the forms of work and play stiffen into a cult (which is neither good theory nor good practice), the child will respond day after day to his inner demands, bringing them, under guidance, to more mature, external standards. Thus the growing child will not be *empty;* he will, if need be, find beauty, love and intellectual power even under austere conditions. In the midst of a luxury era that precedes a possible 1984 disaster, this strength from within is no small virtue. It serves to highlight what is worth preserving at all costs, and, in so doing, to intensify the search for peace and security.

We have now briefly explored certain theoretical features of the new plan. At this point, some attention should be paid to the significance of the word *new*. What, for example, is *old?* Let us turn to a description of the self-contained classroom in American schools.

4

THE SELF-CONTAINED
CLASSROOM

WHAT IT IS

Beatrice Davis Hurley gives a compact description of the self-contained classroom. This device was itself a promising departure from earlier classrooms that were devoted less to specialization than to fragmentation. Thus the language arts were once taught as separate subjects: speaking, reading, writing, spelling, and penmanship. The contemporary use of the term "social studies" covers subject matter more familiar to older generations as geography, history, and civics, with added segments in anthropology, psychology, economics, and sociology. To quote Hurley:[1]

Among organizational plans deserving mention here is the self-contained classroom-unit plan, a plan growing in favor. Basically, this plan assigns a socially compatible group of children to one teacher for the major portion of their instruction and guidance. It is postulated that the commonality of interest of such a group makes possible the development of large group activities operating around a central core, hence the term core-curriculum. The group, thus organized, lives and works together as a classroom unit on curriculum enterprises of central concern. All modern knowledge about newer, more flexible grouping practices, provision for individual talents to flower, and opportunities for maximal range of choices for individual and group pursuits are employed. Care of the classroom as well as responsibility for planning with the teacher

[1] Beatrice Davis Hurley, *Curriculum for Elementary School Children* (New York: The Ronald Press Co., 1957), pp. 91–92.

48

the social and academic program are both implied in this plan of organization.

The utilization of specialists in art, music, physical education, health, or science in this plan is on quite a different basis from that held in earlier organizational schemes. The author prefers to designate such specialists as "collaborating teachers." As the term signifies, this core of specialists plans *with*, works *with*, and evaluates *with* the basic classroom unit comprised of a teacher and her children. The curriculum that results incorporates the special talents of all the teachers, and children as well, to further children's growth. For example: the collaborating teacher in art works shoulder to shoulder with the classroom teacher and children to implement curriculum plans arrived at jointly.

Thus every classroom is to be fully equipped (perhaps with the aid of service centers to which the children may go), and every teacher —by himself or *jointly with* a specialist—will teach every subject. Inevitably this system leans heavily upon the structuring of the problems of the day into an orderly curriculum; the future is contained in the child's daily life. What is to happen in future, for example, in terms of life's *differential* demands on the learning habits and achievements of adults, is not emphasized. Life in school is not radically different from life outside; problems are met as they arise. Skills improve. The curriculum, one might say, is omnipresent. It consists of the experiences of the child that have some relation to the school's program. Still, since the school *has* a program, there are selective, cultural forces at work. Thus parents, before the child is five or six, generally have sought to aid the child in hygiene, physical fitness, oral English, and ethical conduct. The home as a classroom for the preschool child is indeed self-contained; the trouble is, so many things *not needed by the child at the time* are overlooked; without schools, they would continue to be left out, year after year.

The self-contained classroom, or the unitary grade plan, is the common school experience of Americans in Grades I through VI of the elementary school, and frequently up through Grade VIII. It is often called the children's home at school, but it differs from his true home in certain important respects. It is a social artifact, superficially similar to grades or forms in other countries. The concept of social interaction, of learning through doing, and of interplay be-

tween school and community events is carried much further than
is the case in Europe. Nor is it fully self-contained: even in the early
grades the teacher is unable to offer music, art, or shop in a fashion
interesting to children, and is therefore dependent upon special
teachers. In theory, these specialized supervisors are called in to
assist the teacher, but in practice they themselves teach while the
classroom teachers look on. Consequently, there is a duplication not
so much of effort as of time; of the two teachers in the room together
only one is effective. This is not a total loss, for the classroom teacher
may need the rest and a change of pace. She will also learn something of the response of her pupils to other teachers dealing with
specialized subject matter.

WHAT HAPPENS IN IT

In the self-contained classroom there is much group activity. Action is easily confused with learning. As I have said elsewhere, *we
learn to do neither by thinking nor by doing; we learn to do by
thinking about what we are doing.* In a good self-contained classroom the teacher is aware of this. The preparation for a visit to farm,
factory, or courthouse carries with it, through immediate motiva-
tional devices, some systematic clustering of items so as to provide
an ascending scale of learning. At times the energy requirements for
such action components are so great as almost to bury the hard core
of intellectual comprehension. Children may visit factories, farms,
and courthouses, or they may walk through the woods, play on the
beach, and gaze at the stars—all without moving upward intellectually. Adults who have had such experiences a hundred times over
have not necessarily learned to transmute them into knowledge or
artistic achievement. Compare such visits under a teacher who has
only a superficial awareness of what is there to be understood and
appreciated with visits under the guidance of an expert who is
equally fond of children. A walk through a factory in the company
of a skilled mechanic, engineer, or foreman who, sensing the wonder
of young children, is able to track through from early processing
stages to the refined output, may prove to be inspiring. Furthermore,
consistently with contemporary thought, we can encourage such a

tutor or guide to take full advantage of printed and graphic materials, films, and prepared demonstrations by way of highlighting the things and processes being observed.

SOME ILLUSTRATIONS

In similar fashion, consider the farm. Farmers and farm children are friendly to the city pupils and teachers who visit them, but frequently they regard these visitors as picnickers. The experienced elementary or high school teacher counteracts this attitude by arranging study seminars in advance, together with special work by individual pupils or groups. This may, or may not be, education in depth, but the pupils have a cheerful time of it—anything for a change, a lark, an expedition! Such outings are inherently good; they are especially good outside of school hours, for they can be arranged by parents, Scout leaders, or welfare workers. Some matters in agriculture are best learned, however, by a process which begins in the elementary schools and persists through the high school and college years. I am not referring to the Future Farmers of America, but rather to the future adults of America. There are matters that the child can begin to understand early which will permit him to get on the main line of intellectual, emotional, and social events, as it were, and by so doing make him increasingly aware of the true nature of agriculture and of rural life. As he grows up, a child should not have to look back to a few expeditions as the principal source of ideas and attitudes.

Where are these intellectual beginnings to be found and at what child ages can they be introduced? It is not my purpose to outline the cross-hatching threads of such a curriculum, but to express a doubt as to their being found at all in a layer-cake system of Grades I–VI (or I–VIII). Certainly the teachers are friendly and they converse with one another from time to time, but they do not often get together to knit the work of one grade closely with that of another, nor have they had the specialized education to do so in all areas.

Thus in agriculture, I would expect the grade teacher to help in all the language aspects of the expedition, to assist the pupils in finding references, photographs, and film strips, and to prepare carefully for the physical hazards of the trip. Millions of children come happily home from such expeditions, weary like the teacher herself, but with a sense of having had a good day of it. Nobody would want to take from them this rare exhilaration. Quite the reverse: let us think of ways to enhance it, to have it lead to an ascending series of integrated experiences which have at their hard core some of the realities of science, technology, economics, and sociology. In the early grade years pupils are not aware of such academic designations, but right at the start, as they observe crops, animals, insect control, the processing of food and fiber, record keeping, and selling, there can be inserted the beginnings of science, of machine and food technology, of transportation, communication, and a business life different from that of the city. How is this to be accomplished? In the self-contained classroom a great deal is left to the variable brightness of the children themselves and to their cultural background. We might well be less opportunistic in these matters. Every time a farm is visited, the visit can be structured by someone who knows a great deal about the technical, economic, and social aspects of agriculture. Generally this is not feasible in the self-contained classroom. In the Dual Progress Plan it will call for co-operation between a core teacher of the social studies and a teacher of science. Thus the science teacher can go far in the preparation, supervision, and later utilization of experiences, calling upon the full resources of his science classroom. On the other hand, with respect to visits to a courthouse or polling booth, we should expect the teacher in either the self-contained classroom or the graded portion of the Dual Progress Plan to be able to do all that is required. History, law, and government—these are cultural imperatives for all adults and required study for all pupils; they do not depend upon esoteric formulations.

SOME IMPLICATIONS OF ORTHODOX VIEWS

It is well known that children like to visit farms, factories, and zoos, and perhaps to see the city government at work. Most pupils delight in getting ready for such activity, forming committees, writing letters, asking questions, and so on. But it is not clear to me that this chain of experiences will yield what the children most lack. In fact, teachers may unconsciously downgrade the concepts and abstractions of the classroom as being of less consequence. At this point we need some criteria of inclusion and exclusion for a school's curriculum. *The school cannot do everything.* Its day is short and its year is short. What, then, should the school choose to do, and according to what criteria? A few principles come to mind.

The school day should be different from the out-of-school day, particularly with reference to the systematizing of knowledge and to the expectation that the child will devote himself to improvement in learning and achievement. When school-directed experiences are much like nonschool experiences, we are probably wasting the time of the child. Of course, children learn through expeditions, visits, and parties. Furthermore, in playing games and refining special skills, they learn to do what they like to do. For hundreds of millions of children in the world today, such learnings do not depend upon schooling; they take place in an illiterate society. On the other hand, a school in the midst of a free and literate society has a social contract: the school undertakes to bring each child to maturity and life adjustment through systematic, evaluated learning, so that he may be well prepared as a person, a worker, and a citizen. The pupil himself should come to see this with increasing clearness, and it is crucial that he do so if the school is to achieve a lasting measure of success. What the child will choose to do needs to be conditioned by what he is expected to do, now and later. There is a purposive element that emerges on the first day of school and carries through to the last, such that the last days of schooling, as determined by law or individual choice, are partially foreshadowed from the start. In our culture pattern, the child learning to read is learning eventually to read difficult passages to be found in newspapers, journals, books, and government documents—if he can. Novels, plays, poems, and speeches, he is learning to absorb whole—if he can. It is foolish to pretend that he is just reading so that he may better describe the cow, the store, or the factory product. These items are sides in their preparatory role.

Education *is* preparation, as well as a series of events in day-to-
of momentary psychological interest, but their real importance re-

day life. It is not, or should not be, the repetition of things already learned or their unthinking use in aggregative experience. Innocent mental acceptance characterizes the habit patterns of millions of American adults whose education failed to take hold. At the mercy of the slanted article or the unexamined argument, they are easily swayed by political orators, salesmen, and smooth talkers on radio and television. They lack defenses against such devices and pressures; they are undone by specious arguments and oft-repeated blandishments. They are meat for the mass-producer and for all agencies, public or private, that crave a mass-response. Such non-education drives us, year after year, to devote vast amounts of money and energy to appearances—to slogans and escape mechanisms—as against the more lasting benefits that accrue to the free and prepared mind.

In a mature society, well-rooted down through the high school and elementary school system, what is now called "high-brow" would characterize the expected interests of average persons. We are accustomed to this in sports and luxury items. Everybody wants the best athletes, the best roads, cars, and horse races, but it takes enormous initiative to get the best schools, libraries, museums, courthouses, and art centers. However, there are some promising bright spots. While much of journalism and commercial television is nothing to be proud of, everybody is hopeful that things will improve, with educational television out in front. By and large, social progress is a characteristic of the American scene. As slums are cleared, the new buildings are a notable improvement, and this can be said of new forms of transportation and communication. In schools and colleges and TV stations the pursuit of excellence is more likely to be recognized now than it was only a short time ago.

ON LEARNING AND CREATIVE ACHIEVEMENT

The question is, are these moves toward better learning and a more creative life well started in the framework of the self-contained classroom? It is doubtful. The creative acts of children are all too rarely school-centered. Later, up through adolescence and early adulthood, there seems to be more of a convergence between creativity and the scholastic process, a phenomenon related to the increasing curricular specialization in high school and college. Where such stimulation is lacking in academic circles, the painter, the musician, and the writer turn away from school even in a school-centered society. Up to the recent past in a few advanced countries, creative works were largely the product of persons who were either self-taught or taught in a master-disciple studio. The essence of such teaching is found in concentration and perseverance; these attributes linked with genius produce the masterpiece, but linked only with talent their yield is impressive.

The key concept in high achievement is the ability to accept a task and to drive through to its completion. If we place the goals low, the happiness ("life adjustment") of pupils is readily attainable and may become cloying. Often the end result is a progressive dissatisfaction, not only with the slowly ascending program of learning but also with the scarcity of individual projects that really stretch the mind. At any age, to be only a member of a group is to be less than a complete person. Every alert child knows this before he goes to school. He engages in a constant tug of war with all persons, things, and events that keep him from expressing himself. In the preschool years he is willing to pay a prodigious price in energy and parent censure in order to achieve some self-directed purpose. It should be the function of a school not to smother these drives but to channel them into learnings, achievements, and spiraling aspirations.

Since in mathematics and science we need to develop both interest and proficiency, the first little steps forward should carry enough practical application, be enough of a "game," to hold the child's attention. Then, over the years, certain mental habits are formed. The child becomes increasingly skillful in solving problems through a knowledge of their parts and of the way these parts, in themselves manageable, fit into a larger whole which is perceived with increasing clarity.

This is a concept of life adjustment that need not be set aside when a child leaves the classroom. It is not foreign to his need for solutions to problems, for new experience, and for a better response to his numerous confrontations. The habit of thinking gets allied to the habit of facing, encountering, engaging; it is an antidote to a whole series of escapes from mental tasks and therefore from reality. When we use the expression "escape from reality" we do not refer to the process of abstraction. *Abstraction at its best informs reality and builds upon it.* In a creature with a highly developed cerebral cortex, the true escape mechanism is one that discounts appropriate cortical activitiy. In our time, with a vast spread of knowledge laid out before us, to fail to partake of it according to one's talents is, paradoxically, to escape reality by immersing one's self in a here-and-now flood of objects and events that are best made *real* by the process of abstraction. Everything is made more real by understanding. The insightful illusion, as in art or geometry, synthesizes observations that otherwise might carry little meaning.

Now all this is, of course, incompatible with any theory of a *lump of learning*, itself a fallacy. There is not just a package of learning that can be stored in a child's brain and nervous centers ready to be called upon at some future time. The mind has to be more open and facile than that; any fixity is relative, being greatest for facts whose accuracy is constantly verified. Facts can be put together in many ways to form a hypothesis to be tested. This means that the efficient brain should be plastic, capable of taking on new impressions, making new analyses, and setting new problems.

The magnificently developed horse could not evolve into the crudest form of a machine; inventors discovered that the new principles to be relied upon were not in horse anatomy but in heat engines and other mechanical forms. The one logical category that includes both horse and automobile is *transportation*. This is a concept to be found in the minds of men. The engine was not linked to wheels or planes until some men thinking about transportation restated the problem and solved it by solving the smaller problems, tying together sub-solutions in order to get over the ground, over and under the sea, in the air, and into the airless space beyond. These familiar examples are not lost upon young children. It is essential to cause the dynamics of the world to enter into the new thought of the child, as if this had never before happened in the history of the race—as, indeed, it had not in this example of the human race which is the unique child growing, learning, and reaching out.

Perhaps we can establish a hierarchy of thought processes, recognizing that any classification is arbitrary and not entered into with equal meaningfulness at all child levels. These levels are merely suggestive; they go from top to bottom:

1. creativity; the emergence of originals;
2. reasoning, problem-solving, and intellectual achievement—especially when resistance through tradition or emotional involvement is encountered;
3. appreciation, enjoyment, taste;
4. organized information;
5. physical prowess and motor skill.

The difficulty with all such schemes of classification is that they fail to show organic interpenetration; these traits rely on organs of the total functioning organism. For example, the motor skill of a ballerina partakes of the highest degree of human awareness, for it is creative. In like fashion, some abstractions do not appear in usable form without a vast supporting body of information that has already led to lesser abstractions. Masterpieces in science or art do not appear out of a blue sky. The saint for all his seeming innocence is wise in the ways of human nature. Intuition, essentially a fast way of solving a problem or getting something done, comes with a frequency exceeding chance to the prepared and seeking mind.

In all these considerations there is a common factor that is easily lost sight of: whenever there is thinking in a group, it is a private experience of a particular person. Committees and classes do not think, but some persons may think better in such an environment. Moreover, persons in a group responding to a problem set for all its members may arrive at sub-solutions or tryouts that can be woven into a productive whole; this is the essence of teamwork. We can arrange the conditions conducive to thinking but not the thought process itself. The classroom is itself an artifact, theoretically ranging in size from one to tens of thousands—or tens of millions by way of radio and television—but always with a convergence upon one person. The teacher's classic question is, "Tommy, how is it with you?" Tommy, for all his prior subservience to the group, is now on his own. In this way, showing his own strength and confidence, like the batter who gets a hit when it is needed, Tommy may take hold.

All education is process but not just any process; all education involves content but not just any content. Accordingly, we need not abandon the aim of *life adjustment* (I prefer *life fulfillment*); rather, we should endow it with substance and meaning. We enrich our lives through systematic thought that prepares for and accompanies action. Action in turn leads to a reconstruction of experience and so to improved forms of both action and thought: one tests the other. Before research exposed the fallacy, this reciprocating chain of events was thought to demand a positive transfer of training, a mental discipline, through which the mind, like a muscle, hardened itself and was better prepared for its next problem-solving venture. But, it turns out, the best preparation for new solutions is the reverse of this hardening process; it is a nonhardening, plastic condition through which solutions are arrived at in pragmatic fashion and then abandoned for better solutions that are validated in the same pliant manner. To the question, *Is it true?*, we add the further question, *Is it still true?* To the question, *Is it good?*, we add the question, *Is it good for us, in our time, and our condition?* To the question, *Is it beautiful?*, we add, *Does it seem beautiful to us now (as perhaps it once did to others) in our culture pattern?*

It is to be noted that the culture pattern is on a short-time scale compared to the genetic pattern which, as far as we know, has scarcely changed at all in the span of human history. What we face is the fact of a brain no better than it was five thousand years ago, setting and solving problems in science, art, and social structure that were unimagined in more primitive days. Obviously the brain has developed new external aids, as in the microscope, the telescope and the machine; more importantly, it may now utilize the *methods of science*. When we seal off any intellectual area against these new processes, the outlook is as gloomy as it ever was in the past. The prime example is our utter inability, up to now, to establish peace among nations, a problem suddenly transformed in the atomic age to the saturating one of human survival.

FURTHER OBSERVATIONS ON THE SELF-CONTAINED CLASSROOM

Now let us look more closely at the self-contained classroom (the unitary grade plan). In most cities the trend has been to progress from rather stiff, nonsocial groupings to genial workshops. There is a great deal of simulation, and this draws upon the imaginative powers of teacher and child. It is amazingly easy for the young child to draw or make boats, bicycles, rockets, or other contrivances, and to go through the motions of running them. The classroom store, post office, garden, aquarium, newspaper, repair shop, or Indian camp seem very real to the children involved and, for all I know, to the teachers themselves. The theory is that segments of learning will be agglutinous if brought together in these little enterprises. Or, we might say the self-contained classroom is homeopathic: it reorganizes what children and adults do outside the school, often in a haphazard fashion, into teaching situations. The school becomes a slice of life, or at least a slice of friendly life, for the activities are expected to proceed in an atmosphere of mutual helpfulness.

The self-contained classroom is expected to follow and to serve the needs of the community. The emphasis is on activity. The children are accepted as workers and companions; the classroom is a busy place, organized into numerous committees and groups. There is a verisimilitude to life except that, as I have indicated, violence, hatred, and jealousy may not enter. Nobody would want horrifying intrusions in any action program; for young children, as for adults, they can be allowed to enter only at the ideational level. The hope is that, with an emphasis on co-operative activity, some of the misfortunes of life will be counterbalanced by agreeable experiences. The activities are expected to be healing in their influence, the school joining the home as a place where the child can find understanding, companionship, and affection.

It is important to retain these virtues which have been built into the self-contained classroom. Any new form of organization, whatever it does to accelerate learning, must at the same time demonstrate that it preserves these essential values. In so doing it may get beyond the mores of the community, for some communities are noticeably indifferent to humane considerations. Today in the United States there are neighborhoods, cities, and states in which large numbers of persons, in school or out, are not accepted as equals. There are also bias-ridden cities in which the welfare of children is regarded chiefly as the concern of sentimental women. For a school placidly to parallel both the virtues and the defects of a community would make for a poor school. There is always the larger humanity to be served. What we condemn as totalitarian or tyrannous among nations can hardly be said to be good when it is rampant in community or classroom.

In brief, schools cannot play "follow-the-leader" vis-à-vis their respective communities; to serve a community well they must themselves lead. Communities, in turn, should expect the schools to be only a segment of community life. A school is as special in its prerogatives and responsibilities as the nervous system is to the human body. To plan otherwise, is to guarantee both a poor school and a deteriorating community, regardless of other indicators of "progress."

These general considerations do not indicate what kind of environment is appropriate for effective learning. Thus, to mean much, the school store must differ from the local store and the school newspaper from the local newspaper. These local services are end-products; often they are not local, but only links in a chain enterprise devoid of local roots. The thinking and decision making may be confined to a small group of persons far away. In the school store or newspaper, every child is expected to do some thinking and some work on behalf of the enterprise. The child is not running a store or learning how to run a store. The teacher is using the pretense of running a store as a means of arousing interest in words, sentences, and meanings. The pupil may learn a little about human behavior, but not much, for in the school store nobody is overcharged or otherwise exploited. In the schoolroom, hidden factors such as finance, competition, and obsolescence stay hidden. There is much myth-making and the charm and gaiety that go with it.

While these enterprises are defended by experts in elementary education as a concession to the present learning needs of the child, this is a dubious premise. At this age children do not need to run stores or live in foreign villages; they do not need to get ready to do so in this manner. The problem in child education is analogous to the bodily condition whereby the child must function effectively in the present while preparing for a different physiological mechanism in future. This is what the body is designed to accomplish: a normality in the here-and-now combined with a steady growth toward a more mature normality, the latter slowly shading over to deterioration in all bodily functions. But there is a difference. There is no definite conscious purpose at the physiological level, discernible to the body itself; it is only observed in terms of the experience of others. If the oldest persons in the world were six-year-olds and there were no record of the past, nobody could extrapolate their physical, emotional, or mental development.

WHAT IS NEEDED?

In any culture both fixed and changeable patterns are laid down. Something is expected of the child, and the whole of education is devoted to helping him to reach these expectations. These goals are not the same as those the child would set for himself; it is unlikely that he would set out to excel in English, mathematics, science, art, music, family life, or government. At every learning point he is moving into a future which is somewhat prescribed by the adults around him and by the academic tradition which they represent. The child is sure to be deflected and controlled. He is fortunate if he is brought up in a society which does not completely brainwash him, let us say along tribal, political, or religious lines. Truly this is the little man in the egg: it would be a forbidding thought, were it not for the gloriously resisting powers of individual children.

What we seek to do, then, is to invest the school pattern with segments of life that go beyond repetition and assimilation. The good self-contained classroom does this, but only incidentally. The investment in the future is often seen as a by-product rather than as an essential part of the train of thought and action being developed in the segments selected for organized instruction. The enrichment of today's experience for child or adult is uncertain unless it contains within it some regard for the future. This does not imply a lack of interest or sense of achievement until a fixed future time is reached; such a state of mind would indeed be scarifying. We might better say there are little futures—the next moment, the next hour, day, or month—each with its own validity and appeal. In fact, there is no sense to the idea of one future point when all is miraculously achieved. The difference between sentimentality and genuine maturity is found right here: escapists want everything to follow upon simple happenings. At some point, as in the fairy tale, they are to "live happily ever afterward." The "victories" of life have a way of regressing unless they are sustained by more "victories," i.e., accomplishments. No deed is good enough by itself alone to determine the full virtue of any person. We may always ask, Was the deed truly representative of inner character, or was it perhaps accidental?

We would do well to ask ourselves at every point in the school's program: how much of the future is a proper ingredient of the present? It is rational to eliminate teleology in genetics and cosmology, but it is difficult to do so in human behavior. We should not be unaware of the billions of children steeped in illiteracy who, at one time or another, lived happily upon this earth. (Other billions died prematurely.) In the stern world of the twentieth century we are unwilling to promote child happiness at that price. To be happily illiterate now, one must assume the posture of mental defect, pathology, or social backwardness. Are there any other options? Certainly not many. Hence we cannot wish away such thorny realities as language, social studies, and vocational fitness.

The only acceptable choice is to make learning as alluring as possible to the growing child. Since society regards learning as important up to a point, professional educators are expected to organize learning in such a way as to arouse the present curiosity of the child in behalf of both his present and future needs. Otherwise, the child may choose a carefree life today, avoiding hard tasks, only to be progressively defeated by growing bigger but not better. It is good pedagogy to assist the child in becoming intuitively aware of a future which he can experience vicariously in the lives of the persons about him in whom he has confidence.

In some school systems (for example, in Europe) the sense of getting prepared is so overriding as to derogate the immediate purposes and pleasure of childhood. This is the other extreme, and we should not turn to it as a guide. The balance is properly struck, as it is in the growing organism itself, by watching for and encouraging learning that is good now and good as a step toward a desirable future.

It can be said, therefore, that the self-contained classroom is defective not because it is centered in experience, but rather because the experience to which the children and teachers often devote themselves is trivial and unproductive. It clearly will not help anybody if the learning is inconsequential. Reading is more than a subject matter; it is a child and adult need. In our society reading is like conversation—no more to be decried than speaking is for all children who are not deaf and dumb.

Under primitive conditions, hunting, fishing, planting, weaving—subject matters all—were child and adult needs, developed without benefit of schools. Was there anything artificial in expecting the children of hunting, fishing, and agricultural tribes to become proficient in food-getting skills and arts? Was the tutelage of the elders therefore subject-centered rather than child-centered or tribe-centered? I think not. The induction of the boy into full maturity through special rites at adolescence usually demanded of him not only useful skills and information but also a demonstration of such tribal virtues as patience, stoicism, and loyalty.

In the schools of today we are hopeful that the child will regard the task of learning as worthy of his best efforts. The hope does not rest forever—or for very long—upon a simple acceptance of the word of parent, teacher, or counselor that something good will come of scholastic achievement. It is buttressed by a shorter range of satisfaction on the part of the child himself. Out of something abstruse in mathematics, he learns to make change or compute interest, and this is all to the good. What is *not* defensible, but is fairly common practice, is the attempt to deduce a systematic structure of mathematics from a wholly unsystematic series of skills and exercises. The process of deduction, even for young children, calls for observations each of which illustrates the law or principle involved, however different the surface phenomena may appear. It took the human race a long time to comprehend this distinction, but when it did, it began to appreciate the full power of the scientific approach. In every case, once the principle was established, the applications were vastly greater in number and significance than could be derived from any sweeping together of any aggregations of facts. Thus the advancing knowledge of the structure and motion of molecules, atoms, electrons, nuclei, and nuclear particles has recast the forms of thought in the modern world, providing a systematic approach that ranges from the smallest object to the galaxies. Life itself, as an understandable phenomenon, is the next scientific target.

It is a part of the future of most children to get some grasp of all this. Can the grade system with its stairsteps of self-contained classrooms meet this aim? Again the answer is, *No.*

In American education, the idea of a school grade is only about a century old. As in other nations the earlier forms of organization were less structured. On the whole, the grade may be regarded as a good invention, but like so many other inventions it has become obsolete. To the extent that a grade embodies appropriate attention to individual differences, is based on common cultural demands, and is capable of being competently taught, it is a useful device. It is consistent with other guideposts of maturity such as age, size, weight, and mental maturity.

When the grade idea was applied only to common learnings (i.e., the three R's), it was closer to its ideal than it is now. We have no common learnings in abstract mathematics, science, music, or art; in these areas not much is expected of the American adult, even by way of appreciation. On the other hand, a great deal is expected of the adult in terms of the language arts and social studies, *so much so, that they form practically the whole content of our standardized tests of intelligence.* Tests of general mental ability scarcely get beyond reading comprehension; they make only a bow to science or the arts, or to originality in any form.

Somehow there has developed throughout the grade system a distrust of the specialist. Perhaps there was felt to be little need for specialized training. Engineering and other technologies scarcely entered into the planning of the elementary school; before the Land-Grant College movement, such studies were not the general rule in higher education. The average American child, while often adept in mechanical manipulation, remains essentially indifferent to pure science. This indifference is not a necessary by-product of his nervous system; it is more often a result of his schooling. An interest in three-dimensional, mechanical features was to be expected in the days when craftsmanship meant so much and machines designed by a few persons had to be operated and repaired by large numbers of skilled and unskilled workers.

The same social process has marked other professions. It took a long time for the specialist in medicine to gain recognition. The truly honored medical man was the general practitioner who was prepared to do anything and did it well, according to the standards of the day. The emergence of the specialist has raised standards so that the general practitioner is no longer expected to be at once superior in diagnosis, research, and the various surgical specializations. We do not ask the specialist to replace the general practitioner, but rather to supplement him. Having done so, we tend to place him on a high professional level. Similarly, we tend to give special honor and a higher salary to the specialist in education who finds his niche not in the self-contained classroom of the elementary grades but in high school or above. This is not defensible, for the teacher of the young child is as important a professional person as the teacher of the high school or college student.

As we move from the self-contained classroom to the Dual Progress Plan, we should not entertain the thought that the specialists in the ungraded section are more praiseworthy than the teachers in the core section devoted to the language arts and social studies. In fact, the latter also become specialists, though the range is broad. We might with justice say that in the new plan all teachers are both specialists and generalists. They are specialists because they are expert in certain areas. They are generalists in the sense that, no matter what the specialty, the English language will continue to carry great weight; it is the unifying force. They are also generalists in child development and in the art of teaching.

Since learning to some extent will be oriented toward what society regards as important, the situation leads immediately to a study of the social organization that makes demands upon the growing child. In the United States today, a child may be unmusical, inartistic, and unscientific but he cannot in good conscience (unless compelled to be so by massive defect) be illiterate or be ignorant of history and government. In order to appraise the value to society of any specialization, we bring to bear upon it a full understanding of the cultural imperatives. We then come to a better understanding of the place of science and art in the growth of intelligence and the improvement of social structures. The physical scientists have made it a condition of survival to unite the world in a single system of efficient and fair government, but as scientists they are unable to go further. The next steps will have to be taken by leaders, officials, and authorities in the art of government.

The advocates of the self-contained classroom are well aware of these problems and emergencies. They seek to prepare the child for them by graded experiences that take place within the school or under its aegis. The "cardinal aims" of education invariably speak of healthy children who learn to lead a better life in their families and in civic circles. Children are expected to get ready for a vocation and for the leisure time that most vocations permit. Nobody will quarrel with such generalizations. The difficulty is in the means by which children become physically and mentally healthy and do indeed grow steadily into more mature and well-prepared persons. It is curious to note that leaders in the elementary field are often willing to accept as worthy aims these conditions that carry such a strong future reference. After all, the only present vocation of an elementary school child is that of *pupil*. Everything else of a vocational nature lies in his future; in an open, mobile society, it is largely undetermined. He is not making vocational choices as an elementary school pupil and, for the most part, they are not as yet being made for him by parents or teachers. To some extent this is true of "citizenship," which is rather adult in its implications; at least, the term is weak as a description of the child's current family and school activities.

We might say that many a classroom of the homeopathic type contains the ingredients of adult life made easy. As indicated, we should question even the visits to a courtroom as part of a citizenship project unless these visits are accompanied by a study of laws and statutes. It may be held that the children are not mature enough to profit from such study, but if this is the case, they are not mature enough for the visits. Even adults get little out of visits if they go in the mood of tourists.

Of course, the key to all improvements in education at any level is the teacher himself, but *the teacher* should not be taken to mean a confirmed operative whose capacity for change has weathered away. My feeling is that teachers rightly resist change just for the sake of change; they are understandably wary of untried schemes. It is not a case of prevailing upon teachers and supervisors to "go along." The first loyalty of any teacher is to his profession, which is to say, to the pupils, to the community, to society as a whole. Administrative convenience, "economy measures," or any form of "grandstanding" will not furnish a solid basis for the all-important rapport required if lasting progress is to be made. Certainly I am not alone in trying to find out what is expected of the teacher in the self-contained classroom and what the teacher, in turn, is able to accomplish.

IN SUMMARY

Now, a few pages by way of summary. The self-contained classroom, despite its high aims, tends to blur the everlasting need of the child to grow as a person and as a learner. Its advocates play down the structures of knowledge in Western societies and fail to appreciate intellectual growth in a particular child. Truly, all science is contained in the child's early questions and it takes all science, and all human experience, decently to approximate the answers. There is nothing foreign or forbidding about this process, for it is embedded in the nature of the human cerebral cortex. The inexcusable way to answer the questions of a bright child is to ignore or belittle him as a person. More commonly in this country there is set up an elaborate diversionary pattern: through dullness and repetition, the school may play safe. There is so much to learn—to learn, forget, and relearn—before the child gets to the real core of his vital questions that he may never again get around to such matters. The good teacher senses this and keeps putting yeast in the daily bread. Knowledge is not built in discrete layers but in helical figures, enabling a child to move up, in the same field, from c-a-t, cat, to Ph.D., cat—that is to say, over a nineteen-year stretch of supervised instruction, to a scientific study in anatomy, or perhaps to a dissertation on T. S. Eliot's well-documented whimsies.

What we get from the self-contained classroom at its best is a high regard of the teacher for her pupils and a growing sense of communion and co-operation among the children themselves. In a good self-contained classroom the children work hard and purpose-fully without trying to distinguish between work and play. It may be that henceforth we shall make a greater distinction, not in order to make children less happy, but in order to encourage them to build their happiness less upon entertainment and more upon the excite-ment that springs from learning and achieving. In any given grade, it may be hard to tell the difference, but in a succession of grades (or learning levels on the ungraded side) we should be able to elicit and measure the deeper sense of adjustment that sets in when the intellectual components of life are fully taken into account.

While we seek to avoid the extremes of action for its own sake or of thought for its own sake (the one leading to fragmentation and opportunism and the other to a dry scholasticism), the danger is not that we shall have too much thought but that we shall have too much memorization, repetition, and dogmatic statement. It was against this dreary trinity that the progressive schools rebelled, at first with substantial success.

The Dual Progress Plan calls for both active thinking and thought-ful action. It seeks to retain the durable satisfactions that good teachers have developed in the self-contained classroom. Thus, it is all right to extend experience by work outside the school that enhances the school's program. We should ask communities not to expect to be reproduced in miniature in the classroom but, if any-thing, to expect more of the school's program in the community. The ideal school calls for speaking, reading, writing, thinking, creating, composing, performing, behaving, and working in ways that are considered beneficial. All this is good for homes, too. There should be the same companionship at home that we find in our better schools, with a greater opportunity for deep affection. The home, too, should provide standards of maturity, growth, and freedom on the part of the child.

Perhaps in future one test of a good school will be its ability to reproduce certain of its features in home, neighborhood, and city. Such an interchange of instructional and social units as between school and home will be facilitated by the availability of books, recordings, motion pictures, and television. It will be possible to re-produce in any home or auditorium some actual work and play situations of the school. Already the self-contained classroom is far from being self-contained; a further departure from this concept may be viewed with equanimity.

Certainly, since Rousseau we have accepted the view that education *is* life, as well as a preparation for life. The growing child does not respond well to the straight imposition of learning tasks pushed down from an adult world. All contemporary child development points up the significance, the glory, of a child as a child. But one certain thing about the young of any species is that they are growing up. In man the period of infancy is long. Nevertheless, a child who stays at infantile levels too long is a cause for concern; if he persists in the defect, he may become a pitiable creature.

Consequently, as I have indicated, we must consider the way education helps a child to be secure where he is and, at the same time, to move happily through more mature stages. A child cannot be regarded as well adjusted *today* unless his nervous system is reaching out toward the days to follow. The most remarkable ingredient of normal life is its ability, its *necessity*, to project itself into a future that brings into play new abilities and learnings. The vital concern of the school is the growing child; the unceasing drive of the normal growing child is to grow. Thus far we have not systematically linked the phenomenon of child maturation to the social requirement of growth in subject matter. At times precociousness in a child is regarded as a sign of mind-warping—an unhappy by-product of parental ambition. Of course it could be so; we can cite examples, but they are rare. We can ruin a child by matching him to tasks beyond his reach, just as we can ruin a boxer by overmatching, or we can let him regress through standards lower than they need be. Any curriculum that does not allow for a tremendous range in pupil talent is hazardous along such lines.

As child and adolescent, the American student, if average or above average in mental ability, can progress through one scholastic level after another, and, as a young adult, through college. We are charitable to the "late bloomer"; we take the long chance. In the college years especially, we are tolerant of less than maximum intellectual performance on the part of students. Does not an easy-going college of liberal arts (there are many examples) represent the declining stages of the progressive education movement? Now there is something carefree about all this innocence unspoiled by the defects of one's early education. On the whole, the American high schools and colleges have provided an education whose chief strength lies in mental elasticity—in Henry Adams' "suppleness." I, for one, would not exchange it for an intellectual snobbishness based on knowing what to say in what tongue and with what accent. Education in the traditional European style gives us no reliable answer. The English have long neglected their talented youth, but they are changing swiftly. The French have not as yet been able to solve their divisive political problems. Germany is the classic modern example of a nation that was unable, after a century of the "finest" education, to understand other nations or to restrain a murderous drive for power. A nation of the highest accomplishment in science, music, and literary scholarship—all reflected in its schools—the Germany of the recent past failed its people and brought misery to countless millions of persons around the earth. A similar defect in the totality of Japanese education, reflecting the ambition of Japan's war leaders, permitted the adult citizen to "reason" without benefit of insight into the social sciences. Again, the final breakdown was moral.

In these areas of world decision, the education of free peoples proved superior. Often ignorant of fundamentals, our high school and college graduates were fresh to receive the sudden terrible learnings of the wartime period. As a whole, they possessed something not given to Bourbons, Teutons, or Orientals who kept to their past traditions of repeating and respecting whatever had once been regarded as important. The problem facing us is how to design a fresh and vibrant program of knowledge *and* open-mindedness—not to trade off virtues, but to combine them.

5

REPORT OF THE WORKING PARTY: THE CO-OPERATIVE STUDY IS SET UP

THE WORKING PARTY: THEORETICAL CONSIDERATIONS

For the record, the *raison d'être* of the working party (see page 79) is contained in conversations and letters exchanged between Dr. Alvin C. Eurich, vice-president of the Fund for the Advancement of Education (Ford Foundation), and myself. These events took place in the spring of 1957, following a formal request on March 22 of that year for Ford financial assistance in undertaking a co-operative study of teaching. This co-operative study, then, is the matrix of the working party. The latter, in turn, laid out plans for a full-scale experimental study. The way in which these plans were revised—transformed would be closer to the mark—is described in the latter portion of this chapter.

Let us examine first the "prospectus" of March 22, 1957, submitted to the Fund jointly on behalf of the School of Education of New York University and the school systems of Long Beach, Ossining, and Scarsdale (all in New York state).

Part One—The Plan

A. The demand for a breakthrough in educational practice and tested achievement has reached the intensity of the ancient search for the philosopher's stone. The compelling reason is a desire to master the forces of nature and society as a means of enriching life. It is unnecessary to enlarge upon the relation between the progress

71

of a nation and the liberal, technical, and professional preparedness of its citizens. In turn, the latter depends directly upon the quality of the schools.

Today there is no assurance that able young persons will be attracted in sufficient numbers to mathematics, natural science, and engineering. In any event, such decisions are likely to depend upon early scholastic experience. Similarly for the social sciences, humanities, and creative arts: in principle, it is foolhardy for a nation to achieve world economic and military leadership without a correlative strengthening of its cultural system.

What happens in the million classrooms of the United States is properly a matter of national concern. Yet the American classroom lags behind; in fact, in some school districts, it is about to be overwhelmed. In a time of plenty unmatched in our history, *we are again beginning to ration education.*

B. The classroom teacher generally resists a division of labor, fearful that intimate contacts with the pupils may be lost. Apart from the textbook, there is a limited utilization of equipment. The aids and incentives to learning have for the most part come from outside the classroom; the teacher has shared in them, but rarely at the level of invention or initiative.

Inside the classroom the typical teacher is swamped with chores. She is supposed to act as a tutor, even with thirty pupils in the classroom, but she does not really know their minds. Technical aids are a luxury. We have spent billions of dollars on kitchen and other household equipment in order to "free" the homemaker, but to "free" the teacher is often regarded as wasteful. A teacher may be supervised from above, but is only rarely assisted from below.

At the precise moment of learning, everything that happens is in the mind of the learner. Learning is a private experience, even in a group. But we have not developed methods of teaching that permit a full application of this basic principle of learning. Thus learning often calls for self-study, group practice, and audio-visual aids; it calls for dramatic experiences in order to point up the desirability of gaining a deeper knowledge of a subject. Where self-study is called for, it may be conducted in cubicles with the aid of films, records, and tape recordings that may help to iron out common errors, and may increase the confidence of the learner. Mechanical aids to learning are impersonal; they do not embarrass the learner at a time when he is tempted to withdraw into a nonlearning shell. On the other hand, they are unable to show an affectionate interest in the child.

C. This memorandum will focus on curricula, methods, and evaluations—on what is taught; under what plan; by what methods; with what success; at what cost; and with what sense of the future in education.

In the School of Education it is proposed to embed these questions in experimental situations, to relate them to the principles involved (perhaps implicitly), and to test alternative procedures. Starting with a re-examination of philosophy and educational psychology, we propose a stream of controlled events as follows:

1. The design of experiments on individual, cluster, classroom, or school experiences—as in motivation, learning, retention, intellectual progress, application, behavioral adjustment, and creativity.
2. The "mock-up" of classrooms—studios, carrels, "social centers," and stagings.
3. The organization of demonstrations that fit research parts together so as to form a teaching whole. These demonstrations would be the subject of student-and-teacher observation, publication, radio and TV programs.
4. Consistently with the basic plan in each school, the running of field tests, based in part on the experiment-demonstrations, to take place in the three participating school systems.
5. The massive presentation of basic findings, techniques, and results through standard professional channels in education, special reports, films, and TV programs.

D. In order to focus on leads that are promising, the following "targets" are suggested (they should be reviewed in the spring conference later described):

1. The teaching of reading, writing, and speech.
2. The teaching of social studies.

3. The teaching of mathematics and science.
4. The maintenance of mental hygiene.
5. Studies of the range of pupil talent, general and special, together with its implications for individual growth.
6. The dynamics of the classroom as a whole.
7. A revision of the elementary grade plan.

Although the seven "targets" listed above appear as separate items, there are obvious interrelationships among them. For example, the maintenance of mental health must serve as a continuing thread. The teaching of reading, social studies, mathematics, or science cannot be studied effectively apart from mental health factors such as participation, belonging, achievement, and respect for personality. Likewise studies of pupil talent are vital in any subject field. The investigation of such relationships makes possible the study of the dynamics of the classroom.

E. The present system of elementary grades will not be incorporated in these experiments and demonstrations except as a criterion. For example, as a part of the basic demonstration in the School of Education co-operating centers, it is proposed to extend downward to the first grade, on a half-day basis, a plan of specialized instruction.

The pupils in Grades I–VI will remain with their respective home-room teacher for the half-day devoted to reading, writing, speech, and the social studies. The rest of the day will be under special teachers in mathematics, science, music, arts and crafts, recreation and health, these teachers to work as a team responsible for instruction up through the grades. Thus a special teacher will offer work on a longitudinal basis, regrouping the pupils according to the learning needs of each child rather than on an age-grade distribution. He will also help pupils to form social clubs, based on content interests. Home-room and special teachers will meet together regularly to discuss common problems.

A pupil's grade standing (an over-all maturity concept) will be determined by his home-room teacher, but the pupil will be free to pursue a specialty according to his aptitude and rate of achievement.

A typical day:

Morning (or afternoon)	*Afternoon (or morning)*
(Home-room teacher)	(Three special teachers)
The language arts and literature	Mathematics and science
Social studies	(a) Music, (b) arts and crafts—on alternate days
Individual and group projects	Recreation and health

Perhaps a diagram will help.

Grades　　　　　　THE CHILD AS A LEARNER

Grades				
VI	The Language			
V	Arts and	Mathematics and Science	Music, arts, and crafts	Recreation and Health
IV	the Social			
III	Studies			
II	Year by			
I	Year			

As far as we know, this diagram pictures for the first time in education the ambivalent nature of the child in a given culture pattern. This is the way child, youth, and adult are really tested in our society. The graded steps—regular school grades, made more elastic—should represent the accepted, averaged *core*. That these steps rest essentially on a grasp of the language arts and the social studies has been lost sight of. A concept of maturation in general mental, physical, and social ability is retained in the new plan. Certain aspects of science and the fine arts penetrate these "core" layers or grades, but the nature of the penetration is in descriptive terms—knowledge *about* science and technology, music, arts, and literature. Thus mathematical terms, physical equations, singing, composing, sculpturing, acting, and dancing are really special in our culture; taken by themselves, they should neither retard nor advance the scholastic progress of the child. In order to give these disciplines free play, they should be exempted from the concept of age-linked grades.

This plan, in essence, would give up the unsuccessful, century-old struggle to find grade teachers who really like mathematics, science, art, and music, and are sufficiently competent to guide pupils in every one of these studies. It presents a means of progress for pupils of special talent, without doing violence to present-day concepts of general maturation. It should encourage the home-room teachers to become truly expert in the language and descriptive arts, capable of teaching through the whole spectrum that runs from "remedial reading" and speech correction to imaginative writing.

F. Since the diagram above is in reality not at all simple, it may be well to enlarge upon it briefly:

1. The plan involves a fundamental shift in our concepts of child development and behavior. It applies to the child what is more conspicuous for the adult, namely, that general education is based on a common core in language, social studies, and the descriptive aspects of natural science, technology, and the contemporary scene. Sentence structure, pronunciation, history, literature, and current affairs—these are of the cultural currency; they carry a potential for either embarrassment or personal satisfaction.

   The technical aspects of art, music, crafts, mathematics, science, or recreation—these are wonderful personal assets to those who possess them, but in our society there is no insistence that everyone possess these assets in equal measure. Nobody hands us a violin, a chisel, a mathematical formula, saying *play, sculpture, solve.* As a rule we do not know rocks, plants, animals, or stars in a scientific way. Except as uncomfortable amateurs, we are not even expected to sing, dance, recite poetry, or take a dramatic role. But a few double negatives or historical misquotations and we are put down as ignoramuses.

   Perhaps children know this and respond in a desultory fashion to what should be for many of them immensely appealing and satisfying. In any event, all children should make the best progress they are capable of in the home room, which is the nearest to the parental situation from which they have come at age five or six and to which they return for half of each waking day for 185 days on the calendar. And with a long period of acquaintanceship with the child, the teachers of science, art, and mathematics can discover the fascination of these subjects to the child, creating for them a place in his exciting life.

In this plan we hold that this ambivalence in the child and in the culture should be recognized and provided for. A child lacking in special abilities is not pressed and prodded, but he is helped to go along at his own pace, with no grade failure dependent upon a lack of achievement in this segment. A gifted child, on the other hand, finds the ceiling removed; he may move fast up the longitudinal pathway.

2. It is necessary from the beginning to dismiss the idea that while home-room teachers are expected to love and understand their pupils, "longitudinal" teachers are not. Actually, over the years, the team of teachers responsible for science and mathematics through Grades I–VI will get to know Johnny in a way not given to the teacher in the home-room grades. The discipline itself, with its spiraling intellectual demands, will be a medium for approaching and understanding Johnny as he grows up.

The postulate, which must be made a reality in this project, is that the teachers, home-room or special, (a) are equally competent in the profession and (b) are equally devoted to the long-range growth of children in the attributes deemed essential. These attributes are, of course, the cardinal aims of education as agreed upon in advance.

3. In both the home-room and special areas there is a demand for mobilizing new teaching devices and procedures. The experimental sections and schools will call for new curriculums, methods, and evaluating devices. For example, there would not be a "fifth grade arithmetic," but rather an ascending series of facts, skills, problems, and insights arranged systematically and presented in learning sequences that make sense to the maturing mind of the child. This is new, but it does not preclude the determination of "grave equivalences." An essential ingredient will be the increasing participation of the child himself, with concomitant satisfactions.

4. To match the "experimental" groups, there must be control groups led by teachers doing a first-class job under standard conditions.

G. The experimental setups, "mock-ups" and intensive "runs" at New York University are not direct counterparts of the programs in the co-operating centers. Utilizing children "on loan," fully controlling the dynamics of space and grouping, the research team in the School of Education can be flexible and radical in its approaches.

It will be easy to start and stop studies and to vary the factors. Through joint planning and consultation, aided by a constant exchange throughout the three years—all under a single co-ordinated directorship—it is believed that the project will develop organically and harmoniously.

Part Two—Implementation

The second part of the co-operative study proposal is devoted to implementation. It is to be seen that, at this stage, the School of Education was to design an elaborate sequence of experiments covering the findings in mocked-up learning situations and classrooms and to call upon the three co-operating systems by way of large-scale, practical field tests. It was recognized that the schools would deviate from the New York University demonstrations and from each other. Validity was to be secured through matching procedures. Four principles were considered basic:

1. The maturing elementary school child needs recognition as a whole organism. There is some logic in grade classification, grade promotion, and a substantial amount of supervision by one teacher, but there is also a need for elasticity.

2. The home-room teacher concept (for a single grade), which may be built up strongly around a core of reading, writing, speech, and the social studies is needed for Grades I–VI (and perhaps for Grades VII and VIII also), but it may be well to confine it to a portion of the day. This is the "layer-cake" component.

3. The maturing elementary school child is uneven in interests and aptitudes; he needs special attention and opportunity for

acceleration (or deceleration) in mathematics, science, music, arts and crafts, and physical and recreational skills.

4. A longitudinal plan from Grades I–VI will emphasize those aptitudes—often the urgent demands—that reveal themselves early, and under skillful, humane guidance flower beyond what is expected in our standard, full-day grades.

It was understood from the beginning that the selection, supervision, and retraining of teachers would be an important part of the plan. Also the necessity of constructing new curricular units and sequences would soon become apparent, particularly in the ungraded segment. New materials and new methods of grouping and motivating would, in turn, place unusual demands on any program of measurements and evaluations.

The time schedule called for launching the program in two stages. A working party would lay out the plan in the spring and summer of 1957 and work would begin in all four places at the beginning of the school year. The sum of $1,112,000 was requested for a three-year period. It was soon apparent that this sum would not be made available for 1957 and further that, as a matter of policy, the Fund for the Advancement of Education held that "action" research was preferable to the more experimental, matched-group procedure. Actual demonstration under proper test controls would (1) save time, (2) enlist school personnel from the beginning, and (3) demonstrate both the theoretical and practical outcomes. Such considerations were believed to outweigh the more elegant findings of a matched-group study and to ensure a follow-through in co-operating and affiliated school systems, should the plan live up to its early promise.

FURTHER STEPS

In a memorandum to the officials of the Fund (Clarence H. Faust and Alvin C. Eurich), dated May 10, 1957, the writer clarified four points that were being discussed:

1. the relation of the Co-operative Study of Teaching to the school systems involved and to others that may in future follow the proposed plan;

2. the extent to which the study involves an action program;
3. the changes in the school systems of the nation that might follow upon the development and completion of the study;
4. the changes that would take place immediately and in the long-
range program at New York University.

In his reply of May 17, Dr. Eurich listed a series of "general
criteria" which should be met:

1. The commitment to establish new relationships between a
school or department of education and school systems in which
the potential teaching resources of communities are surveyed
and developed, and out of which programs for better utilization of all available teaching resources, better ways of preparation for teaching and related research would grow.
2. The commitment that the purpose of the new relationship is to
enlist and utilize most effectively all teaching talents available
which carries with it the commitment to seek out ways to reduce the ratio of fully trained teachers to students, while at the
same time raising the quality of learning.
3. A commitment to action rather than merely to studies of possibilities.
4. Plans which make the new developments more than mere projects added to the present programs of a school or department
of education but involve comprehensive reorganization of the
teacher training program.

The March joint request seemed to meet criteria (1) and (3), but
there was not contained in it any "commitment to seek out ways to
reduce the ratio of fully trained teachers to students." In fact, in the
early stages of the project there would be needed new personnel in
curriculum organization and teacher supervision. Also the reorganization of the teacher training program was left for future development.

Accordingly, at this time the project as a whole was not granted
financial support. Rather, on June 27, the sum of $15,000 was made
available by the Fund for a working party which would emphasize
these points:

1. New relationships between the New York University School of Education and the school systems.
2. New possibilities for enlisting and utilizing most effectively all teaching talent.
3. Possibilities for a program of action.
4. Possibilities for a long-range program of the School of Education.

The working party, consisting of nineteen members of the staff of the School of Education, two members from Long Beach (David G. Salten and Thomas W. Guilford), two members from Ossining (Charles M. Northrup and David W. Bishop), and three "outside" consultants, held its final session on January 15, 1958. Its report, entitled *Report of Working Party on A Co-operative Study of Teaching and An Experimental Teaching Center* is dated February 25, 1958. A mimeographed document of 134 pages, it was addressed to the Fund for the Advancement of Education and was given a limited circulation.

The report is based squarely on the proposal of March, 1957, which called for an intensive co-operative study of teaching in the elementary school and for establishing an Experimental Teaching Center in the School of Education. The designation of the self-contained classroom as the *unitary grade plan* is used for the first time and is compared to the new Dual Progress Plan. Also the framework of the Experimental Teaching Center is delineated:

In relation to the study, the Experimental Teaching Center will focus on developing new programs in teacher education, supervision, and assistance; utilization of teaching aids; and methods of measuring pupil progress. It is contemplated that research findings at the Experimental Teaching Center will be continuously field-tested in affiliated school systems and that the school systems will, in turn, continuously "feed back" outcomes of field tests as well as needs for further research to the Center.

While the Experimental Teaching Center will receive its initial focus and impetus from the Co-operative Study of Teaching, it will develop a long-range program at the same time it is executing the study. In general, its program will encompass the laboratory studies, field tests of research findings in school systems, and the dissemination of established findings via various communication media and teacher education programs.

The new proposal again listed the seven major "target" areas for the Experimental Teaching Center's research-to-application program as reported above. Once a clear distinction had been made between the unitary grade plan and the Dual Progress Plan, and hypotheses had been set up covering the potential benefits of the latter, the working party was immediately confronted with the problem of *criteria*. The pupil-centered outcomes would be in the learning of subject matter, but this learning was to take place under sound conditions of mental hygiene. It is well known among school people that the word *experiment* elicits images of pale "eggheads" relentlessly rushing toward intellectual achievement. This group, composed of professors and administrators, took a more balanced view. Systematic learning was accepted as the normal expectation and so was the concept of the growing child as a stable personality who, under proper conditions, would be willing to secure adjustment through learning. New learning is as characteristic of the growing child as increments in height, weight, and motor skill. The teacher also was seen as the chief determiner of the effectiveness of the new plan, as of the old.

In academic content, nine results of instruction were identified as significant:

1. Knowledge of basic facts and skills
2. Understanding of concepts; abstract thinking
3. Problem solving employing facts, skills, concepts
4. Creativity within a subject
5. Integration of knowledge of a subject with knowledge of other subjects
6. Attitudes concerning the subject (expecting success or failure, pleasure, frustration, or boredom)
7. Self-direction in acquiring and applying knowledge
8. Level of aspiration concerning mastery of the subject
9. Centrality of interest in the subject (as related to future goals)

Co-ordinately, in terms of personal growth and adjustment, ten goals were set forth as follows:

1. Emotional security (feelings of belongingness and adequacy)
2. Effective and socially acceptable expression of dependency needs
3. Relative absence of nonconstructive "ego defenses" such as withdrawal, overconformity, and rationalization
4. Spontaneity in expressing feelings and attitudes
5. Co-operative attitudes and behavior
6. Knowledge of social rules and expectations
7. Understanding individual differences in role taking as a protection against disillusionment
8. Problem-solving approach to interpersonal relations
9. Interest in acquiring knowledge of self and others
10. Interest in increasing personal efficiency

The items just listed are not mutually independent, nor do they conform to psychological realities. Each one needs to be carefully delineated if reliable tests are to be constructed along such lines. It may be said that these "goals" are really what the advocates of the unitary grade plan believe to be its inherent virtues—virtues in danger of being neglected if pupils do not spend the full day with a single classroom teacher. In short, the ten goals demand clarification and improved testing devices for assessing either "dual progress" or standard grade progress. It is unrealistic to hold that they are essentially a by-product of school practice, for they are traits whose beginnings go back to infancy; they are strongly developed before the age of six. After school age, the child is still bathed in social situations at home and in his neighborhood that may determine the course of his behavior.

It is sure to be difficult to establish real differences *along these lines* between any two plans. All we can hope for is that no defects in character or personality will be causally related to the new plan. For example, against the possible confusion element of having five regular teachers a day (English-social studies, physical education, mathematics, science, and, alternately, arts and music), is the further factor, less frequently referred to, of a *vertical* continuity over the years. Teachers will get to know Johnnie, year after year, as he moves up through the ungraded subjects. The "at-homeness" of the core classroom devoted to English and the social studies—everybody's currency of communication—is supplemented by a sustained continuous interest in his specialized talents. It is these talents that finally may pull Johnnie out of the crowd, for the imaginative, creative aspects of language are easily lost in a classroom where every subject is taught. As most adults have developed interests, skills, and attitudes that mean much to them beyond any *general* social expectation, so every child should have this enriching opportunity in school on a free-choice basis, once the level of his general and special aptitudes has been accurately measured.

Good outcomes in mental hygiene are postulated along this dual line: on the one hand, maximum accomplishment where the culture demands it, and on the other, freedom to achieve—or not to achieve —along lines that mature adults regard as optional for themselves. Thus, reading is not optional; painting is.

To quote from the report of the working party:

In general, members of the working party regarded the rationale for the dual progress plan as sound and novel and the plan worthy of experimental test. Questions were raised as to whether the distinction between cultural imperatives and cultural electives is not actually less absolute than the plan implies. Thus, it was urged that some aspects of science, mathematics, and the arts are cultural imperatives, while some aspects of language arts and social studies are cultural electives. This is of course true. Another question raised called attention to the marked theoretical advantages of individualizing instruction and asked why these advantages were not fully applied to the instruction of English and social studies within the dual progress plan. In answer to the latter query, it was claimed that English and social studies lend themselves especially well to social interaction of age peers (everybody needs to achieve maturity in language) and are thus better suited to the grade plan than to individualized treatment. The postulate is that age-grading or maturity-grading is a useful social invention.

Further, as to the "newness" of the Dual Progress Plan:

One question considered was whether the dual progress plan is the same as the previously tried "platoon system" of instruction. The working party members agreed that it is not, inasmuch as the platoon system was adopted as an administrative convenience rather than on the basis of a theory of education and inasmuch as the platoon system involves moving entire classes from room to room rather than providing individualized instruction in ability-grouped classes for different subjects. Another question discussed was whether the dual progress plan is the junior-high-school departmentalized plan brought down to the elementary grades. Again, the answer was negative, since the dual progress plan has two segments of instruction based on the distinction between cultural imperatives and cultural electives.

The working party developed eight hypotheses as guide lines for the proposed matching study of the unitary grade plan and the Dual Progress Plan, as follows:

Hypotheses

1. Subject-matter learning in mathematics, science, and the arts, measured in terms of scores and ratings, will be greater within the Dual Progress Plan than within the unitary grade plan.

2. The advantages of the Dual Progress Plan over the unitary grade plan for subject-matter learning in mathematics, science, and the arts will be greatest (a) for superior pupils, (b) for pupils in the upper grades, and (c) as measured by the criteria of problem-solving, self-direction, and creativity. (This hypothesis assumes that superior pupils will gain most from nongraded instruction that permits them to advance in subjects unrestricted by the usual grade barrier. It assumes that pupils in the upper grades will be especially advantaged within the Dual Progress Plan because their greater maturity will enable them to make fuller use than younger pupils can make of the special opportunities provided by the plan. It assumes that nongraded, ability-grouped instruction particularly fosters the advanced forms of subject-matter learning represented by problem-solving, self-direction, and creativity.

3. Subject-matter learning in language arts and social studies, measured in terms of means and variability, will be superior in the Dual Progress Plan. (This hypothesis assumes that the selection of teachers of these subjects within the Dual Progress

Plan in terms of their competencies and interests, and the fact that these teachers may concentrate on teaching only these subjects, will favor the Dual Progress Plan over the unitary grade plan.)

4. Pupils' enjoyment of their school experiences will not differ as between the two plans of the Co-operative Study. (This hypothesis is stated in this form since there are some theoretical reasons that favor one plan, other theoretical reasons that favor the other.)

5. Pupils' personality growth will not differ as between the two plans.

6. Teachers' satisfactions will be greater within the Dual Progress Plan than within the unitary grade plan. (This hypothesis is based on the assumption that the greatest difference between the two plans as they affect teachers' satisfactions is related to the assignment of teachers in the Dual Progress Plan to teach just one or two preferred subjects.

7. Individualization of instruction in mathematics, science, and the arts will be greater within the Dual Progress Plan than within the unitary grade plan. (This hypothesis assumes that nongraded, ability-grouped instruction of these subjects will result in greater use of projects in teaching curricular units and will result in more emphasis on self-directed study.)

8. Teachers' utilization of opportunities for in-service training will not differ as between the two plans.

MODIFICATIONS OF THE PLAN

The practical experience of a year and a half in Long Beach and two years in Ossining throws some light on the validity of these hypotheses. These effects are described in Chapters 6 and 7 but it can be said at this point that children enter into the new program with zeal.

Had the report of the working party been fully accepted and supported as a *modus operandi* for the research program to follow, it would now be appropriate to show exactly how, on a controlled basis, the two plans were to be compared and measured in the two school systems. Instead I will pull out of the report only the findings and recommendations that were carried through to the "action-research" program presently to be described.

The first departure was the recommendation that the study begin at Grade III, instead of Grade I as theory demanded. The group was uncertain as to the effects of the daily shifting on the personality development of six- and seven-year-olds; this was a factor. More weighty perhaps was the question of the readiness of these young children for any kind of specialization. Also there was a need to get started. It would be difficult to measure the special aptitude of beginning pupils, to set up a new program, and to prepare teachers for such work. In future these latter considerations need not be decisive if it appears that six-year-olds are ready to begin the "vertical" approach to mathematics and science. Doubtless some pupils are ready for the dual system by school age; they may already possess incipient concepts of number, size, proportion, and computation which need systematizing. For six years they have been learning fast: their oral vocabularies and sentence usages are impressive. In the first grade we find pictures and mock-ups of planes, rockets, and spaceships that indicate a strong interest in the events of the day. Is it then too early to introduce, gently but consistently, some concepts of what makes things go, as well as a familiarity with their outward forms?

In any case, the theoretical position is clear and, in future, should be subjected to a practical tryout. The time to introduce a systematic approach is at the beginning stages of learning; by first grade it is already late. If the defects in science and the arts are less conspicuous than those in English, it is because so few parents are able to make distinctions outside the core areas. To remedy the situation in the first grade, or the first stages of science and art instruction, calls for a radical change in methodology. Long ago G. Stanley Hall surveyed the contents of children's minds on first entering school. We need such studies today, but they should not be confined to content. Attitudes, interests, drives, and complexes should be analyzed beyond any simple findings in vocabulary or general information. Some clues as to further learning or premature deceleration may be discerned early. A fateful discovery every child has to make is that not everything told him is true. As he learns to read—as previously through listening and watching—he will be subjected to a mighty flood of propaganda and commercial pressure. How soon should teachers begin the unending business of preparing the child to ask for facts, to weigh arguments, to withhold judgment, to bring to bear on any problem he can conceptually formulate his own ability, small though it be, to approach a solution? This is what education is all about—not to impose solutions and finalities, but to offer data, experiences, methods, and evaluative procedures that the child progressively will appropriate to himself as a means of coming into better terms with life as he lives it and with the future. These stages of maturity are not sealed off from one another. Who has not overheard in wonder children and youth discuss complex human relations, unconscious of the delicacy of their observations? Under the right circumstances, what they have is what many adults have lost through fear and anxiety, namely, an unfettered, objective approach to the subject at hand. In intellectual affairs, immaturity is less of a handicap than rigidity. Magic and superstition, for example—devices of demonstrable value in a primitive world—are not today akin to growth; rather they resemble the spoilage of something that, before infection, was promising and fine.

Consequently, we need to follow in children not only the course of mental acquisition but also of straight thinking; not only skills but creations; not only acceptance but criticism. From facts freely fitted and studied emerge new facts—outcomes, as it were, of a new frame of reference, leading to new generalizations; these in turn demand new value systems and new loyalties. As we turn from one historical epoch to another, or from one cultural system to another the same "facts," even in science, take on a different meaning. This phenomenon is not entirely lost upon the child, for whom taboos may preclude learning.

To return to the report of the working party. It was proposed that the first tryout of the Dual Progress Plan not extend beyond the elementary grades. This would yield some comparable measures between the old system and the new with respect to the adequacy of pupil preparation for the specialized work of the junior high school. (Actually, after one year, the plan was extended to Grades VII and VIII.)

The working party had devoted considerable thought to ways of controlling the "nonexperimental" factors in the proposed matched group experiment. While not incorporated into the action research as finally developed, these variables are of interest. They show what the committee regarded as items of consequence in any teaching situation—items of such significance as to weaken any conclusions that disregard them. With some revision, they might still be useful to a school system prepared, on an "all-out" basis, to compare its existing plan with the Dual Progress Plan. Thirteen sets of variables were identified, together with the particular aspects regarded as essential:

1. Financial support
2. Teacher competency and teacher time spent
3. Availability of specialist consultants
4. The ability and achievement of pupils
5. The pupil-teacher ratio
6. Materials, equipment, and teaching devices
7. Instructional time for each subject
8. Emphasis on each subject
9. The "extracurricular activities" of pupils
10. Beyond an initial, transitional training period for teachers on the Dual Progress Plan, equivalent in-service training
11. Communication of information on the study, the hypotheses under study excepted
12. Teacher motivation and morale
13. Community acceptance

Teachers in the matched unitary grade plan, the one to which they were accustomed, were to be free to use any materials or methods of the Dual Progress Plan as long as they did not appropriate the defining features of the latter: (graded and ungraded segments, assignment of teachers to only one or two subjects, nongraded advancement of pupils in specialized subjects, team teaching in the nongraded segment).

Subsequently, six chapters of the report were devoted to the setting up of a controlled experiment designed to test the basic hypotheses and to minimize the influence of the "nonexperimental" variables. These detailed procedures need not concern us now. The main consideration is this: the working party was able to agree upon matching measures with respect to such factors as pupil equivalence, teacher selection, class scheduling, and the time to be allotted to each subject. The recommended instruction time in minutes per week is given below:

Subject	Minutes per Week
Language arts and social studies	600
Mathematics	200
Science	200
Music	100
Arts and crafts	100
Physical education	150
Opening exercises, planning	75
Library, audio-visual, etc.	75
Total	1,500

The chief departure from the current schedules in Long Beach and Ossining was in the allotment of 200 minutes per week to science—about twice that under the existing unitary grade plan. Also, the global allowance of 600 minutes to English and social studies would permit flexibility as between the two subjects.

Some knotty problems were foreseen. Since it was thought that the language arts and social studies would require about two clock hours, it was clear that a teacher could teach two sections. To quote from the report:

True, she would be responsible for approximately 60 pupils. However, if she were prepared to teach, say, both third and fourth grades, she might stay with one class a second year and take on one new class each year. This would mean she would need to get acquainted with only 30 new pupils each year. All in all, it was anticipated that the teacher of the graded segment would normally prefer this assignment to that of the regular teacher within the unitary grade plan.

In the dual progress plan, teachers of mathematics, science, music, arts and crafts, and physical education would teach a succession of classes each day. In the course of a week, the number of pupils they instructed would be large. Estimates based on the proportion of the pupils' time spent with each subject were as follows: science, 150 pupils; mathematics, 150; music, and arts and crafts, 300; and physical education, 200. Obviously, getting to know the pupils individually would be difficult. However, there are several factors that would make these numbers less threatening than they at first appear. Specialist teachers in the unitary grade plan—in music, in art, in science at Long Beach, and in physical education—now teach even larger numbers of pupils. Also, within the nongraded or "longitudinal" segment of the dual progress plan, a teacher of one of these subjects may instruct the same pupil during two or more successive years. Further, it was noted that, while the unitary grade plan teacher has only 25 to 30 pupils to instruct, she must know them and their work in all subjects of the curriculum. The teacher in the dual progress plan may concentrate her attention primarily on knowing her pupils' talents, interests, and accomplishments in just one subject.

It was held that under either plan the equivalent of one class hour per day be reserved to the teacher for consultation and other non-teaching purposes. Under the Dual Progress Plan this schedule was suggested:

Language arts and social studies	2 classes of 120 minutes each per day
Mathematics	6 classes of 40 minutes each per day
Science	6 classes of 40 minutes each per day
Arts and crafts	6 classes of 40 minutes each per day
Physical education	8 classes of 30 minutes each per day

The actual schedules set up in Long Beach and Ossining during the first year (1958–1959) of the study are given in Chapters 6 and 7. All the schedules are regarded as strenuous by the teachers themselves. Still, each teacher is devoting her time to her favorite subject matter in which she has undertaken special training. Under the standard plan the classroom teacher "watches and waits" while specialist teachers in music and art (sometimes science) take over the classroom. This does not seem to allow her either an effective teaching or rest period.

For the co-operative study of teaching the working party distinguished six types of in-service training:

1. general orientation of the faculties of the co-operating school systems to the study;

2. summer workshops for teachers and specialist consultants of the study on curricular materials and teaching methods;
3. workshops on instruction of each subject in the curriculum;
4. conferences between specialist consultants and teachers;
5. in-service courses for credit, on teaching particular subjects or on topics related to instruction, such as child development or mental hygiene;
6. university courses for improving subject-matter knowledge.

The remaining eight chapters of the report of the working party concentrated on the research procedures to be set up in the Experimental Teaching Center in order, through a careful analysis of data, to come out with a clean-cut account of the effectiveness of the two plans under study. Since the data to be secured for the action-research (later agreed upon) differ from the matched group requirements, I need not report further upon the proposals of the working party. Rather, in the chapters that follow there will be presented an account of the procedures, tests, and preliminary findings bearing on the first two years of the co-operative study, together with a brief description of the Experimental Teaching Center.

6

THE FIRST TWO YEARS OF THE
DUAL PROGRESS PLAN
AT LONG BEACH, NEW YORK

After careful consideration, the Board of Education of Long Beach on June 24, 1958, approved a three-year trial run of the Dual Progress Plan, with the understanding that its "classroom use" would begin in February, 1959. The first half of the school year 1958–1959 was devoted to planning and preparation.

While many of the problems of curriculum, administration, and consultation germane to setting up the new plan will be discussed in Chapter 8, it will be helpful to describe briefly what actually took place in the co-operating school systems.

The account which follows is based on the reports of Dr. Gilbert M. Trachtman, research co-ordinator.

The Long Beach City School District includes the city of Long Beach and some adjacent areas in Nassau County, New York. The population of the City is about 25,000 during the school year. Most of the employed persons commute to New York City. The school system serves about 5,000 pupils, with approximately 2,700 in the elementary schools, 800 in the junior school (Grades VII and VIII), and 1,500 in the senior high school.

The school tax rate is $41 per thousand dollars. In 1958 the system had a budget of $3,960,999, or an income of about $786 per pupil.

The schools consist of the senior high school, the junior school, and four elementary schools—East, West, Central, and Lido. Lido Elementary School and the junior school are housed separately in one building.

The Long Beach system operates on a 6–2–4 plan, with considerable variation in curriculum from school to school.

In September, 1958, the pupils and teachers of the four elementary schools were distributed as follows:

| | *September, 1958* | | | |
	East	*West*	*Central*	*Lido*
Total No. of Pupils	650	476	899	597
Pupils, Grades III–VI	373	284	535	346
Classes (Classroom Teachers), Grades III–VI	16	11	20	11
Music Specialists	2PT	3PT	3PT	3PT
Art Specialists	1PT	1FT	1FT	1FT
Science Specialists	1FT		2FT	1FT
Physical Education Specialists	1FT	1FT	1FT	1FT
Reading Specialists	1FT	1FT	1FT	1FT
Speech Specialists	1PT	1PT	1FT	1PT
Foreign Language Specialists	1FT			

(FT = Full Time; PT = Part Time)

Dr. Trachtman succinctly describes the preparatory stages:

In the early fall, literature was distributed to all teachers explaining the philosophy and goals of the Plan, and subsequent discussions were held at several district faculty meetings. A teachers' advisory group was organized consisting of two teacher representatives selected by the faculty of each school; it functioned basically as an elementary school committee. The group met periodically with the Research Co-ordinator, intermittently with members of the New York University Experimental Teaching Center, and, on occasion, with principals and the Superintendent. In October, when Ossining had already begun implementation of the plan, the entire group made a field trip to the Ossining schools to observe the plan in action as an aid to our own implementation plans.

The in-service program for the various DPP subject areas was initiated in October, 1958, and although the program was conducted on a voluntary basis, 90% of the teachers involved enrolled for these courses. The course leaders met periodically with Professor Glen Heathers, Director of the Experimental Teaching Center, to develop co-ordination between Ossining and Long Beach and among the various subject areas.

A testing program for grades 3–7 was conducted late in September and the following tests were administered:

Stanford Achievement Test (grades 3, 4, 5, 6, 7)

Educational Testing Service, STEP Science and Mathematics Tests, Level 4a (grades 4, 5, 6, 7)

Educational Testing Service, STEP Science and Mathematics Tests, Level 3a (grades 6, 7)

Science Research Associates, Junior Inventory (grades 4, 5, 6, 7)

Science Research Associates, "What I Like to Do" (grades 4, 5, 6, 7)

New York University's original test, "Solving Puzzles" (grades 3, 4, 5, 6, 7)

These tests were not utilized by the school system at the time, but the results were turned over to the Experimental Teaching Center to form a body of data to be used as a baseline in evaluating the DPP. Data from these tests, however, were available for the January regrouping necessary for the initial implementation of DPP.

At the start of the Dual Progress Plan there would be needed a corps of teachers prepared to teach in the graded section (English and/or the social studies) or in one of the specializations. (Some teachers could spend a half day in the graded segment and a half day in a specialization, but, except in a large school system, this would raise scheduling problems.)

In Long Beach the teacher assignments in the specialized areas were determined by the principal of the school, although the teachers were consulted and a choice was usually agreed upon. Since reliable measures of art or music ability were not available, the pupils were grouped in these areas in terms of grade placement. At first, the pupils also followed an ability grouping within each grade with respect to mathematics and science. The decisions on grouping were made by a team consisting of the principal, a classroom teacher, the school psychologist, and, frequently, the guidance counselor for the elementary school. The Experimental Teaching Center assisted at all points.

Only a slight augmentation of the teaching staff (in specialized subject matter) was necessary to inaugurate the new plan.

The Teachers Advisory Group continued to function as the plan went into operation in February, 1959. The emphasis was on curriculum, the research co-ordinator assisting with the numerous problems in administration.

At the end of the scholastic year 1958–1959 the research co-ordinator emphasized these items:

1. The teachers were specializing in various subject matters.
2. The pupils' daily pattern consisted of a two-hour "core" period in English and social studies.
3. Mathematics and science were offered daily in 40-minute periods, music and art in 40-minute periods on alternate days.
4. The academic gains of the pupils were similar to those of a standard school year.
5. There was no evidence of unfavorable effects on the personality of pupils.

Looking back on the first year at Long Beach, Dr. Trachtman reports:

In summary, with only the initial steps of implementation completed, the DPP seems to provide exciting possibilities for improving the quality of elementary education. We have already seen some indications in Long Beach of the tremendous potential inherent in this approach to elementary education. However, no plan can be more effective than its structure and organization allow and there are still many mechanical and administrative problems to be ironed out.

We must view all "testimonials" as falling far short of research requirements. They represent opinions and attitudes, habits, emotional conditioning; the immediacy of personal experience has weighted the responses. Teachers, pupils, and parents may, on occasion, react *too* favorably to something new and untried, if only to get away from something they regard as inadequate. When this phenomenon is accompanied by special zeal, we have the well-known halo effect. With this *caveat* fully in view, let us look briefly at the reactions to the Dual Progress Plan during its first trial year.

TEACHERS' REACTIONS

These informed reactions are generalizations that reveal "growing pains." They may, or may not, persist as the new plan develops. In future, it should be possible to foresee some of the difficulties and to take steps accordingly.

(1) *It took hard work to get the new plan underway.*

Comment: Perhaps this reaction is to be expected. The program is more than a standard year organized in a new fashion; it is a trial run and it is, to some extent, experimental. The situation is comparable to the field testing of a newly designed automobile, in that the whole operation is loaded with testing devices and a generally critical approach. Teachers are not accustomed to assuming this combined role of teacher-demonstrator-evaluator. Eventually there should be some relief from clerical work and academic chores. More first-rate materials in textbooks, study manuals, apparatus, examinations, films, and the like, will be made available. The request of core teachers for an "extra free period a day" was certainly reasonable; as of 1959–1960 almost all DPP teachers had two of the eight periods free of assigned teaching duties. However, many of the teachers in mathematics and science stated they had more free time under the plan than previously. The suggestion that clerical help be obtained from parents or high school students is of interest.

(2) *A further definition of homeroom duties is needed.*

Comment: Conceivably some teachers could teach in both the graded and ungraded segments (there are examples of this), but increasingly, with an adequate teacher supply made available from the colleges, a choice would be made between the two. English and the social studies are to be taught by persons who know these subjects thoroughly; after all, the total grade placement of a pupil depends on his achievement in this comprehensive area. However, the teaching of two long core classes a day needs to be cushioned by free time, new curricular materials, and teacher aides. Some core teachers will prefer to teach pupils in a single grade, although the assumption is that the core specialist will be prepared to teach at all elementary grade levels. Also the business of marking and keeping attendance needs further study.

(3) *On the whole, homogeneous grouping gets a favorable response.*

Comment: The narrower range of ability in the classroom permits a more orderly pace setting; there is less danger of concentrating on the needs of a small cluster of pupils, to the virtual exclusion of the others. Although disciplinary problems may appear at any level of student talent, they are more prevalent among slow learners who may progress from frustration to failure to delinquency. We assess not only a pupil's progress but his character on the basis of his willingness (or ability) to follow fixed curricular demands. School failure, if we are not watchful about it, may become to the child an inadmissible failure that calls for drastic diversionary measures. Of these latter, truancy, rebellion, and delinquency are the most common, although a slow withdrawal into a private world of phantasy is an equally dangerous outcome. The answer lies in adjusting curricular demands to the measured potentiality of the child; it calls for a new, informed magnanimity toward the slow learners. Are we not all *slow learners* in some respects?

(4) *The new plan appears attractive to teachers of mathematics and science.*

Comment: Apparently, with the aid of the science consultant, these teachers have improved the course of study, although there is still much to be done. While it may be postulated that the new emphasis on science will be hampered unless adequate facilities are available, this should not be taken to mean that a school must go "overboard" in its expenditures. In fact, the same expert teachers and supervisors who develop specialized science curriculum can show how to maintain the course, year by year, without a huge stockpile of scientific apparatus. To get first things first in science, is to guard jealously the progression in abstraction through the utilization of mathematics and other symbolic processes.

(5) *In a given year, it is more difficult to know pupils intimately under the Dual Progress Plan.*

Comment: The comparison is, of course, with previous experience in a self-contained classroom. It is a *teachers'* observation made against the background assumption that each teacher in the elementary grades should know the pupils well, even if this means that the contacts of the pupils with other teachers is thereby restricted. The balance of values will need to be scrutinized in terms of pupil learning and pupil adjustment. In a half day devoted to English and the social studies, the teacher of the future, *experienced in this core situation,* may discover that these disciplines carry the main weight of cultural communication. Nevertheless, opportunities for teacher conferences across all subject matter lines should be encouraged as an adjunct to the regular teaching periods. The problem is different in the ungraded segments. There it should be feasible to continue the contact with the same teachers over a period of years. In fact, an outright teacher team plan might extend straight through from Grade I to Grade VI, or to Grade VIII if physical conditions permit. Hence the *total* contact of a pupil with a teacher, up through the grades, is not markedly diminished; rather, the time spread is different.

(6) *The marking system needs further study.*

Comment: The questions of the teachers indicate the need for a thorough overhaul of marking and reporting systems. This is recognized in the co-operative schools and the Experimental Teaching Center, and new systems are being tried out. (Could we not reserve the term *grades* for the annual stairsteps, and use *marks* for the numerical or descriptive reports of pupil progress?) For example, "Does an A in a high group mean the same thing as an A in a low group?" The underlying question is, what has an A in a subject *ever* meant in the elementary schools? What should it mean? Perhaps the new plan will underscore the need for a new approach to marking and evaluating schemes, varying from practically no objective information to rigid test-based scores or rankings. At this point, I can offer only a few postulates for systematic study:

(a) At appropriate times, and particularly at the close of the school year, there should be made available to teachers, counselors, and parents *two* marks, one based on comparative achievement standards and the other on objective measures of the pupil's ability. The first mark shows where the pupil stands in *achievement,* regardless of his age, mental ability, special aptitudes, or interests. Achievement quotients, on the other hand, are ratios of performance to general and/or special ability. Presumably parents will be able to benefit by information of both kinds. Rough standards can be expressed in centiles on *grade* norms for the core and in centiles on *age* norms for the special subjects. A single parents' meeting should serve to clarify the meaning of these terms. Thus the work of Mary, a bright ten-year-old in the fourth grade, might be reported as follows (Table I):

Mark 2, can be styled "effort." The hypothetical Mary, on the basis of her work in Grade IV and under the specialized teachers,

TABLE I

	Mark 1: Achievement (Centiles)	Mark 2: Achievement Quotient (AQ)
The Grade IV core (English and social studies)	85	70
For age 10:		
Mathematics	40	80
Science	60	80
Music	10	100
Art	95	130

emerges as follows: She is doing excellent work in the core, and is solidly established in her grade: she will be found in the top section of either a two- or three-section grade. Nevertheless her Achievement Quotient (AQ) of 70 indicates that her ability (in this case, all-round intelligence), warrants a higher achievement in the core than she has shown. (A mark of "100" in AQ is *average*.) Mary does well in art, standing in the upper one-twentieth of ten-year-olds; here she is showing a zeal for work that exceeds her group. Mary is slightly below average in mathematics and should do better; while above average in science, there, too, she could do better. Since in music she works as hard as can be expected (AQ, 100) and still stands near the bottom among her age group, it can be said that music is not her forte; *if* the tests of aptitude, achievement, and interest continue to show this deficiency, there is not much point in pressing Mary to meet fixed standards in music. It would be better to build up her other deep-seated abilities, while devoting her musical experience to appreciation.

These two types of marks call for careful testing and evaluation of the pupil's work. At the same time, the objective measures could be turned over to teacher aides for administration, analysis, and report. Also *Mark 1* can be related to norms for the school system and the state, as well as to national standards if the latter are available.

And, now, back to the question, Who gets an *A*? Under the scheme just outlined (it is not new), *nobody!* Grade norms having been compiled over the years—and revised, hopefully upward—what happens in the grade can be carefully evaluated and compared. The parent will know from the report where Mary stands in the grade and, therefore, where she stands with respect to the likelihood of continued success and promotion. The other marks, equally revealing, round out the picture of Mary's specialized accomplishment and zeal for study.

All such reports are *cumulative*. It would be misleading to stake everything on a particular school year, with its particular cluster of teachers and pupil associates. Moreover, there are the factors of stability, personality, and physical development to be considered; there is the factor of *creativity*, so poorly measured by most tests.

It should suffice, *in the report to parents,* simply to list observed strengths, weaknesses, and interests in health and physical education (marks appear to be out of order in this field). The aim is to suggest nutritional or medical attention, where indicated, and to give clues as to out-of-school ways to build up the health and recreational features of the child's life.

The teacher's internal record of the child's talents, achievements, and behavioral responses is a technical and professional matter. Similarly, the counselor's records will stress personality items. All taken together will form the basis of a series of parent conferences, individually or in groups. It would add to the usefulness of reports and conferences if each child were allowed to give his reactions to a partially structured set of questions, and also, briefly, to "freewheel."

TEACHERS' ANSWERS TO THREE QUESTIONS

How do the teachers react to the Dual Progress Plan? The answers to three questions are pertinent:

1. "Indicate your feeling about the fact that, in the Dual Progress Plan, teachers specialize in teaching the children one subject area."

	In favor (%)	Don't care (%)	Opposed (%)
September, 1958 (preview)	70	14	16
June, 1960 (1½ years of DPP)	71	14	15

2. "Indicate your over-all reaction to the Dual Progress Plan as a way of conducting instruction in the elementary schools."

	In favor (%)	Don't care (%)	Opposed (%)
September, 1958	69	7	24
June, 1960	57	1	41

3. "If you were given the opportunity, would you choose to return to teaching in the 'self-contained' classroom plan?"

	Would return to SCC	No preference	Would not return to SCC
June, 1960	46%	9%	45%

THE RESPONSE OF PUPILS

On June 11, 1959, all the pupils present in Grades III-VI wrote twenty-minute essays; they were requested "to write down all the things that say what you think about the dual progress plan and how you feel about it." (The teachers were asked to refrain from any suggestions.) Lois Beilin and Richard Anderson have analyzed the results; they are summarized in Table II.

TABLE II

PERCENTAGE OF LONG BEACH STUDENTS EXPRESSING FAVORABLE AND UN-FAVORABLE ATTITUDES TOWARD THE DUAL PROGRESS PLAN BY GRADE AND ABILITY GROUP (BEILIN AND ANDERSON).

Ability Group	Grade				
	3rd	4th	5th	6th	Total
High Ability					
% favorable	67	49	58	61	59
% part favorable, part unfavorable	15	20	30	22	22
% unfavorable	18	31	12	17	19

Average Ability

% favorable	46	56	41	68	52
% part favorable, part unfavorable	19	25	29	22	24
% unfavorable	35	19	30	10	24

Low Ability

% favorable	80	53	57	67	64
% part favorable, part unfavorable	8	22	12	21	16
% unfavorable	12	25	31	12	20

Total

% favorable	60	53	51	66	58
% part favorable, part unfavorable	15	22	25	22	21
% unfavorable	25	25	24	12	21

Note: The data in this table are based on the responses of 1,281 students.

As indicated previously, we must discount the validity of all such responses—they are simply indicators of trends. It would appear, at least, that prior fears regarding the attitudes of third-graders (60 per cent favorable) and of the slow learners (64 per cent favorable) may be unwarranted.

Beilin and Anderson undertook an intensive analysis of the 371 papers of two high-ability and two low-ability groups in each of the four grades, with the following results regarding specific features of the plan:

1. Sixty-six per cent of the 258 pupils mentioning this aspect enjoyed changing classes.
2. Eighty-six per cent of the 64 pupils commenting on specialist teaching believed they learned more from specialized teachers, and they found the instruction more interesting.
3. Eighty-nine per cent of the 27 students who commented on grouping on the basis of ability favored it.
4. All 47 students (largely in the high-ability groups in the fifth and sixth grades) who mentioned preparation for junior and senior high school preferred the Dual Progress Plan.

5. Of 40 students who mentioned science, 82 per cent preferred the Dual Progress Plan.

Among the complaints most often listed was the lack of a private desk (should desks of a twin type be provided in the homerooms?) and overlapping between teachers in assigning homework.

THE RESPONSE OF PARENTS

Anderson and Beilin have analyzed the reactions of the Long Beach parents to the first half-year of the Dual Progress Plan. Ninety-five anonymous responses to a questionnaire mailed to 254 parents were received in June and July of 1959. This sampling covered all schools, Grades III–VI. The results are shown in Table III.

TABLE III

PERCENTAGE OF NINETY-FIVE LONG BEACH PARENTS WITH CHILDREN IN GRADES THREE THROUGH SIX DISPLAYING FAVORABLE AND UNFAVORABLE ATTITUDES TOWARD THE DUAL PROGRESS PLAN AND ITS MAJOR FEATURES (1959).

	% Strongly in favor	% Moderately in favor	% No preference	% Moderately opposed	% Strongly opposed
Q.1 The DPP in general	36	38	5	11	10
Q.2 All teachers specialists	53	33	1	4	9
Q.3 Ability-grouped classes	67	23		5	5
Q.4 Child having different teachers	53	31	1	7	8
Q.5 Promotion on *core* progress only	25	17	1	27	30
Q.6 Nongraded advancement in mathematics, science, arts & crafts, music	58	27		9	6

A separate analysis was made of the responses of parents who indicated an over-all unfavorable attitude toward the Dual Progress Plan in order to uncover reasons for their opposition. Table III shows that, though the proportions are not as high as in the whole group, at least 50 per cent of the parents who indicated over-all opposition to the DPP (Question No. 1) favored specialist teaching, ability grouping, departmentalization, and nongraded advancement. As in the case of the group of parents as a whole, most of the parents generally unfavorable toward the plan were opposed to having promotion depend entirely upon marks in the core. Seventy-four per cent of the parents favored the Dual Progress Plan in general. Of those who reacted unfavorably to the plan as a whole, the principal opposition was to these three features: all teachers specialists; different teachers for the child; a promotion based on the "core" program only.

Certainly promotion only on the basis of English and the social studies is strange to the parents; it may strike them as unfair. Part of the blocking may be semantic: grade *promotion* has always been largely based on these two subject-matter areas plus skill in arithmetic. (It is to be doubted that the self-contained classroom either holds back or accelerates pupils except in terms of reading comprehension.) Conventional "self-contained" arithmetic simply does not involve the basic ingredients of a proper grade classification. As for physical education, art, or music, there never has been much attention paid to these as determiners of grade placement.

In future, if science were to be accepted as a genuine cultural imperative, a further shift in the organization of the elementary schools would be indicated. As long as science is regarded as having no fundamental bearing on *every* field of human thought, the imperative is lacking. Thus, parents who want mathematics and science transferred to the core as a part of the grade system, may really be ahead of the times. Most of our American leaders of thought are *literary* in their background: they downgrade science in such fields as psychology, sociology, economics, government, ethics, and religion; to them an emphasis on social science is often a dangerous business. It is, indeed, this cluster of prejudices that lies at the center of the bitterness toward John Dewey: what alarms the critics most is his "outrageous" proposal to apply the tools and structures of thought to regions of thought and behavior considered "out of bounds."

SUPPLEMENT IN 1960

I can now briefly supplement the 1959–1960 data reported above. The new data were obtained from seventy-seven teachers divided as follows:

Language arts and social studies	38
Mathematics or science	23
Art, or music, or physical education	16
Total	77

Two-thirds of the teachers favor the testing of the plan in the Long Beach school system and about the same per cent are glad to take part in the plan.

The following explanatory paragraph and table (Michel Radomisli; June, 1960) is of particular interest, inasmuch as it reveals a dichotomy of preference to some extent consistent with the theory of the plan. A majority confirms the validity of regarding language arts, social studies, and physical education as grade-related, while only about half the group feel the same way about mathematics, science, art, and music. Still, up to two years previously none of these teachers had the experience of teaching or observing either mathematics or science as a specialized subject in the elementary school. In art and music, having had the experience of specialized supervision combined with "self-contained" teaching at a grade level, one-half the group favor retaining the grade level. To quote:

The plan provides for grade-level and non-grade-level instruction depending on subject area. Teachers were asked to indicate their opinion on how 7 different subject areas should be taught. The table shows the percentage of teachers who preferred grade-level instruction for each subject area.

Only 57 per cent of the teachers reported that the plan provided "well" or "acceptably" with respect to reporting student progress to parents or for conferences with parents. As indicated previously, the

PERCENTAGE OF TEACHERS PREFERRING GRADE-LEVEL
INSTRUCTION FOR SEVEN SUBJECT AREAS

Teacher group	Lang. arts	Soc. stud.	Math.	Science	Art	Music	P.E.
Lang. arts & S.S.	91	87	41	33	49	46	69
Math., science	86	90	46	41	50	50	80
Art, music, P.E.	86	79	61	50	57	56	71
All teachers	88	85	49	41	52	51	73

procedures will need careful study. Certainly the teachers have the needed data, especially in the graded segment. For the ungraded subjects it may be that adequate conferences with parents will have to wait upon cumulative reports showing progress from year to year.

Many teachers felt that the new plan did not provide adequately for nonclassroom activities such as assemblies, band, library, and field trips. However, more recently the plan has been shown to be flexible in this respect. My general point of view is that some of these activities have made unreasonable inroads upon the small amount of school time available for systematic learning. The question revolves about a better *integration* of "activities" and abstract learning.

Ninety-one per cent of the teachers stated the Dual Progress Plan provided "exceptionally well" or "adequately" for the gifted pupils, and 81 per cent placed the Dual Progress Plan in these categories in regard to average pupils. However, only one-third of the group gave this approval to the plan with respect to the "slow learners." Of course a prime purpose of the plan is to remove restrictions on the rate and depth of learning in all subjects. Since most observers agree that, in the past, the chief neglect has been in teaching the gifted pupils, it is gratifying to have this tentative expression of teacher confidence: similarly, for the average pupils.

What, then, is wrong with the teaching of the "slow learners"? (It should be noted that none of these responses is comparative as between the self-contained classroom and the Dual Progress Plan. The question asked was this: "How well does the Dual Progress Plan provide for academic learning by pupils of different levels of ability?") At Ossining I have observed the teaching (under the plan) of pupils low in ability and have been impressed by the lack of tension in the class and the apparent concentration of the pupils on subject matter adjusted to their ability. It does not seem that the plan is *inherently* unsuitable for the slow learners; in fact, the whole concept of grading is designed to remove undue pressure on such pupils. Similarly, in the specialized vertical segments, the slow learners are expected to go at a slower pace and to turn to the descriptive aspects of subject matter—to nonabstract activities, for example—in so far as their mental status would otherwise postulate *confusion*. It is a matter of degree, for all students are capable of some abstract thinking. Is it possible that some of the teachers are unwilling to let slow-learning pupils remain in these lower categories of learning? What a strange paradox it would be, if teachers long accused of *neglecting* the theoretical for the concrete, even for bright pupils, should now shift to an *unreasonable* demand for abstract performance on the part of the dull!

Of course, there may be other limiting factors in the plan. We have seen that it is, indeed, more difficult to schedule "activities" under the plan and it is these activities that most easily fill the day for pupils who shun abstract formulations. Since the pupils are sectioned on the basis of aptitude, in the lower sections there is, or should be, an opportunity for meeting acceptable standards in handwriting, spelling, grammar, simple computation, and other memoriter accomplishments, not to mention a more meticulous approach to manners and customs. Responses in behavior and character can be nicely distributed along the whole range of mental ability *provided* neither the school's nor the parents' ambition identifies "goodness" with scholastic success in a uniform program. Under the Dual Progress Plan, the bright achieve and the dull achieve, but not in relation to a fixed standard for all pupils.

This observation applies with equal force to the teachers' opinion of the ease with which the plan permits "teaching the relations of your subject area to other areas of the curriculum (integration)," and to its effectiveness in "meeting the emotional needs of pupils generally." In both cases about two-thirds of the teachers were negative.

For reasons developed elsewhere in this book, I am unable to feel much concern about superficial "integration"; outside of school there is a surfeit of demands on the child. His hard lines of insight and proficiency are blurred as he responds to constant stimulation through casual reading, motion pictures, radio, and television. The question is, what does he have by way of useful transfer from one field to another? A child cannot go far in science without an interplay between science and language; there is a "built-in" integration. Much of art and music also depends on insights into human nature and the social structure. Art is culturally determined. The integration we seek may be below the surface of observable daily tasks, and it may take a span of years for its fruition.

As noted, about two-thirds of the teachers report that the plan did not properly provide for the emotional needs of pupils. Fortunately, the testers have prepared a follow-up question that relates the answers (a) to the grade placement of the pupils and (b) to their status as gifted, average, or slow. Perhaps the resulting analysis reveals where the trouble lies. Thus, the teachers report the plan is adequate for meeting emotional needs, in these percentages: third grade, 7 per cent; fourth grade, 39 per cent; fifth grade, 57 per cent; sixth grade, 59 per cent. It was adequate also for gifted pupils, 76 per cent; for average pupils, 52 per cent; for slow learners, 13 per cent. Since in studies of child psychology there has not been noted any remarkable spurt in growth or maturity as between the ages of 9 and 10 (they are relatively stable years for both sexes), the difference in the observed adaptability as between Grades III and IV is more likely related to the organization of the classroom or of the school itself. The question remains, what really happened in the classrooms of third-grade pupils to elicit this negative rating?

Similarly, we need to analyze the situations which led three-fourths of the teachers to report that "conduct or discipline problems" were more frequent under the Dual Progress Plan. (A series of external observations of pupil behavior indicates that most of the disturbances could be classified as "talking," "noisiness," and "moving about"; clearly these are not reliable indices of the underlying causes.) For example, the proportion of teachers who felt their teaching under the Dual Progress Plan had improved (over the previous self-contained classroom plan) was exactly three to one; for the areas of language arts, social studies, mathematics, and science, it was four to one. However, the teachers of art, music, and physical education—a total of twelve—gave a slight edge to the older teaching plan. We may surmise that differences here are somewhat overlaid by the fact that teachers in the latter scholastic areas had long enjoyed some recognition of their specialized subject matter. Hence, it seems legitimate to ascertain the probable causes of the disciplinary upsets—their character, severity, and, above all, their progress toward a rational resolution. In these analyses, to be pursued further, we must take care not to equate good behavior with meekness or conformity; acts of aggression or arrogance that spring from insecurity are another matter, as is any tendency to withdraw from reality. A resolution of the important behavior questions raised by these teachers will call for carefully constructed measures of testing and observing.

On the basis of a small number of blanks returned by parents (78 out of 354 sent out) in July, 1960, it is possible to supplement the data already reported for 1958–1959. The first six questions are the same as before, and, on the whole, the responses confirm the first-year impressions. Thus the *general* response to the Dual Progress Plan, which was 74 per cent favorable in 1959, is 85 per cent favorable in 1960. The table that follows permits an item-by-item comparison of percentages.

With respect to Grades III and IV, the sampling (N = 29) shows a favorable response of 96 per cent—contrary to predictions of the attitudes of the parents of the younger children. Two-thirds of the parents (representing all four grades) believe their children are learning more under the new plan. Eighty per cent report that their children enjoy school, but not all of these relate the pupils' enjoyment to the operation of the new plan. There is a consensus that the competence of the teachers is a deciding factor in the excellence of any school, regardless of the plan in force.

As before, we should be cautious about attaching much validity to these small samplings of subjective data. Variability is likely to be found and it is not necessarily closely related to virtues that can be reliably established—or disestablished.

TABLE IV

PERCENTAGE OF SEVENTY-EIGHT LONG BEACH PARENTS WITH CHILDREN IN
GRADES III–VI DISPLAYING FAVORABLE AND UNFAVORABLE ATTITUDES
TOWARD THE DUAL PROGRESS PLAN AND ITS MAJOR FEATURES
(1960)

Topic of Question	% Strongly in favor	% Moderately in favor	% No preference	% Moderately opposed	% Strongly opposed
Q.1 The DPP in general	45	40		9	6
Q.2 All teachers specialists	60	22	6	5	6
Q.3 Ability-grouped classes	63	28	3	3	4
Q.4 Child having different teachers	64	15	9	8	4
Q.5 Promotion on *core* progress only	22	24	12	15	27
Q.6 Nongraded advancement in mathematics, science, arts & crafts, music	55	35	5		5

THE SUPERINTENDENT OF SCHOOLS REPORTS

It is appropriate to close this chapter with a statement prepared by Dr. David G. Salten, superintendent of schools for the Long Beach City School District. It will be recalled that Dr. Salten was a member of the working party described in Chapter 5; he was, in fact, a very active and farseeing member of that group. Here I shall simply record that Dr. Salten, his staff, and the members of the Long Beach Board of Education deserve a tribute for their courage in approving a five-year demonstration. As Dr. Salten remarks, the Dual Progress Plan is a heavy dosage! We have seen, too, that the pupils' parents, representing a good cross section of the city, while remaining critical of certain features, are loyal to the first proposal to give the plan a try. This attitude, backstopping, as it were, the staff and the board members, is not to be lightly accepted, for most American communities are conservative, if not gun shy, when it comes to anything that might be called "controversial" or "experimental."

Dr. Salten's statement of September 1, 1960, follows:

Unlike many other attempts at improving the quality of education, the Dual Progress Plan rests on a new conception of the relative value of different kinds of knowledge. Stoddard's theoretical formulation represents a fundamental change in the design of the total educational scheme. Consequently, implementing the plan in an on-going school system requires more than a tinkering with the present mechanism. It presents some of the difficulties one would face in designing and building a better airplane without shutting down the plant for retooling and changes in the production line. Although a few features of the plan can be adopted piecemeal, the basic theory cannot be tested without a radical reorganization of the school. One cannot cross an abyss in two jumps.

The plan is all-embracing and total in its effects. First, and most importantly, it calls for a more precise assessment of each youngster's potential and achievement in each of the major categories of the school's program. Also affected are the scope and sequence of each subject in the curriculum, selection of new teachers with a mastery of a subject matter field as well as a knowledge of child development, in-service education of present teachers, cooperation with university faculties in the development of new teacher education programs and the construction of more valid and reliable instruments for appraising individual potential as well as achievement, pupil grouping procedures, space utilization and teacher assignment.

Developing such a structure without damaging the present levels of pupil achievement and staff morale requires consideration of a large number of administrative variables. Before the plan went into operation, Long Beach, unlike most of its neighbor school systems, already had a large core of specialist teachers in the elementary schools. Nevertheless, we found ourselves pioneering in largely unchartered territory. Under the circumstances, a five year demonstration period may be just barely enough time to put the plan into effect and arrive at a preliminary comprehensive appraisal.

A full-scale evaluation of the plan cannot be made before the mid-60's. However, a number of gains are already ascertainable. Teacher specialization improves the quality of teaching almost immediately. When elementary school teachers of common branch subjects are assigned as specialists on the basis of interest and background, a decided gain in pupil learning and teacher morale results. This gain is evident even when teachers use essentially the same method and materials they employed when they were teaching the entire complex of elementary school subjects. Accompanying this improvement in motivation and instructional skill of the teacher we observe that children react with immediate enthusiasm and improved performance to novelty, physical movement between classes and exposure to a greater number of personalities during the school day. It might be assumed that this enthusiastic response to a novel situation would lessen with the passage of time. After a year and a half, however, this eagerness appears to be increasing rather than diminishing.

Teachers have been stimulated to increase their knowledge in their specialized subject areas. The science or mathematics teacher is more alert to developments in his own field. The mere act of labeling a teacher as a specialist markedly affects his perceptual set even before he begins advanced study in his field of specialization.

As soon as the school staff began to study the Stoddard Plan, and prior to its actual implementation, a number of weaknesses in our traditional policy were exposed. Teachers at all levels became aware of the necessity for articulation between the primary, intermediate and secondary grades. Later, when non-graded advancement was actually introduced, the staff was sensitized to the problems involved in effective pupil placement which had been present for a long time and almost consistently overlooked. The staff became more fully conscious of the inadequate knowledge we had of the individual child's capacity and potential. Inconsistencies in evaluating pupil progress were brought to light. As soon as we knew more about each child's present position and rate of progress we found the traditional methods of marking and reporting to parents outdated. We have not as yet succeeded in devising a method which will record pupil progress as clearly as we should like. However, the wholesome discontent which has developed with outworn procedures augurs well for more effective innovations in the near future.

To the extent that our appraisal of pupils is less accurate than we wish, our grouping procedures are occasionally arbitrary. Nevertheless, our present practices, admittedly in need of further refinement, are yielding early gains for the brighter groups. Although the slower groups have not benefited as promptly, or as markedly, there is reason to believe that additional teacher training will be helpful with these children.

At the earliest level at which the plan becomes operative—the third year—it is apparent that we do not know our primary school children as well as we should. If the Dual Progress Plan is to become the design for the intermediate grades in the school of the future, the primary school years will be recognized increasingly as the period for diagnostic and child development focus. At the upper end of the DPP, at present the eighth year, the evidence supports our earlier assumptions concerning the need for modifications in the organization and curriculum of our high school. These changes in purpose and organization will strongly affect our ideas of school building design in the years ahead.

Another early outcome is a general recognition of the fact that extensive research in related educational and psychological areas must be undertaken in order to implement the plan with optimum efficiency. Use of teacher aids, television and other mechanical and electronic teaching devices, team-teaching approaches, social and psychological effects of ability grouping when differentiated by subject without regard to age and grade lines, to mention only a few, deserve intensive study.

Certain local needs in Long Beach have brought about modifications which depart from the initial plans for implementation. Some of these adaptations involve temporary measures undertaken while comprehensive administrative solutions are being investigated; others may be more permanent. Next year, for example, all children will receive an additional forty minute period of developmental reading daily in addition to the functional reading which is part of the language arts—social studies core. In grades five and six, twenty minutes of the core period will be devoted daily to foreign language instruction. But these additions to the original plan represent functional modifications rather than 180° reversals. In mathematics and science children are currently following non-graded ability groupings. However, in music and art, children this coming year will be grouped in terms of core placement—an example of a modification dictated by administrative expediency rather than basic rationale.

If asked for a brief accounting of our present position, I would say that the enterprise and the ideas it embodies have already proven themselves viable, adaptable and productive. Compared with the massive investment which has been made in terms of skilled professional effort, our present gains may appear small, but they are positive, substantive, and give every indication of growth as we proceed with the plan. It is too early in the life of the undertaking to expect returns commensurate with the initial effort which has been made. It is not too early, however, to recognize several of the broad conclusions emerging from the data. Some of these are well developed, others still inchoate. Yet all suggest strongly that the broad hypotheses underlying the plan will be sustained by future experience. Without falling into the presumption of prophecy, I believe the available evidence indicates to me that time is clearly on the side of the Dual Progress Plan.

Some who admire the elegance and comprehensiveness of Stoddard's basic formulation will argue that insurmountable difficulties lie in the way of its practical application in any American public school system. Others do not understand the plan well enough to be confused. Nobody who has had close contact with the demonstration would deny that some of the programming problems have an awesome complexity. Yet our own experiences up to this point embolden us to believe that our Long Beach staff, and our colleagues in Ossining and the Experimental Teaching Center of New York University are inventive enough to unravel, or cut, the administrative snarls without impairing the unique human values of the plan. There are difficulties still to be overcome, but in the words of Spinoza, "all good things are as difficult as they are rare."

I should like to reiterate that attitudes and subjective responses do not take the place of objective data and comparative analysis. Decisions are not to be equated with statistical findings, the latter of necessity forming a tight circle that does not include all values. What we need, and are steadily obtaining through the combined efforts of teachers, researchers, and administrators, is a synthesis of test results and value judgments that will serve to enrich the educational experience of all students. To date, all findings are tentative.

7

THE FIRST TWO YEARS OF THE
DUAL PROGRESS PLAN
AT OSSINING, NEW YORK

Ossining is a Hudson River city of 20,000 population, located 35 miles from New York City. Unlike most Westchester County communities, it displays a wide range along economic, social, and ethnic lines. Many persons commute to nearby cities. In 1958 the total school enrollment was 3,650, and the staff, 190 persons.

The following data and the quoted comments are from the July, 1959, report of David W. Bishop, project director.

After full discussion among the teaching and supervisory staff, board members, and public groups, the administration decided to

TABLE V

GRADES III–VI, INCLUSIVE, OSSINING, 1957–1958

School	Pupils	Teachers*	Pupil-Teacher Ratio	Range of Section Size
Brookside	244	10	22/1	17–33
Claremont	189	8	20/1	11–27
Park	297	12	22/1	13–34
Roosevelt	324	13	23/1	14–31
Washington	209	8	22/1	14–31
	1,263	51		

* Five arts and crafts teachers and three physical education teachers augment the classroom teaching staff.

TABLE VI

1958–1959 ENROLLMENTS (SECTIONS)

	Brookside	Claremont	Park	Roosevelt	Washington
Grade III	59 (3)	46 (2)	81 (3)	90 (4)	58 (2)
Grade IV	59 (2)	57 (2)	77 (3)	81 (3)	57 (2)
Grade V	64 (2)	37 (2)	67 (3)	66 (3)	49 (2)
Grade VI	62 (3)	49 (2)	72 (3)	87 (3)	45 (2)

proceed with the installation of the Dual Progress Plan at the beginning of the school year in September, 1958. (Dudley Hare, superintendent of schools, in 1956 had worked on the plan with the writer and others at New York University. Following Mr. Hare's death, Roger Garrison, a member of the school board, played an active role. Subsequently the new superintendent, Charles M. Northrup, and David W. Bishop have carried forward the project.)

PREPARATORY STEPS

A substantial amount of preparatory work was completed during the summer of 1958. One of the helpful outcomes of this period was the decision to lengthen the school day by fifteen minutes. This permitted a time block of one hundred and twenty minutes for the graded core and thirty minutes for physical education. The other half day was neatly divided into three periods of 40 minutes each for the ungraded segment. Every teacher carried a six-period day or its equivalent—a tight schedule. In the words of Mr. Bishop:

Shortly after the opening of school, the problems inevitable in any new program began to develop. Many problems that we had anticipated did not. Our children began to show fatigue. The DPP teachers were exhausted from their efforts to adjust their teaching and thinking, and from the plethora of necessary but tiring demands on time and effort in faculty meetings, subject area meetings, in-service programs, and meetings with the New York University staff. Even the high school teachers, with nothing at all to do with the program, were tired. The administration became fatigued, as well, from coping with problems as they arose, from meetings of all kinds, and from answering the same questions of parents over and over in P.T.A. meetings and individual conferences. By midyear, this condition had disappeared in both children and teachers and did not reappear as we started school this year (1959–1960).

The first "shakedown" trial showed that: there was a need for more materials and facilities; a "break" was essential in the teaching day; teachers generally should not be asked to teach in two subject-matter areas. It was also evident that special methods should be set up to teach the slow-learning pupils. On the whole, it proved easier to have the children move from one room to another than to have the teachers move. Aware of some weaknesses in grasp of subject matter, forty-eight of the fifty-nine teachers in the four grades voluntarily participated in in-service programs.

A SUMMARY REPORT

In summary, Mr. Bishop reports for the first year:

The results of a vastly increased testing program show no significant increase or decrease in the learning of those things so measured. Neither do they show the maladjustment and emotional upset *supposedly* inherent in a semidepartmentalized elementary program. For this first year, these results are acceptable to the system. We know that there has been a great deal of growth in our students and our teachers that is not measured by our testing program. One need only to observe the changes that have taken place, the questions raised by teachers, the intelligent activity of children, the surprised reactions of parents to their children's discussions and attitudes, to know, subjectively, but nonetheless validly, that the Dual Progress Plan represents a step forward for our elementary program. Most significantly, the Dual Progress Plan has brought to the surface the submerged problems of the "self-contained" classroom to which elementary teachers everywhere have been paying only lip service: "individualized instruction," "starting where the children are," etc. The Dual Progress Plan has fostered an aggressive frontal attack on these problems and presented a practical and realistic path to solution.

TEACHER RESPONSES

The Ossining teachers' reactions to five of the items in an anonymous questionnaire are indicated in Table VII. (My comments are based on Dr. Richard Anderson's analysis of these data.) The restrictions on opinion polls which I referred to in Chapter 6 apply here; favorable or unfavorable, the replies are simply indicators that are subject to considerable fluctuation.

TABLE VII

PERCENTAGE OF OSSINING TEACHERS EXPRESSING FAVORABLE AND
UNFAVORABLE ATTITUDES TOWARD THE DUAL PROGRESS PLAN
(DPP) AND ITS MAJOR FEATURES IN JUNE, 1959*

	% Strongly in Favor	% Moderately in Favor	% No Preference	% Moderately Opposed	% Strongly Opposed
Over-all reaction to DPP	13	40	6	22	19
Test of DPP in Ossining	30	31	7	15	17
Specialist teaching	42	36	11	9	2
Teaching several grade levels	24	41	9	15	11
Ability grouping of children	33	30	4	20	13

* The percentages in this table are based on data obtained from an "Inquiry on Teachers' Attitudes toward the Dual Progress Plan" and an "Inquiry on Teaching in the Dual Progress Plan." A total of fifty-four teachers responded though not all teachers answered every question. Percentages may not add to exactly 100 per cent because of rounding error.

After a year's trial, 53 per cent of the teachers favored the Dual Progress Plan, and 41 per cent did not. Sixty-one per cent thought it desirable for Ossining to give the plan a three-year trial; teachers with over five years of experience were more favorable than others. In this regard, the most striking testimonial was given in New York in February, 1960; at a meeting of the Women's City Club, Mrs. Lillian Chase, a teacher at the Washington School with forty years of experience, said, in part:

The introduction of the new system produced a unique situation for both teacher and student. Let us consider the child first. Under the old system the child spent the whole day with one teacher who taught every subject in the curriculum. Supervisors in art, music, and physical training came once a week and children in need of remedial reading reported to the remedial reading teacher. Under Dual Progress, children from the third through the sixth grades were changing rooms and being taught by different teachers. They seemed to enjoy this fully. They felt very grown up, like their older brothers and sisters in Junior High. The changing from class to class was done in an orderly fashion. Each child was issued a card giving him the name of the teacher, the subject, and the room to which he was to report. By the end of the second day all was well. The children had a chance to work with and become acquainted with more children because the groups did not move as units from one class to another. . . . From the viewpoint of the teacher a new and interesting experience had opened up. Instead of teaching all subjects she could now concentrate on the one of her choice. She undoubtedly put in more time and effort in research in her chosen field and in the preparation and planning of the day's work. Latent abilities were tapped and brought into use. There were new areas to be explored and new situations to be met. It was an exciting challenge.

Each child could now move at his own pace. The more talented in the field of science could work out more difficult and complicated projects while the others could work out projects on their own level of ability. What a splendid chance for creativity! Experiments became the order of the day and even the youngest "eager beaver" kept the teacher on her toes. Research was done by the children. Newspapers and magazines were scanned for new developments in science. Most of all the wonderworld of science was unfolding for the children. There were no limits on how far the child might advance. The number of science books, microscopes, chemistry sets, telescopes, rock collections, etc., requested by the children for birthday and Christmas gifts pays tribute to the children's interest in science. With almost forty years of teaching experience in the elementary field, I find the teaching of science under the Dual Progress Plan stimulating to the teacher and very rewarding in the interest, response, and development of the child.

As the answers to the questionnaire indicate, other teachers are strongly opposed; perhaps they could produce equally eloquent statements. All we know from enthusiastic reports such as the one above is that, from the teacher's viewpoint, the plan *can* be made to work effectively.

Turning to various specific features of the plan, we find the percentage of approval somewhat higher than for the plan as a whole. Thus 78 per cent of the teachers favored specialist teaching, although one teacher remarked plaintively, "The only difficulty with specialist teaching is that I am not a specialist yet." On the other hand, a teacher commented, "The primary concern of the elementary school is the *child,* not the subject matter. I am positive the continual relation with the group is more worthwhile [than the contacts under the new plan]."

The questionnaire, "Inquiry on Teachers' Attitudes Toward the Dual Progress Plan" was also administered to twenty-six teachers in the kindergarten and first two grades and to forty-seven high school teachers. The comparative reactions of these teachers "on the margins" and teachers in the plan are given in Table VIII.

TABLE VIII

PER CENT OF OSSINING DPP, K-2, AND JUNIOR-SENIOR HIGH SCHOOL
TEACHERS EXPRESSING FAVORABLE AND UNFAVORABLE ATTITUDES
TOWARD THE PLAN AND TOWARD TWO ASPECTS OF THE PLAN
IN JUNE, 1959

	% Strongly in Favor	% Moderately in Favor	% No Preference	% Moderately Opposed	% Strongly Opposed
Over-all reaction to DPP					
DPP teachers	13	40	6	22	19
K-2 teachers	4	50	19	27	
Junior-Senior High School teachers	4	30	19	34	13
Meeting children's emotional needs					
DPP teachers	2	26	26	30	16
K-2 teachers		20	24	48	8
Junior-Senior High School teachers		7	50	43	
Specialist teaching					
DPP teachers	42	36	11	9	2
K-2 teachers	19	50	16	12	3
Junior-Senior High School teachers	23	41	11	18	7

In general, it can be said that the reactions of the teachers unaffected by the plan (except in a marginal way) do not markedly differ from those of the Dual Progress Plan teachers. All groups are somewhat fearful that the new program cannot meet the children's emotional needs. The feeling is prevalent that children need the comforting security of an all-day teacher to whom they may turn as to a mother at home. How much of this feeling is in accord with the measured responses and patterns of personal growth in children constitutes one facet of the present study, and an important one.

In view of my comments in Chapter 6 on the Long Beach findings, it will be unnecessary to insert their counterparts here. It will suffice to report, with brief annotations, the other major returns on the questionnaire to teachers.

Most of the teachers thought the program required more time and energy (than the unitary grade plan); this led to the reasonable request that a free period be provided each day.

The reactions on the adequacy of the plan for various levels of pupil talent are given in Tables IX and X.

As far as these teachers are concerned, the case is clear for the gifted and the average pupils: the plan is fairly effective. What to do with the slow learner in the elementary school remains a problem—a problem to be attacked through various approaches that trace the all-round development of *each child* up through the school years. In the Dual Progress Plan, we shall need cumulative records of the learning and behavioral growth of slow learners under cir-

TABLE IX

TEACHERS' RATINGS OF THE ADEQUACY OF THE DUAL PROGRESS PLAN
IN TERMS OF THE ACADEMIC LEARNING OF GIFTED, AVERAGE,
AND SLOW STUDENTS, JUNE, 1959

	% Provides Exceptionally Well	% Provides Adequately	% Provides Inadequately	% Provides Quite Poorly
Gifted pupils	42	42	9	8
Average pupils	15	66	13	6
Slow learners	13	26	34	26

TABLE X

TEACHERS' RATINGS OF THE ADEQUACY OF THE DUAL PROGRESS PLAN
IN TERMS OF THE EMOTIONAL NEEDS OF GIFTED, AVERAGE,
AND SLOW STUDENTS, JUNE, 1959

	% Provides Exceptionally Well	% Provides Adequately	% Provides Inadequately	% Provides Quite Poorly
Gifted pupils	37	37	14	12
Average pupils	10	56	17	17
Slow learners	10	25	27	38

cumstances that really remove the pressure to advance very far along abstract lines. Many years ago the Bureau of Child Guidance of New York City reported that the single factor most often associated with juvenile delinquency was failure in reading comprehension. To teach a child to read properly, up to his full potentiality, is just about the best thing any teacher can do. Success in this great sector of learning is deep-seated and comprehensive; failure often appears to be associated with feelings of frustration, humiliation, and rebellion.

Hence, for the slow learner, we may well consider the suggestion of some of the Ossining teachers that there be less mathematics and science and more reading. The meetings of the specialized classes, perhaps every other day during the week, could be devoted to an all-out attempt to strengthen facility in the mother tongue. With a stronger base for mental operations, as it were, the child could later be returned to the regular meetings of the lower sections in the ungraded subjects. (Some rearrangement of schedule would be needed. In the Long Beach eight-period day one period each half day is available for remedial reading.)

In the practical classroom situation, even with three sections formed on the basis of pupil ability, the range of talent is high; under good teaching conditions, it increases. One might well hope, as do the Ossining teachers, that classes for the slow groups be made smaller than is the general rule. Since the pupils who are average or bright need just as much individual attention as the dull, we are faced with the over-all question, What is the optimum class size? It is doubtful if any combination of research and experience will arrive at a single, fixed size. (Dr. Alvin C. Eurich has dug up evidence to show that the custom of having twenty-five students in a class perhaps stems from the size of the rooms and alcoves available in ancient times!)

Since the Ossining teachers did not feel happy about the curriculum in mathematics and science, specific steps were taken in the second year to improve the situation. In the core areas there was widespread satisfaction. The general frustration associated with the setting up of special programs should be lessened when there are free periods for the teacher, together with some scheduling changes. As indicated previously, I am hopeful that large-scale field trips can be relegated to "after hours"—to late afternoons, weekends, and the long, rather empty summer vacation.

PUPIL RESPONSES

The reactions of the pupils toward the new plan are summarized in Table XI.

TABLE XI

PERCENTAGE OF OSSINING STUDENTS EXPRESSING FAVORABLE AND
UNFAVORABLE ATTITUDES TOWARD THE DUAL PROGRESS PLAN
BY GRADE AND ABILITY GROUP (JUNE, 1959)

Ability Group	3rd	4th	Grade 5th	6th	Total
High Ability					
% favorable	72	74	64	79	72
% part favorable, part unfavorable	13	20	17	10	15
% unfavorable	15	6	19	11	13
Average Ability					
% favorable	83	85	84	77	81
% part favorable, part unfavorable	5	9	8	16	10
% unfavorable	12	6	8	7	9

TABLE XI (Continued)

Ability Group	Grade 3rd	4th	5th	6th	Total
Low Ability					
% favorable	80	71	59	71	71
% part favorable, part unfavorable	1	11	19	15	11
% unfavorable	19	18	22	14	18
Total					
% favorable	78	74	66	76	74
% part favorable, part unfavorable	7	15	16	13	13
% unfavorable	15	11	18	11	13

Note: The data in this table are based on the responses of 1,032 students.

As Beilin and Anderson point out in their analysis of these results, "in the average Ossining class of 23 students, 17 were favorable to the Dual Progress Plan, three had mixed feelings, while three were unfavorable." In view of the predictions of teachers, it is astonishing that low-ability third-graders (at the bottom of the whole group in ability) registered a favorable vote of 80 per cent. From the same analysis, we may add a few items of interest:

1. Four-fifths of the pupils who mentioned the topic preferred moving around to remaining in the same room all day.
2. Specialist teaching, mentioned almost exclusively by high-ability groups, was favored by a count of fifty-eight to two.
3. Of the forty-six high-ability pupils in the fifth and sixth grades who mentioned grouping on the basis of ability, forty-two were favorable.

Pupils who expressed negative reactions especially disliked not having desks of their own; they also hoped the teachers would get together on the piling up of homework. There was, in addition, a sprinkling of minor complaints some of which could readily be met in another year. In short, there is a basic pupil acceptance of the new plan. (If there is a "halo effect" here, it should be counteracted later in the project.)

PARENT RESPONSES

The reactions of the parents of the children are given in Table XII. The questionnaire was mailed in June, 1959, to 252 Ossining homes having one or more children in Grades III–VI; they furnished a fair sampling, covering all five elementary schools. The answers were to be submitted anonymously; eighty forms were returned.

TABLE XII

ATTITUDES OF OSSINING PARENTS TOWARD THE DUAL PROGRESS PLAN (DPP) IN GENERAL AND TOWARD ITS MAJOR FEATURES[1]

	% Strongly in Favor	% Moderately in Favor	% No Preference	% Moderately Opposed	% Strongly Opposed
The DPP in general	55	33	4	5	3
All teachers specialists	63	22	1	7	7
Ability-grouped classes	66	24	1	7	2
Child having different teachers	60	25	6	8	1
* Promotion dependent on *core* progress only	22	25	6	31	16
Nongraded advancement in mathematics, science, arts and crafts, music	62	28		9	1

[1] The figures give per cents of parents answering each question who checked the given attitude (N = 80).

* Based on only forty-one returns; question five was misprinted on the remaining thirty-nine returns.

The evenly divided opinion of parents on a grade and promotion plan based on English and the social studies (here the sampling is defective) should be further analyzed, for 90 per cent of the parents approved non-graded advancement in mathematics, science, arts and crafts, and music. It seems unlikely that these parents wish to abandon the grade system entirely. Still, to anyone who does not accept the validity of the difference between a "cultural imperative" and a "cultural elective," the promotion scheme may appear arbitrary.

Eighty-one per cent of the parents felt that their children learned more under the new plan than under the old, and 90 per cent reported that their children now enjoyed school more. The same number noticed a positive effect on children's interests in learning, with special reference to science.

SOME 1960 OBSERVATIONS

The Stanford Achievement Test reveals nothing significant. The 1960 STEP tests indicate a steady grade-to-grade progression, as expected but no differences from the 1959 ratings for each grade. The pupils' attitudes toward the new plan is as favorable in 1960 as in 1959. Only 20 per cent of the questionnaires mailed to parents in 1960 were returned (as against 33 per cent in 1959). Seventy-eight per cent of these parents now favor the Dual Progress Plan in general, with the approval of various facets of the plan, with one exception, running from 80 to 82 per cent. The exception is again to having grade standing and promotion based entirely on the core (in 1959, as indicated previously, 47 per cent of the parents were in favor; in 1960, 36 per cent).

To the questions asked of the teachers, "If you were given the opportunity, would you choose to return to teaching in the self-contained classroom plan (SCC)?" The Ossining returns were as follows:

	Would Return to SCC	*No Preference*	*Would* Not *Return to SCC*
1959	51%	19%	30%
1960	35%	11%	53%

In June, 1960, 87 per cent of the teachers favored specialization in one subject-matter area, and 8 per cent were opposed.

FURTHER RESPONSES OF THE TEACHERS

What basic changes in teacher attitudes took place in the Ossining program during the second full year of 1959–1960?

Michel Radomisli's report (July, 1960) analyzes the data on teachers' reactions to the Dual Progress Plan for 1959–1960. Sixty-four teachers filled out the questionnaires.

The over-all reaction to the plan as a way of conducting elementary education yielded a favorable percentage of 71 (twice as many teachers in 1960—compared to 1959—were "strongly in favor" and only half as many were "strongly opposed"). Nevertheless, only slightly over half the teachers, given the opportunity, would *not* choose to return to the self-contained classroom; for the language arts and social studies, the proportion was nearly two-thirds. Teachers in the combined category of art, music, and physical education tended to favor a return to the previous plan (39 to 30 per cent).

Three-fourths of the teachers favored the testing of the Dual Progress Plan in Ossining, and 71 per cent favored their own participation in the research.

Eighty-eight per cent of the teachers favored the subject-matter specialization of teachers under the plan. Not one was "strongly opposed." Nearly three-fourths of the group liked the idea of teaching a subject area at all elementary school levels.

Eighty-four per cent of the teachers favored ability grouping; only one teacher was "strongly opposed."

Grade level instruction was strongly favored for the language arts and social studies (the core) and, to a lesser extent, for physical education. For mathematics and science, ungraded instruction was strongly favored, and the group, as a whole, favored ungraded instruction in art and music. (At the same time 57 per cent of the art teachers and 64 per cent of the music teachers favored grade-level instruction—a curious reaction in view of the commonly observed disparity between a special aptitude in music or art and general maturity for a grade.)

Only 60 per cent of the teachers felt the Dual Progress Plan provided "acceptably" (or better) for reporting to parents and conferences with them. For "conducting nonclassroom activities—assemblies, band, library, field trips, etc."—the comparable percentage was

41; no teacher thought the plan did this "very well." (My remarks with reference to the Long Beach situation are applicable here.)

The teachers strongly felt the plan adequately provided for academic learning among gifted pupils (92 per cent). For average pupils the teacher vote in this respect was 71 per cent favorable, and for the slow learners, 59 per cent favorable. Thus, while the trend is the same as in Long Beach, there is not the emphatic feeling in Ossining that pupils below average are neglected. If further reports are consistent for the bright pupils, we can at least gain a measure of reassurance, for the sharpest criticism of the American school system has been directed toward the failure to "do right" by the gifted. It is no part of the theory of the Dual Progress Plan to rectify this deficiency *at the expense of* the average or the dull, but quite the reverse: so to organize the curriculum, the teaching methods, and the competence of the teaching staff as to bring out the best in pupils at all levels of general and special ability.

Again, the "integration" of subject matter across the scholastic spectrum gets a low rating under the plan (40 per cent "fairly well" or better).

The Ossining teachers were about evenly divided at the two extremes of the question on meeting the emotional needs of pupils generally: one third favorable, another third unfavorable. The others thought that emotionally the pupils "will manage." (In Ossining the unfavorable votes were piled up in Grade III; for Grade VI the response was 89 per cent in favor of "adequately" or better.) As in Long Beach, the teachers felt that disciplinary problems were greater under the Dual Progress Plan. Hence the case for an analysis of the factors involved is strengthened.

The one unanimous agreement among sixty-one teachers was that the new plan made a greater demand on a teacher's time and energy than the older plan. It is hard to tell how much of this experience is ascribable to two nonrecurrent factors: (1) the newness (the transitional stages) and (2) the difference in teacher training and experience as between the two plans. Any *change*, either way, calls for new energy. The extra demands, in the opinion of these teachers, produced results: 55 per cent of the teachers felt they were now teaching "somewhat better" or "much better" than before, while only

18 per cent felt they were teaching "not quite as well" or "not nearly as well."

FURTHER RESPONSES OF THE PARENTS

A total of 240 parents representing all five schools and each of the Grades III–VI responded to a questionnaire in June and July, 1960. The attitude toward the Dual Progress Plan in general was 78 per cent in favor and 22 per cent opposed. The parents of children in Grades III and IV were slightly more favorable than the parents of children in Grades V and VI. On other features of the plan the following percentages were obtained:

| | Per cent | |
Parents' Responses*	Favorable	Opposed
All teachers specialists	82	10
Ability-grouped classes	82	16
Child having different teachers	81	12
Promotion on "core" only	39	54
Nongraded advancement in mathematics, science, arts and crafts, music	80	13

* Other parents reported "no preference."

Again we find an anomaly in the negative attitude toward promotion on the "core," in juxtaposition with a favoring of nongraded programs for other subjects. It may be related to the traditional view of mathematics (arithmetic as a basic subject—one of the "3 R's").

About two-thirds of the parents felt their children were learning more under the new plan than previously. Eighty per cent thought their children had enjoyed school, but one-third of the parents in this group did not regard Dual Progress Plan as a factor. About two-thirds of the parents reported their children had shown an increased interest in learning; the increased interest in sciences was especially noted.

THE PROGRAM IN MATHEMATICS

Although still in its early stages, the program in elementary mathematics prepared by David W. Bishop and his associates in

Ossining appears to be carefully constructed. Many, but not all, of the understandings and operations expected of the pupils will be familiar to the experienced teacher of arithmetic in the self-contained classroom. By recognizing three general levels of mathematical achievement—*elementary,* "which all children must learn in order to be arithmetically operative as adults"; *intermediate,* for utilization by a person of average ability; *advanced,* for children who are above average—Bishop is able closely to approach the idea of mathematics (above the simple tools or skills) as a cultural elective.

Already, in actual practice, these procedures and aims result in some assignments that will startle anyone who thinks of the elementary grades as unsophisticated! For example, in the Ossining Schools, we find the slide rule being used by mathematics sections that contain pupils in the fifth and sixth grades, and a prior introduction to the *meaning* of such terms as *root, power, exponent, coefficient, characteristic,* and *mantissa.* A study of the decimal system is accompanied by some attention to the binary system. In algebra, basic concepts usually introduced at the high school level are not beyond the grasp of selected pupils. Also the plan of nongraded ability grouping has intensified the demand for supplementary books, articles, and magazines.

THE PROGRAM IN SCIENCE

Of the new science program in Ossining, which is supervised by Mr. Lawrence J. Heldman, Mr. Bishop states: "No other facet of our elementary program has aroused such bewilderment, wonder, and enthusiasm in the parents of our children. No other area elicits the same degree of satisfaction and interest on the part of our students." There are two fully equipped science rooms in each of the five elementary schools. The large equipment includes bioscopes, microscopes, oscilloscopes, various types of scales, terraria and aquaria, models and charts, textbooks and supplementary books, sets of slides, and experimental animals. Rockets and atomic power plants have proved to be within the intellectual grasp of a surprising number of the pupils. As in mathematics, the aims in science instruction go beyond observation, immediate experience, and manipulation to some insight into *process* and some understanding of the structure of knowledge that underlies any series of data or events. In a sense, these pupils seek their own answers to conditions and problems; the teacher is simply there to help.

GRADES I AND II

The following statement (September, 1960) by Mr. Bishop clearly indicates the place of the primary grades (I and II) in the Ossining Schools. His advocacy of the ungraded feature of the Dual Progress Plan for these grades is of particular interest.

With the introduction of the Dual Progress Plan in Grades III–VI in the Ossining system, the administration considered the immediate role of Grades I and II in relation to the new elementary whole. In effect, though not so specifically stated, it was decided that we in Ossining would continue our present efforts in these grades with no particular added emphasis here because of the DPP in the upper elementary grades. This is not to say that the Dual Progress Plan has not had, or will not have, an impact on Grades I and II, but that this impact has been, and will be, incidental to normal articulation between these grades and those that follow.

This means, then, that the primary grades (below Grade III) continue to be essentially self-contained, meet the current curricula for those grades, and, in essence, are as separate from the program begun in third grade as they have traditionally been separate. Further, it brings Grade III into focus as the transitional grade between the unitary grade plan of the primary classes and the fully implemented classes in the Dual Progress Plan. Third-graders follow the mechanical operation of the plan relative to semidepartmentalization, are very generally grouped in core classes, but do not meet nearly as much cross-grading in the non-graded subjects of science and mathematics as their older fellow students.

Though supervisors in core subjects, mathematics, and science are assigned to Grades III–VI specifically, primary teachers have asked and received their assistance. In two of our five elementary schools, primary music is serviced by the DPP music teacher outside the plan. The system head of the art and arts and crafts department assists and supervises the art program of the primary grades. The physical education personnel serve all elementary grades. Inevitably, then, through the sharing of personnel, the primary grades are drawn close to the DPP in striving for the goals of the elementary system.

If we may be permitted a personal observation, it seems to us that a completely logical extension of the DPP downward into the primary grades falls within the realm of its non-grading rather than within its specialization through departmentalization. A non-graded primary program would, we believe, provide for differences in social, emotional, physical, and mental abilities without doing damage to modern theory relative to early childhood education and child development, provide a foundation commensurate with the aims of the DPP, and provide the time-progress flexibility which primary teachers have come to consider so highly important.

OBSERVATIONS OF THE SUPERINTENDENT OF SCHOOLS

Dr. Charles Northrup, the superintendent of schools, in October, 1960, at the close of the first two years of the trial run of the plan in Ossining, stated:

When I assumed the duties of Superintendent of the Ossining Schools on August 1, 1957, I found that my predecessor, the late Dudley Hare, had been working with Dr. George Stoddard of New York University and the superintendents of two other school systems on a plan for the reorganization of the elementary school program. This plan was to be known as the Dual Progress Plan.

With Mr. Hare's untimely death in February of 1957, there was some consideration given to the dropping of the Ossining Schools from the study. However, the Board of Education had become so interested that they decided to continue the study with one of the board members serving as the local co-ordinator until the appointment of Mr. Hare's successor.

After carefully exploring the philosophy, reviewing the work that had been done, discussing the proposal with Dr. Stoddard, local board members, and members of the administrative staff who were familiar with the plan, I determined that I was in sympathy with what the plan proposed to do. I agreed to work with, and give my support to, the initiation of the program in Ossining.

By March 1, 1958, we were assuming that there was a very strong chance that we would be operating the Dual Progress Plan in the Ossining Elementary Schools the following September. We started immediately to survey our staff, to inform them about the program, and to find out how we could best use our existing staff in the changed program. We discussed with them our hopes for the education of our children under the new organization and worked with them to determine how they would best fit into the change.

As vacancies occurred, we kept in mind the information gained through our staff survey and did our best to fill the vacancies in such fashion as to take care of our greatest needs. Each teacher interviewed for an elementary position was told about the plan and informed that we might be using it the following September. We were pleased to find that most teachers interviewed were not only interested in the proposal, but eager to be a part of it. All applicants were informed that, at the beginning, the program would require many extra meetings and much work.

During the spring months we encouraged community groups, including P.T.A.'s, to invite us to describe the program. At these meetings, we discussed the plan and let the people know that our schools might possibly be using it the following September. The people attending these meetings asked many questions that we answered to the best of our ability. From the beginning we found great interest on the part of our teachers and the public.

Before the end of the school year, we carried out on paper the work of grouping our children for the core program as required by the plan. School was out for summer vacation when we learned that the grant funds had been provided for the introduction of the Dual Progress Plan into the Ossining Schools. During the summer months the administration worked long and hard to do the best possible job of grouping and scheduling all children in the special areas.

The following September, with the first day of the new school year, Ossining launched the program in Grades III–VI. It has since been extended to Grades VII and VIII.

We are now starting our third year of the program. Our pupils like it, our parents like it, our teachers like it, and our administrators like it. We believe the education of our children has benefited because of the plan. We have great hopes for our total educational program in Ossining. The Dual Progress Plan plays an important part in these hopes.

As in the case of Long Beach, definitive results will not come in until the demonstration has run five years and, even then, there will be many an unanswered question.

8

CURRICULUM, TEACHING
METHODS, AND SCHOOL DESIGN
IN THE DUAL PROGRESS PLAN

The two preceding chapters based directly on the two-year experience at Long Beach and Ossining have entered into the subject matter of this one. All I propose to do in this chapter is to clarify some concepts and indulge in a few generalizations. A general theory of curriculum in the Dual Progress Plan can be approached from various angles. In choice of subject matter the plan is not radical. The departures appear in the *organization* of subject matter; in the teacher's day, and his preparation for it; in the attempt to integrate the past, present, and future development of the child; in the assumption that subject matter is of unequal significance, both to the child and to society. If, under the plan, the school day *seems* to be more subject centered (it certainly is more systematic in its intellectual demands), we should remember that the child's *out-of-school* day is unsystematic and opportunistic. For example, it may be heavily devoted to commercial radio and television programs of dubious quality. Through the ages, out-of-school experience, *if exclusive,* has produced, for the most part, primitive societies unable to advance the human condition. In modern times, illiteracy results in defective individuals and inadequate social organizations.

Perhaps at this point, a few "ghosts" could be laid away. The theory of the new plan is consistent with the theories of John Dewey and to the school practices he endorsed. It does not call for laissez faire. In its long-range view of the curriculum, it allows for much variation in content, method, and pupil evaluation. The fact that *any* long threads are to run through the whole pattern will signify to some teachers that determinism has set in and that scholastic authoritarianism most likely will follow. Such an outcome would be a shameful abuse of the plan, and, as we have seen, it has not appeared in either Long Beach or Ossining.

I am reminded of an episode some years ago at the University of Iowa. Kurt Lewin was running his classic experiment on authoritarianism, democracy, and laissez faire as competing principles in classroom organization. Professor Charles H. Judd, of the University of Chicago, on spending an hour observing in one of Lewin's "classrooms," was enthusiastic. He said, "Professor Lewin, this class is the most accurate representation of the typical American schoolroom I have ever seen." Lewin, somewhat embarrassed, replied, "But, Dr. Judd, you have been observing our rendition of an *authoritarian* situation!"

Doubtless, the authoritarian attitude in some teachers will not be eradicated by the new plan. Some teachers will continue to resent the idea that one set of classroom tasks is not as good as another. The plan itself should avoid either authoritarianism or laissez faire. For the child who continually "wants a reason" for doing something —especially something hard—the reasons, both in the core and in the ungraded segments, are there at hand. The child is not only being introduced to new intellectual content in new ways. He is also discovering for himself new approaches to the art of learning that should invest his immediate life with new strength—with purposes he himself can understand and embrace.

As for society as a whole—shaping and shaped by our educational structure from bottom to top—let us hope that there are fit, fertile choices between the common habit of muddling through, on the one hand, and the imposition from above of rigid doctrines, on the other. Many nations of the world today are notoriously unprepared for democracy; they go easily from one form of tyranny to another. Their citizens do not stand up fearlessly as informed, free persons. It was no different in Italy under the Fascists, in Germany under the Nazis, in Japan under the war lords; it is no different today in Russia, Red China, or Cuba.

A sorry corruption of the Dual Progress Plan would be to turn it over to political "leaders" for whom learning is simply a power-serving device. The emerging youth we have in mind—under this plan or any other that puts a premium on freedom through knowledge and day-to-day experience—is no simple reciter of facts or solver of problems. On the contrary, he is expected increasingly to exemplify the virtues of freedom, knowledge, and love in human affairs.

Unfortunately, our measures of friendship and affection in the schoolroom are largely negative: a failure to increase the child's insecurity or loneliness is regarded as a good sign. For the time being we are accepting such tests, but it is to be hoped that more positive methods of assaying "mental hygiene," "personality," and the like, can be built up. In valid tests of this sort the two basic factors will be: (1) an expectation of achievement adjusted to general ability and specialized aptitudes, and (2) a complete acceptance of, and regard for, the sovereign personality of the child—no matter what he does or fails to do. The first attitude will make for *fairness* and the second for *friendship*. Love is thereby more likely to manifest itself as a positive force in the child's approach to others: not to be loved is bad enough, but not to be able to love is worse. To raise the level of expectation of a child as he slowly matures is not a form of punishment; it is, rather, a subtle recognition of the fact that he *is* growing up and, in the process, taking the first steps toward emancipation. In a literate society any unnecessary illiteracy is a form of child neglect.

THE VERTICAL SEGMENT

Dr. Glen Heathers, director of the Experimental Teaching Center, has outlined the meaning of nongraded advancement in the Dual Progress Plan (February 16, 1959):

In every curricular area, educators have developed courses of study that outline a recommended sequence for the learner to follow, year after year, as he advances in the subject. Ideally, these sequences would provide for an orderly progression of understandings where learning each new understanding is aided by having learned those that went before. In actuality, many of the courses of study that are in use do not offer true sequences of understandings, but rather offer arbitrary arrangements of topics that could just as well have been placed in a different order. In the discussion that follows, we assume that a true sequence of understanding is outlined in the course of study, and that students follow this sequence. . . .

For each non-graded subject area, grouping requires, first, determining how far the student has already advanced along the sequence of understandings in the subject. This may be determined by achievement tests and teachers' judgments. *This present level of advancement* sets the starting point for the next phase of advancement. Students are assigned to levels of work on this basis. Note that the levels spoken of here are *not* grade levels. They are simply positions along the sequence of understandings outlined in the course of study. Students of different ages, and with different numbers of years of schooling, will be found at the same level of advancement.

When students' levels of advancement in a subject area have been determined, the second step in grouping is to sort students found at a given level into classes according to their *ability to advance further in the subject*. This is ability grouping. Ability in a subject may be estimated from measures of I.Q., tests of special abilities in the subject, tests of creative thinking, and teachers' judgments of ability. The number of ability groups that are formed at each level of advancement depends on the number of classes that may be taught in the school. This depends on the number of periods of instruction and the number of teachers available.

UNGRADED SCIENCE

The "guidelines" for the elementary science course of study follow Dr. Heathers' memorandum of April 22, 1960:

The Dual Progress Plan calls for an elementary science course of study suited to nongraded grouping and advancement. The course of study should provide a sequence of learning materials suited to the needs of the least and the most advanced pupils in Grades I–VI. It should be designed to meet the needs of *all* elementary children, regardless of ability. *All* pupils should be required to attain a reasonable level of mastery of any given topic in the sequence before being introduced to the next topic.

It is assumed that pupils will be grouped for instruction in science without regard to grade placement according to their *actual* level of advancement in the course of study. It is assumed that, at each general level of advancement, pupils will be grouped according to their ability (or learning rate). Finally, it is assumed that pupils in different classes, and within the same class, will advance at different rates along the curricular sequence.

The science course of study as outlined by ETC will be organized in terms of stages in learning *the scientific process of acquiring knowledge,* rather than in terms of acquiring knowledge (vocabulary, facts, principles) in the content fields of science (*e.g.,* physics, biology, astronomy, geology). The sequence will recognize, at all levels, that the essence of the scientific approach involves asking questions about relationships of cause and effect (antecedent-consequent, independent-dependent variables), stating hypotheses about assumed relationships, testing hypotheses, and stating outcomes of such tests. In other words, the essence of the scientific process concerns *explanation.* Description enters inasmuch as explanation calls for hypotheses or principles that relate *variables.* Description has to do with identifying, naming, classifying, and measuring variables.

It is proposed that children's questions related to explanation are of two main types:

Type 1. This happened; why? (Going from effect to cause.)

Type 2. If this is done, what will happen? (Cause to effect.) It is proposed that Type 2 is more fundamental since answering Type 1 questions calls for setting up and testing Type 2 questions.

It is proposed that children's questions related to description are of three main types:

Type 3. What is this? (Assigning a class name.)

Type 4. What is this like? (Abstracting essential qualities.)

Type 5. How is this similar to, or different from that? (Comparing and classifying.)

Answering these questions calls for abstracting and generalizing, and for measuring quantities related to the qualities abstracted.

A sequence will be developed in terms of *stages of advancement in the scientific processes of inquiry.* Dr. Heathers' report of plans for developing such a sequence, when given recently at a conference conducted by the American Association for the Advancement of Science in Washington, D.C., received enthusiastic endorsement. The Dual Progress Plan, with its provisions for nongrade-level grouping and advancement, appears to be well suited for a process-centered elementary science program.

EXPERIMENTAL TEACHING CENTER PROJECTS

The Experimental Teaching Center of the New York University School of Education is the keystone of the structure for research and development of the Dual Progress Plan, as, indeed, it will be for other studies in education. Dr. Glen Heathers, director of the center, lists twelve project areas in which the center was active during 1959–1960, all directly or indirectly dependent on the grants from the Ford Foundation (brief reports on some of these projects will be found in appropriate chapters in this book):

1. Participation in the second year of the five-year Co-operative Study of the Dual Progress Plan. The center is responsible for helping the Long Beach and Ossining school systems implement the new plan, and for evaluating the plan.
2. Initiation of a two-year, longitudinal study of personal-social adjustment of pupils in four school systems, two (Long Beach and Ossining) with the Dual Progress Plan, two (Hastings-on-Hudson and Roosevelt) with the self-contained classroom.
3. Development of an adaptation of the elementary mathematics course of study for nongrade-level grouping and advancement in the Dual Progress Plan.
4. Development of an elementary science course of study adapted to the requirements of the Dual Progress Plan.
5. Revision of Dr. Kaya's test of creative thinking in young children, the ETC "Solving Puzzles Test."
6. Conducting two DPP administrative internships in co-operation with the Department of Administration and Supervision (Professor Borgeson), and the Long Beach and Ossining school systems. One intern was provided for each of the two systems.
7. Initiating a three-year research program on the teaching of foreign languages in elementary and junior high schools.
8. Developing a master's program for the preparation of elementary teachers with a specialty in mathematics, science, or language arts-social studies.

9. Developing the ETC Affiliates Program involving research relationships between the center and school systems in the New York metropolitan area that are interested in the Dual Progress Plan, or in introducing and evaluating other innovations in their schools.

10. Conducting a questionnaire study of attitudes of public school superintendents in the New York metropolitan area regarding employing and utilizing elementary teachers with a specialty in mathematics, science, or language arts–social studies.

11. Participation in several New York University projects as a way of providing the services of this research center to the University.

12. Publicizing the center and its work through talks to organizations, publishing reports of its work, and distributing written materials to individuals and organizations requesting information about any of its activities.

Of the twelve projects listed, all but three (1, 5, and 12) were new in the year, 1959–1960.

The 1959 Ford grant permitted the annual employment of two administrative interns, one each for Long Beach and Ossining. The first appointees were graduate students in Educational Administration and Supervision at New York University. Under the guidance of Professor Frithiof C. Borgeson, they aided in the day-to-day administration of the plan and collected data on its implementation. Such interns will form a nucleus of experienced personnel as the plan is taken up in other school systems.

It is to be noted that the Experimental Teaching Center is an integral part of the School of Education—a research arm for testing and demonstrating new ideas "in theory, organization, leadership, curriculum, materials, methods, and teacher education." This means that eventually its work will extend beyond the Dual Progress Plan. Already, it is clear that new studies are needed in preschool education; in programs for the kindergarten and Grades I and II; in high school curriculum and methodology; in tests and measurements; in personality and adjustment; in comparative instructional costs; in the use of special devices, such as films, recordings, radio, and television; in new concepts of higher education; in the design of buildings and facilities. Studies of this type are already under way in various departments and research institutes; for the School of Education, the center increasingly is expected to become a centralizing force in such activity. To do this effectively would appear to call for a second unit, namely, a Child Research Center. This outcome, like the establishment of the present center, was recommended in the 1956 self-study of New York University.

At numerous points the work of the Experimental Teaching Center calls for a close co-ordination with research groups and departments outside the School of Education—psychology, sociology, the physical sciences, and the humanities, for example. However, co-operation *in general* does not mean much: it is only when university professors are really concerned about the quality of teaching below college, and in their chosen technical fields, that a true working relationship is established. Thus the work of the center, in future, should throw light on *why* pre-engineering subjects appear to be neglected, and *why* engineering as a career is so often distasteful to American young men, and almost beyond the pale for the women.

KLINE ON THE TEACHERS OF MATHEMATICS

In the preceding chapter, as in the plans of the Experimental Teaching Center referred to above, some attention was paid to new ways of presenting mathematical and scientific concepts to the child. It was indicated that the content itself was not a radical departure from what scientists themselves had long advocated. There is danger, however, that a zeal to improve teaching methods in order to intensify the children's interest in learning will divert us from the true aim of education. The aim is not indiscriminate learning, but learning devoted to important subject matter and to increasing competence, insight, and originality on the part of the learner.

Today many experts, particularly in mathematics and other branches of science, are taking a fresh look at what happens in the face-to-face teaching situation at the secondary and elementary levels. Often they do not like what they see, and they are not always reassured by the proposals for reform.

Mathematics, according to the distinguished mathematician, Morris Kline of New York University, is already suffering from a rash of new "methods" that dilute the learning process and restrict the competence achieved. He states[1]

The modernists would replace material currently taught by such topics as symbolic logic, Boolean algebra, set theory, some topics of abstract algebra such as groups and fields, topology, postulational systems, and statistics. I have no objection to the introduction of statistics, but I should like to examine the value of the other subjects from the standpoint of their central position in the body of mathematics and from the standpoint of application. As for importance in the body of mathematics, I believe it is fair to say that one could not pick more peripheral material.

Professor Kline holds that of the topics mentioned only statistics has a rightful claim as a subject to be taught in elementary mathematics. When it comes to *application*—in itself a sound concept—Kline notes that the "modernists" leave out of their discussions the applications [of orthodox mathematics] to:

Mechanics, sound, light, radio, electricity, atomic and nuclear theory, hydrodynamics, aerodynamics, geophysics, magnetohydrodynamics, elasticity, plasticity, chemistry, chemical physics, physical biology, and the various branches of engineering. If there are ten people in this world designing switching circuits, there are a hundred thousand scientists in these other fields. And what mathematics is used in these fields I have mentioned? Because I work in a large institute devoted to applied mathematics, I believe I can tell you. The subjects are algebra, geometry, trigonometry, co-ordinate geometry, the calculus, ordinary and partial differential equations, series, the calculus of variations, differential geometry, integral equations, theory of operators, and many other branches of analysis.

Kline has some positive views on curricular reform:

Genuine improvement of the curriculum does call for drastic revision, though not of course by resorting to modern mathematics and not by merely reshuffling the traditional mathematics. Just what should we be

[1] Morris Kline, "The Ancients versus the Moderns, A New Battle of the Books," *The Mathematics Teacher,* LI (October, 1958), 418–427.

doing? Let me begin by stating that we have not thus far correctly analyzed the weakness in the present curriculum. The trouble is not that we are teaching outmoded mathematics, except for one or two topics. Rather, the trouble lies in the way in which we approach the material we teach. I shall try to indicate the principles which would guide a revision of our present approach. . . .

My first principle, then, is that we must begin our teaching of mathematics by seeking to arouse interest in the subject. If this is agreed upon, then we should select material which will serve the purpose of arousing interest. But what interest can young people find in simplifying fractions, in factoring, in exponents, in the quadratic formula, and in all the other dirty, intrinsically meaningless, boring processes that we teach in first-year algebra? The fact is that we have been guided in our choice of material not by the effort to arouse interest but to teach the mathematics that will be needed in the subsequent study of the subject. Our concern, in other words, has been with preparation for the future. But with such an introduction to mathematics, few students want a future in the subject. . . .

My second principle is that regardless of how we arouse interest in mathematics, even if it be through games, we must supply motivation. . . .

Third, since even the great mathematicians think intuitively, we must all be sure that the intuitive meaning of each mathematical idea or procedure is made intuitively clear to the students. This intuitive side of mathematics is in fact the essence of the subject. Mathematics is primarily a series of great intuitions. The way to make the meaning of an idea clear is to present it in the intuitive setting that led to its creation or in terms of some simple modern equivalent. Physical or geometrical illustrations or interpretations will often supply this meaning. Thus $s = 16t^2$ is not just a quadratic function. It is a law of falling bodies, and s and t have definite and clear physical meanings. The fact that $s = 16t^2$ and not $16t$ also has an important physical significance and makes the quadratic feature impressive. Numerical examples, and especially examples wherein the process or theorem fails, help to make meanings clear.

Kline's observations here and elsewhere constitute an indictment of any teaching reform in mathematics that substitutes esoteric games for the fundamentals. While the advocates of games and a new symbolism stress the arousal of interest on the part of students they have not, in my opinion as a nonmathematician, got to the root of the arguments. Boredom comes not only from repetition but also from a sense of futility. Kline stresses mathematics as a means, as a way of thinking and doing, that brings order into natural and social events. Its operations, since they are useful (that is, problem solving), are capable of arousing interest and appreciation: they encourage intuition and stimulate the imagination. This is the paradox: the impact of mathematics does not come from the abstract, all-encompassing generalization, but from a close attention to the concrete case, the particular solution, the measured work that is done. The abstractions follow and gradually they are revealed in their full power.

From the standpoint of the educational psychologist, I venture to predict that the future lies with Kline and his like-minded associates. The scientific demands of the day cannot be met without a widened and deepened approach to the teaching of mathematics. It will not do to move from an interminable emphasis on the trivial on the part of the uninformed (the general classroom teacher) to a new emphasis on games and tricks. We know already from the Long Beach and Ossining demonstrations that a sound program in mathematics, offered by experts in the subject, does indeed arouse interest. To hold, as I do, that mathematics is not a cultural imperative is simply to recognize that it does not—and perhaps cannot—achieve that status in a word-minded society. That mathematics in its higher stages is inevitably esoteric should not in the least reduce our need for it or our respect for the thousands of scientists for whom it is a *sine qua non*. The lack of something that is, or should be, common (literacy is the prime example), we rightly deplore and vigorously work against. The lack of something specialized, as in a mastery of science, music, or art, we tend to ignore, while intensifying our regard for those who stand out; we go vicarious. The test of a cultural imperative is that there is no substitute for competence in it on the part of any person. Perhaps, in future, the need for *general* scientific and mathematical competence will be so great as to push it across the elective-imperative barrier. In the meantime, for mathematics viewed as essentially an elective, two observations are in order: (1) the early computational stages (simple arithmetic) are needed as a common language, and (2) since we do not know from prior tests which students will prosper in mathematical studies, all students deserve a tryout.

SCIENCE TEACHING

Glenn O. Blough and others[2] present some arresting views on the place of science in the elementary grades and its significance in today's world:

In this century, characterized as it is by scientific and technological advances, scientific attitudes are not the motivating attitudes of a majority of our population. Most people accept scientific knowledge as valid within small spheres of their life and look to other sources of knowledge for behavior guide lines in many aspects of living. This results in a real dilemma. Children, who in science are taught to be open-minded, to be tolerant of various points of view, and not to jump to conclusions, are confronted on every hand with decisions which are not to be questioned, superstitions and magic, advertising that is false and authoritative, and other evidences of unscientific beliefs and behavior. One of the greatest cultural problems which elementary science teachers face is that of helping children see the spheres where scientific inquiry and behavior are appropriate, though perhaps sometimes not acceptable.

Apparently *scientific* answers in the self-contained classroom rarely rise above the level of enumeration and description. The sense of search, hypothesis, operation, and verification is lost, or at least enfeebled. The static item so neatly designed for a later insertion in quizzes—in college "Boards" and "Regents" tests, for that matter—is already firmly entrenched. (In the Dual Progress Plan some questions and answers remain descriptive, but they are relegated to the lower ranges of one's intelligence and aptitude; they are brigaded with the skills which they resemble without being as useful as skills.) In such a climate information grows by proliferation; thinking is shunned, for it is difficult, disturbing, and controversial. Growing into adulthood, the children of such classrooms are easy marks for propa-

[2] Glenn O. Blough, "Developing Science Programs," *Rethinking Science Education*, 59th Yearbook of the National Society for the Study of Education (Chicago: University of Chicago Press, 1960), pp. 112–115.

ganda, demagoguery, and dogma; often they clutter their minds with the unimportant while wearing the badge of the educated person. As education in the United States moves away from its preoccupation with "recitations" of this type, a countermovement in testing, measuring, and evaluating is urgently in demand. Standardized tests have not as yet tapped the ability to think at any level of intelligence or special aptitudes.

This chapter is not meant to be more than suggestive of changes in method and curriculum that are consistent with, and to some extent instigated by, new proposals in elementary education. Insofar as the Dual Progress Plan is concerned, a definitive statement along such lines cannot be formulated before the close of the five-year demonstrations in Ossining and Long Beach. The new place of mathematics and science is stressed only because their removal from the domain of the self-contained classroom is a striking feature of the plan.

ON THE TEACHING OF READING AND OTHER SUBJECTS

At the same time, there is ferment in every discipline or area. For example, in reading, a hardy perennial in all teaching, the controversy over what is auditory and what is visual is giving way to sober plans for instructional improvement along all lines. The teaching of writing similarly is getting its full share of attention. Outside the profession of teaching, few persons realize that *phonics* as a prior emphasis in the art of reading had been tried for a half century in American education and found to be defective. The new synthesis which should improve the effectiveness of the "core" in the Dual Progress Plan is described by Alvina Treut Burrows, an authority on reading:[3]

One of the immediate anxieties which has shown nation-wide symptoms results from the accusation that schools do not use phonics in teaching beginning reading. In this heated attack a false controversy has been dramatized. On a narrowly visioned stage two characters have been

[3] Alvina Treut Burrows, "Controversy over Reading," *Education Synopsis,* New York University (1960), pp. 9–11.

posed: one representing *Good* (phonic methods) and one representing *Evil* (sight methods). This is a primitive over-simplification. It distorts the facts that both sight and sound and a host of psychological factors are involved in learning to read.

The dualistic argument ignores the truth that good schools teach children to analyze words phonetically as soon as they have got the basic idea of reading for meaning. A minimal sight vocabulary is developed from communications of real importance to the young initiates. In many schools children are introduced to reading instruction by use of their own briefly dictated stories, by using signs, directions, captions and labels. From these original "compositions" they progress to easy repetitive texts, magazines, and trade books. They attach meaning to symbols from their very first efforts. In known context they isolate and identify a few words and gradually add to the list they know by sight. When this kind of learning is well under way phonics teaching appears to help and is quite generally employed. However, the instigators of an "either-or" controversy brush aside the fact that curriculum guides and text books include a great number of phonic techniques as soon as the learners have adapted themselves to reading for ideas and have stored up the beginnings of a sight vocabulary.

Both history and research support the practice of using appropriate phonic assistance, along with other techniques, to insure accurate perception and independence. No valid research supports young children's having to memorize isolated letter and syllable sounds as a forerunner to the reading of words and sentences.

Speech, of course, is as important as it ever was, but elocution is not. Silent reading without external "mouthing" has its own validity and a vastly expanded usefulness in a world that is flooded with publications. The impact of motion pictures, radio, and television on this world of the printed page has not been fully assessed. Certainly we should not disparage the place of the spoken word and the moving image; what counts is not the medium of communication but its effectiveness and appropriateness. Any device that strengthens thought and opens channels of communication has value, however much it is subject to abuse. In total footage or poundage the printed page yields its share of what is ephemeral or confusing, and it lacks the virtue of confrontation. In short, literacy taken at its leanest is surely an inadequate goal for any core curriculum.

Music and the arts (graphic and performing) also are vulnerable along the same lines; a truly defensible curriculum in these forms of specialization must go far beyond what is found in the daily life of the American people. In fact, I feel they have a unique part to play in the future of the American school at every scholastic level. Their further development, like that of science in recent decades, may take on the dimensions of a cultural renaissance.

ON THE DESIGN OF CLASSROOMS AND SCHOOLS

The question is often asked, Are schools and schoolrooms architecturally designed to make the most of the Dual Progress Plan? In general the answer is, *No.* But then, thousands of existing school buildings were not designed properly to serve any educational purpose. The trouble is not where the random critics of contemporary education generally place it. The real wastefulness in buildings is not in their high cost (is not everything expensive?), but in the concept of every classroom as an interchangeable part. However, contemporary designs show more freedom. There is a superior use of light, color, and texture; there is provision for flexibility with respect to curriculum and teaching devices. In spite of the loose journalistic talk about "palaces" and "showplaces," I have yet to see a single school that would so qualify; for magnificence, you must still turn to banks, hotels, theaters, courts, churches, monuments, and mausoleums; these somehow seem to escape the wrath of the critic.

We should not downgrade the elements of quality and beauty in human affairs. If we are to design beautiful buildings and grounds for any purposes, I nominate the schools for inclusion in the select company, asking only that "form follow function." Consider the impact of buildings on any social enterprise of vast scope. Human nature endows its ideals and aspirations with physical structures. In religion we have the quiet, gracious chapel and the splendid cathedral, temple, or mosque. We erect monuments to persons, events, and ideals as a constant reminder of times of greatness. Government —local, state, national, or international—tends to take on the dignity and mobility of its physical surroundings; this is especially true of the courts. The modern hospital is more than a functional outcome of medical progress; it also epitomizes our respect for hygiene, personal health, and a long life. Imaginatively designed theaters, halls, and museums lend excitement to every performance or display. Through good design, color, and landscaping, our homes lift us up from the shack, the tenement, or the pretentious monstrosity.

Now, all this is to the good. It is good a hundred times over when applied to the design and construction of school buildings. Schools are more than monuments to a glorious past; they are an investment in the future of the human race. They should exemplify not past mistakes and deficiencies, but our best efforts in the encouragement of learning and the art of communication. A poor structure may exert a deadening influence and, in the long run, be an enemy of child growth. Moreover, an old schoolhouse may be surprisingly expensive if measured in terms of educational outcomes. A building should facilitate and encourage—indeed *invite*—the full participation of pupils in programs deemed desirable; otherwise, like the lobster's rigid shell, it retards progress.

Schools are the workshops and the daily living accommodations of *all* children for the most sensitive period of their lives. *What to teach, how to teach,* and *where to teach* should be regarded as parts of a single cultural whole. To ignore the basic needs in this finest sector of human affairs is to do more than hold back the national economy; it is to lose faith in our future. My feeling is that, far from losing faith, the American people are seeking a new leadership in which economic, political, and cultural affairs will be, for once, thoroughly blended.

9

THE EDUCATION OF TEACHERS FOR THE DUAL PROGRESS PLAN

Although we find specialized teachers in standard elementary school systems, they usually are supervisors who assume complete or partial classroom responsibility for a limited portion of the student's week. They may be regarded as "additives." Teachers of physical education, shopwork, and business courses (when offered) are exceptions to the rule. However, there is a growing tendency to introduce specialized teachers. Of course, such teachers are necessary in the Dual Progress Plan. The school systems of Long Beach, Ossining, and Pennsbury have relied, in part, on in-service education during the period of adaptation to the new plan. As new teachers are added, their strength in specialized areas is ascertained.

Paul Woodring[1] has written a compact account of the course of teacher education in the United States, with emphasis on the proliferation which has taken place in the last few decades. He shows how a perversion of the teachings of John Dewey led to the false assumption that the teaching of the whole child did not require excellence in subject matter or any consistent philosophy of education. Woodring's comments on the way out of this morass should give comfort to all engaged in implementing the Dual Progress Plan:

[1] Paul Woodring, *New Directions in Teacher Education* (New York: The Fund for the Advancement of Education, 1957).

The solution appears to lie in requiring a broad liberal education for all teachers and school administrators and at the same time greater attention to educational philosophy during the period of professional education so that each teacher may see beyond his own field. The liberally educated teacher will see his subject in broader perspective. His aim will be, not knowledge of a subject, but the wisdom which follows knowledge. He will teach his subject better because of his ability to see beyond it. In no profession is liberal education more important than in teaching and in few does it play so large a part. The teacher's need for such a background is not dependent upon the subject to be taught or the age level of the pupils with whom he is to work. . . .

The total education of teachers consists of four interrelated parts:

1. Liberal education;
2. An extended knowledge of the subject or area taught;
3. Professional *knowledge*, as distinguished from professional skills;
4. Skills in managing a classroom, working with children and young people, and in the supervision of the learning process (10–11).

Woodring describes the deeply felt dilemma in which the "academic" world holds that only knowledge of subject matter really counts while the teachers college (now transformed into the college or university) maintains that the *sine qua non* is teaching skills together with enough subject matter for teaching *at a particular grade* level. Of course, with a better understanding of the demands of the educational profession these extreme views approach one another. In this rapprochement, the Fund for the Advancement of Education of the Ford Foundation is playing a leading role; it does not "take sides" in the numerous controversies but endeavors to strengthen teaching in accordance with an agreed upon philosophy. This, too, is shown by Woodring's writing:

If we assume that teacher preparation must include *both* liberal and professional education and that these two must be brought into harmony with each other in some organized pattern, there would appear to be four ways of approaching the problem:

1. A fifth year of professional training and experience can be provided for liberal arts graduates.
2. Liberal arts colleges can be encouraged to incorporate essential professional training into their programs in ways which will not vitiate the liberal arts program.

3. Universities can be encouraged to devise new programs which represent the best thinking of both academic and professional faculties.

4. Teachers colleges can be assisted in providing better liberal arts programs and in reorganizing their professional courses in such a way as to eliminate proliferation and duplication (24–25).

Thus far the fund has principally supported proposals in the first three categories above. In the first group, the essentials that cut through many variations are cited by Woodring as follows:

1. All teachers should have a background of liberal education similar to that represented by a degree from a liberal arts college.

2. A considerable number of liberal arts graduates wish to become teachers and offer an important source of teacher supply.

3. All professional education essential to beginning teaching can be provided in a one-year program following a four-year period of liberal education.

4. A study of essential professional areas of knowledge can effectively be combined with an extended internship during the one-year program. (Some assume that a summer of university work in education is necessary while others offer only late afternoon or Saturday classes or seminars.)

5. Such a combined program makes for better integration of principles and practice than is to be found in existing programs.

6. A concentrated fifth-year program can avoid much of the duplication and proliferation of professional courses allegedly found in traditional programs of teacher education.

7. Professional education should be closely related to the work of the public schools and should include extended experience in those schools—more experience than is normally provided by practice teaching (31).

While some of the above propositions are well backed by experience, and increasingly by research and demonstration, they are still in a hypothetical state. We can, for example, approve a fifth year of professional education (with supervised practice) as one means, perhaps an excellent means, of teacher education without expecting it to carry the chief burden of teacher supply. There is something to be said for an earlier declaration on the part of the student as to his choice of a career. Engineers make a choice in their first college year—undoubtedly a premature choice on the part of many students. The student in medicine, dentistry, or law commonly shows a collegiate preference and may be intensively engaged in preparatory work by his junior year. Graduate students in the liberal arts and science generally follow a major proclaimed one or two years previously. In a profession as significant as education, how casual should the neophyte be? Allowing for the basic need for a strong sequence in the liberal arts, to be overlapped with and followed by supporting subjects (e.g., psychology), there is much to be gained by an early declaration of purpose—of dedication, if you will. My feeling is that the beginning of the junior year of college is a good time to make firm commitments. They are not irrevocable, but neither are they fortuitous. For teaching, at any level from kindergarten to college, it is hard to recruit first-class talent. Perhaps an early contact with the profession would counterbalance prevailing attitudes as to its lack of "a future."

The plain truth is, many capable young persons like to teach, once they have some taste of it; they should be oriented toward teaching before the blandishments of the business world take hold. Perhaps one way out is to project a three-year master's degree in teaching, following the promising plan developed by Dr. Oliver C. Carmichael and his associates. Under this plan, the student embarks on his master's program at the start of the junior year.

The area of agreement in the last ten years, as outlined by Woodring, is impressive. Not much time is given to strictly methodological courses in our teachers colleges and schools of education, and the state requirements, on the whole, are modest (the lowest of any certified profession). In my view, the main defects are found in the fragmentation in *both* the liberal arts and education sequences. This is coupled with a residual contempt on the part of college professors for anything in the department of education and a strong feeling among the staff in education that professors elsewhere shun responsibility for teacher preparation. Here, as indicated, the times are fast changing, and Woodring's view is also of interest in this respect.

A sound program of teacher education must prepare teachers for the schools of the probable future rather than for those of the certain past. However obvious this principle may be, it has not provided the basis for most of our teacher education. In the great majority of our colleges, teachers still are being prepared for the self-contained classrooms of 1940 or 1950 rather than for the kind of schools which most probably will come into existence in 1960, 1970, or 1980 (71).

Woodring then sums up what might be entitled *the insurmountable task* of the all-purpose teacher:

Being responsible for the teaching of all subjects taught in the elementary school, she [the ideal teacher?] should command a scholarly knowledge of mathematics, literature, history, science, geography, government, music, and art. An elementary knowledge of these fields is not sufficient, for in each sixth-grade class there will be a few children with mental ages of sixteen, eighteen, or higher and some of these will have marked aptitudes in special fields. The ideal teacher must have advanced knowledge in all areas if she is to provide maximal learning opportunity for gifted children. She would be an expert in the teaching of reading and able to diagnose reading difficulties. She must teach handwriting, spelling, and many more skills. She should have a thorough grasp of language and should know how to teach children to use it effectively, both in speech and in writing. Probably she should know some language other than her own for foreign language instruction is increasingly becoming a part of the elementary curriculum (71–72).

All that on the side of subject matter! As a result, we have accepted teachers who can do *something* in all these fields, propped up by a few specialists and the ever-ready textbooks and canned examinations; we have, at least, demanded a humane person who generally likes children and gets along well with people. Clearly, the problem is to combine learning in depth (by restricting the content spectrum) with the humane and proficient approach, on the ground that good intentions are not enough. I feel that the team approach, together with specialization fed by a strong program in the liberal arts, in future, will be looked upon as so rational a combination as to make students wonder what the midcentury conflicts in teacher education were all about.

CARTWRIGHT ON TEACHER EDUCATION

A well-known educator observes the trend in teacher education for our own time:[2]

If I were the principal of an elementary school, I would want each of my teachers to be a specialist in some area of knowledge, whether arithmetic, art, geography, health, history, music, psychology, reading, or some other. And I would want the faculty as a whole to have some balance in this regard. This line of reasoning does not necessarily lead to departmental organization, but it might do just that. . . . Thus, I would have both the undergraduate and the graduate education of elementary schoolteachers include a concentration of work in a particular field, even though the formal majors in these programs might well be in education.

THE KLEINMAN REPORT

I am indebted to Dr. Lou Kleinman for use of his preliminary report to the Experimental Teaching Center on developments in elementary teacher education programs in selected institutions. His statement, based on correspondence with fifty-four colleges and universities and on a 1959 report of the National Commission on Teacher Education and Professional Standards, includes these items:

1. Elementary teacher education programs offered by teachers colleges, liberal arts colleges, and universities are becoming increasingly similar. Three factors may account for this trend:
   a. Many teachers colleges have been reorganized as multipurpose institutions. Consequently, academic subject-matter departments at such colleges are being strengthened and general (liberal arts) education requirements for teachers extended.
   b. Liberal arts colleges are accepting a fuller share of the responsibility for preparing high quality elementary teachers to help ease the current shortage.
   c. At a number of universities, responsibility for making policy in teacher education has been turned over to a university-

[2] William H. Cartwright, "The Graduate Education of Teachers—Proposals for the Future," *The Educational Record*, 40, No. 1 (January, 1959), 151.

wide council on teacher education. Such a council usually represents the interests of the university and its several colleges, key academic departments, and professional education specialists (in schools of education).

2. There has been a re-emphasis on general (liberal arts) education for all teachers, including those preparing to teach at the elementary level. Thirty-one states specifically require general (liberal arts) education credits for elementary certification, the average being 49 semester hours. The 294 institutions accredited by the National Council for Accreditation of Teacher Education (the recognized national professional accrediting agency for teacher education) require on the average about 46 semester hours in general (liberal arts) education of elementary education students (a range of 11 to 97 semester hours). Among the areas included in general (liberal arts) education are English and communication arts, humanities, social studies, physical and biological sciences, mathematics, religion and philosophy, physical education, American history, and foreign languages and literature. While most general (liberal arts) education requirements are completed during the freshman and sophomore years, they are being extended into the junior and senior years.

3. It appears that professional education requirements for elementary teachers are becoming standardized. State certification requirements range from 16 to 36 semester hours (average 23 semester hours). Most of the institutions accredited by NCATE require from 20 to 40 semester hours. According to a NCATE report, only three of 294 reporting schools require as many as 60 credits in professional courses. Professional courses generally required are in the areas of philosophical and social foundations of education, human growth and psychology of learning, general methods of teaching, and methods and materials for teaching particular subjects.

4. At a growing number of institutions, "special methods" courses are being taught by subject-matter specialists from appropriate colleges and academic departments. While such courses constitute a combination of content and methodology, they are usually reported as professional education courses.

5. Specialization in one or more subject matter areas (in addition to the work in general and professional education described above) is being required of elementary education students by a small, but significant, number of institutions. Some insist on a full major in a subject-matter area, while others accept a minor. Several schools enable elementary education students to complete the equivalent of the subject-matter major on the basis of general education courses and electives.

6. Increasingly, state departments of education are approving programs for certification rather than specific courses. In such cases, certification is based on the recommendation of the preparing institution. This is particularly true in relation to experimental programs. In order to encourage such programs, a number of state departments of education are willing to give blanket certification to those completing approved experimental programs.

CARNEGIE STUDIES

While it is too early to report upon the outcome of the AAAS-Carnegie Study on the use of special teachers of science and mathematics in Grades V and VI, the very title of the project would have been unusual ten years ago. The abstract that follows outlines this promising demonstration:[3]

One of the major activities in the extended Science Teaching Improvement Program of the American Association for the Advancement of Science, under the new three-year grant to AAAS by the Carnegie Corporation of New York, is to be known as the Study on the Use of Special Teachers of Science and Mathematics in Grades V and VI. The cooperation of the public school systems in Cedar Rapids, Iowa; Lansing, Michigan; Versailles, Kentucky; and Washington, D.C., has been obtained for this project. In each of these school systems, at least one special teacher of science and at least one special teacher of mathematics will teach only science or only mathematics in Grades V and VI to at least four different classes. The teachers have been selected by the school systems as those having special training, competence, and suc-

---

[3] Abstract from *Science Education News*, September, 1959, contained in *The American Mathematical Monthly*, 66, No. 8 (October, 1959), 270–271.

cessful teaching experience in the areas to which they are assigned.

While the use of special teachers of art, music, and physical education is fairly widespread in American elementary schools, the question of special teachers in the academic disciplines such as science and mathematics remains highly controversial. Majority opinion of experts in elementary education, both administrators and teachers, seems to favor strongly the retention of the "self-contained" classroom at this level. On the other hand, many scientists favor the use of specially prepared teachers particularly because of the new and anticipated demands on the elementary teacher. It is quite impossible under the present methods of training elementary teachers for the elementary teacher to take what appears to be a necessary minimum of course work in science and mathematics, or in the other academic disciplines as well. The National Science Foundation sponsored curriculum studies, which are giving attention to the science curriculum at the elementary level, will stress how serious is the problem. Both the School Mathematics Study Group and the Biological Sciences Curriculum Study are concerned with grades from kindergarten to Grade VIII, as well as with the high schools, and there are also other privately sponsored activities which are working on materials at the elementary level.

An attempt will be made to provide a careful evaluation of the Study so that interested persons will have available objective data to support their cases or to persuade them of weaknesses in their present point of view. It is anticipated that the Study will be conducted during a two-year period beginning in the fall of 1959 and it is to be hoped that the Study might be extended to more schools during the second year.

The Carnegie-sponsored STIP Study is timely, for illustrations of the lag in science-teacher education are all about us. Perhaps the experience of Nathan S. Washton of Queens College is characteristic:[4]

The effort to improve, or in many cases to introduce, science teaching in the elementary schools faces a serious stumbling block—elementary school teachers fear and hate science. This was one of two major conclusions reached by Dr. Nathan S. Washton, professor of education at Queens College, after a five-year experiment with teachers taking a graduate course. The second, he said yesterday, was that something can be done about it—that these same teachers can be made to appreciate

[4] Reported by James J. Morisseau in the *New York Herald Tribune,* March 7, 1960.

science and to enjoy teaching it. But he warned against introducing "crash" programs in science in the elementary schools with teachers who are unprepared to run them.

The inadequate preparation in science of most elementary school teachers was underlined, he said, when he gave a standardized ninth-grade science test to 100 of his teacher-students over a five-year period.

Sixty-three scored what would be a failing grade for a thirteen-year-old ninth grade pupil. The problem was compounded in the teachers colleges, where most of his students had no more than one year of science, if that, and where courses in elementary school teaching methods were taught by professors who themselves had little or no background in science.

After a graduate course by Professor Washton which stressed "actual participation in the setting up and demonstration of scientific experiments," the teachers markedly improved in their grasp of science.

FOREIGN LANGUAGES

Another area in the elementary grades in short supply is the teaching of a foreign language—any foreign language, although French is the most common. In a report to the Experimental Teaching Center, Dr. Anna Balakian states:

The interest in Foreign Languages in Elementary Schools (FLES) has been increased all over the United States in the last ten years at a galloping speed. General public encouragement and pressure from parent groups have given the movement unusual impetus. It has proved impossible to keep statistics up-to-date because of the rapid changes in figures with every successive term. A current example will demonstrate the scope of this education trend: this fall the University of Utah put on a television series in French for elementary school pupils and had printed 500 copies of its manual, intended for classrooms that might be tuning in. It received 11,000 requests for the Manual.

However, this current enthusiasm for FLES does not produce unqualified rejoicing among specialists in the teaching of foreign languages. The far-sighted realize that the program is developing upon precarious foundations, for the demand far exceeds the supply of teachers capable of making it a sound educational investment.

Balakian goes on to show how the gap between demand and supply has thus far been filled: by calling upon high school teachers;

by asking teachers in self-contained classrooms to "brush up" on a foreign language studied in high school or college; by using teachers whose native tongue is foreign (they are especially useful in televised instruction). State standards for such teaching are conspicuously lacking; in 1959 only the state of Kansas appeared to have developed specific standards for teachers of foreign languages in the elementary grades.

ART EDUCATION

Wherever we turn, the story of inadequacy is much the same. Thus Professor Howard Conant, Head of Art Education at New York University, in an address to the Chicago Art Educators[5] feels compelled to support this statement by the National Council in Arts and Government which appeared in the *Congressional Record:* "The teaching of art, unfortunately, often has to be assigned to persons who have not had adequate art training for this task, or who lack the desired sensitivity and imagination." Conant adds:

Most classroom teachers have had totally inadequate educational preparation for the art teaching responsibilities which many of them are now asked to assume. Probably less than 5% of all elementary and secondary school pupils receive specialized art instruction from properly trained art teachers. Of the estimated 20,000 art teachers in the United States, probably only a few thousand have had what those of us in this room would call an adequate preparation. The New York State art supervisor recently told me that some 40% of the people teaching art in New York State do *not* meet certification or licensing requirements! Many school systems have fewer art teachers per hundred pupils than they had ten years ago. Very few art teachers really understand and implement in their teaching the most important theories of educational philosophy and psychology.

The only psychological information which has remained on the active intelligence level of most art teachers is that taken from art education textbooks which, though they were written by eminent art educators, are not always well regarded by psychologists. One finds art educators firming up behavioral categories which psychologists themselves have not yet been able to identify clearly!

[5] Howard Conant, "The Role of the Arts in Education," *Art Education Bulletin,* 17, No. 5 (May, 1960), 4–14.

In Conant's view, the needed reforms will also carry a new concept of the place of art in life:

Somehow, we *must* realize that art education is not just a matter of providing enjoyable—and, of course, creative—opportunities for pupils to express themselves freely, even significantly, in paint, clay, wood, and various other media. Creative art expression is *extremely* important for people of all ages. But I would like to submit to you the proposition that creative expression in art is *not* the primary function of art education! Creative expression *is important*. It is *essential* for creative expression to play a major role in art education. But it should not be our sole concern, not even our dominant concern. The *primary* function of art education, I am firmly convinced, is to develop consumer taste—a working knowledge of art—in people of all ages who are now suffering from acute aesthetic anemia.

INVITATION TO MEN

As indicated previously in this book, the Dual Progress Plan, especially in its ungraded segment, should encourage a higher percentage of men to enter the field of elementary school teaching. This would be a good thing, mainly for four reasons:

1. It is truly more "natural" for children to spend time with both sexes than to be constantly under the guidance of one, which is to say, women. Inevitably American women have a point of view which is not without effect; witness their conspicuous distaste for engineering or medicine as a career.
2. In some subject matter, science, for example, the recruitment of teachers could draw upon a large population of males.
3. It is hopeless to attempt to meet the shortage of qualified teachers by relying only on women.
4. A large number of male teachers in elementary education would eventually strengthen the supply of supervisors and administrators who had had a firsthand teaching experience.

Accordingly I have found the program of the University of Wisconsin-Milwaukee of interest: it shows what can be done to effect a change in social patterns if conditions are right for it. To quote:[6]

[6] Gerald T. Cleason and Lee H. Mathews, "Preparing Men for Teaching in Elementary Schools," *Phi Delta Kappan*, 40, No. 7 (April, 1959), 285–287.

During the last ten years (1948–1958) UW-M has graduated 1,124 students who had completed four-year programs and were certified to teach in Grades IV–VIII. Of this number 597 or 53 per cent were men! The yearly percentages ranged from 34.7 per cent in 1954 to 64.2 per cent in 1950. During this same period there were 230 secondary education graduates: 130 or 57 per cent were men. For the year 1957–58 men constituted 64.9 per cent of the total university enrollment; 52.8 per cent of the secondary education graduates were men; and 63 per cent of the elementary education graduates were men. The data for the past ten years show that there has been an unusually high percentage of male graduates in the elementary education program. Figures for years prior to World War II show the same trend, but not to such a marked degree.

The authors identify ten factors to account for this phenomenon (they are not in order of importance): excellent placement opportunities ("the good male graduate usually has a number of positions from which to choose"); opportunities for advancement; single salary schedules for elementary and secondary teachers; acceptable social status ("the concept of the elementary school as the domain of women is rapidly being changed"); high status in the university community ("a student does not have to apologize for being an education major"); separate teacher licensing for upper elementary grades (IV–VIII); guidance for entering students; through community recreation activities, young men often have previous experience with young children; extensive use of men in the teacher education programs for the elementary grades; the requirements of a strong program in general education.

The Wisconsin program is robust, and perhaps unique in the United States. To my way of thinking it is an admirable demonstration of the need to combine many factors—and to "mean business" —as against the common practice of giving up easily if men do not respond to "recruiting" tactics. The men, like the women, respond to deeply felt personal, professional, and financial drives; they are making long-range, perhaps lifetime, decisions. Were we to add the placement and growth potentials inherent in the Dual Progress Plan, together with rank and salary differentials based on merit (as in college teaching), there should be less trouble in staffing the elementary years with both sexes. The word "merit" is often anathema to the teaching profession, largely, I believe, because of the teachers' lack of faith in the objectivity of their local administrators and school board members. More radical, but worth trying, is a further differential related to the number of dependents a teacher has; this is really a cost-of-living adjustment applied to a particular teacher. For a nation that finally accepted the idea of married teachers and married college freshmen with children, it does not seem unreasonable to predict a strong return of the man-with-a-family to the teaching profession. The trade unions handily solved this problem by forcing the hourly and yearly wage high enough to support a man with three or four dependents. The teaching profession "solved" it by setting a "salary" below the wages of the plumber, the bricklayer, or the steelworker—with a resultant mass reliance on unmarried women. These devoted women, unmarried or married, are, and will long remain, the backbone of the profession of classroom teaching, but they will not suffer if men (Wisconsin men in the vanguard!) now offer to work with them, side by side.

PROGRAM 888 IN THE SCHOOL OF EDUCATION OF NEW YORK UNIVERSITY

The grant from the Ford Foundation in June, 1959, included funds for the support of a specialist in teacher education in the center and for scholarships for students (graduates in liberal arts) who would undertake a fifth year in the School of Education to prepare them for specialized teaching in elementary schools. The designated specializations were mathematics, science, and language arts-social studies. Dr. Lou Kleinman of the center's staff, aided by an advisory group, co-ordinated the surveys and inquiries that culminated in the new program. It was necessary to meet not only the requirements of a teaching specialty but also the standards already set up for "common-branches certification." Approved in March, 1960, this School of Education program was given the title, *Integrated Graduate Program 888.* Since there was not time in 1960 really to promote interest in this new departure, its full implementation was postponed to 1961.

Before presenting "888" in detail, I should like to summarize the discussions in the School of Education which preceded its approval. There was opposition in certain quarters and especially in the faculty in the Department of Early Childhood Education—a department committed by tradition and experience to the self-contained classroom. Briefly, the factors discussed in the Experimental Teaching Center Advisory Group (which may be of interest to other schools of education and teachers colleges) were these:

1. A belief that children from 8 to 12 years old will suffer if placed daily under as many as five teachers. (In this argument, the counterbalancing effect of team teaching that would return teachers to the same pupils in the ungraded segments was lost sight of, as was the actual experience in Long Beach and Ossining.)

2. The question was raised whether existing curricula in the Department might meet the demands of the Dual Progress Plan. (This was decided in the negative.)

3. There was a demand for matching the Dual Progress Plan and the unitary grade plan, *using the same teachers*. (This was rejected.)

4. There was agreement that, in view of the prior baccalaureate major in a subject matter area, the bulk of this graduate program should be in supporting and professional areas.

5. There was found to be no reason to exclude present elementary teachers from the program, provided such teachers had already developed a specialization and had a strong background in the liberal arts. However, the program will normally be less attractive to them, since they are already familiar with teaching techniques. Of course, teachers desiring to specialize could combine this program with further work in liberal arts. Many of them are already, in reality, "core" specialists.

6. Some faculty members felt that a six-year program (four of liberal arts plus two of graduate work in education) would be superior to the fifth-year plan. (It may turn out to be so, but there is reason to believe that, after five continuous years of college, the teacher-in-training might well turn to the practi-

cal experience of teaching. Possibly a sixth year later or a series of summer sessions would prove to be more rewarding than six uninterrupted college years.)

7. It was emphasized that New York State requires thirty-six graduate hours for certification for the master's degree in elementary education.

8. Some of the faculty felt that each trainee in "888" should also do student teaching in a self-contained classroom.

9. It was thought that a potential source of recruits would be specialists in various parts of a high school program who might prefer to teach younger children, if they could maintain their status as specialists.

10. There was general agreement that "888" should call for intensity in its approach and that, as a start, it should be set up on an interdepartmental basis.

All the points listed above were thrashed out in the fall of 1959. In the following winter, the advisory group continued to discuss the pros and cons and, in March, accepted a joint proposal of Dr. Kleinman and Dr. Heathers which emerged as "888." The paragraphs that follow are drawn from the 1960 announcement of the School of Education of New York University entitled "888 Integrated Graduate Program for the Preparation of Elementary Teachers with a Specialty."

This program is designed for graduates of accredited four-year colleges with a major in mathematics, science, English, literature, or social science. It requires full-time attendance for a regular academic year plus part of a summer and a minimum of 40 credit hours as outlined below. Successful completion of the program will yield a Master of Arts degree and eligibility for common branches certification.

The new program will prepare teachers who will provide for the child as a person and as a learner of subject matter. Each graduate will have developed competencies in relation to the teaching-learning process in general as well as to the teaching of his particular subject specialty. While the program is intended primarily to prepare teachers for roles as full-time specialists in one of three fields within a departmentalized or semidepartmentalized elementary school or on a "teacher team," graduates will be ready and certified to serve as common branches teachers.

Orientation to American education. The aims, organization, and roles of education in our society will be stressed. Major philosophical orientations to education will be studied within their historical contexts. Analysis of diverse organizational patterns for elementary education will be included and the roles and functions of the teacher examined.

Psychological foundations of education. The nature and needs of the learner, his growth and development, theories of the learning process, and educational evaluation and measurement will be studied intensively.

The total elementary program. Curriculum, methods, and materials will be studied in relation to all areas and levels of instruction so that the graduate may be competent to teach the common branches. Furthermore, though the graduate may be assigned as a specialist teacher, he should be able to relate his curricular area to other areas and to the total elementary program.

Curriculum, methods, and materials in the area of specialty. A sound foundation of content courses in the area of specialty is essential. The elementary teacher, moreover, needs to work on the integration of subject matter with materials and methods appropriate to teaching the area to young children.

Further background courses in the area of specialty. Some students in the program will need to remove background deficiencies in the major area.

Field experiences. The translation of theory into practice is the key task of any program of professional preparation. Concentrated field experiences (participation activities with children and practice teaching) will be intimately blended with course work.

Individual and group conferences. Integration of course work with field experiences will be assured by continuous use of the conference method. Weekly group conferences and frequent individual conferences will be held.

The program will begin with a six-week summer session and a four-week postsession devoted to educational foundations and orientation prior to the regular academic year. The student will enroll, under the guidance of his adviser, in two foundations courses, one in educational psychology and one in educational philosophy. The former will emphasize the nature of the individual, theories of the learning process, and evaluation and measurement; the latter, philosophies that have affected educational practice in this country. Work in child development and introduction to elementary education will round out the student's general orientation.

During the ten-week orientation period, the student will maintain close contact with his adviser to discuss and plan his program. During these conferences, attention will be given to the nature of the new program and to career planning.

During the fall semester, the student will observe and participate in the field one and one-half days per week and attend related conferences one-half day per week. Field experiences will be carefully structured by the staff member responsible for the course in close cooperation with other instructors. The related three-hour weekly conference will feature analysis of field experiences in the light of principles studied in other courses.

All students in the program will take a course focusing on curriculum, general methods, and materials in all levels and subject areas for which the elementary school is responsible. In addition, each student will elect special methods courses related to his area of specialty.

Many students will have particular interests, needs, or deficiencies based on special background factors. Each student, therefore, will have the opportunity to elect, under advisement, a course intended to round out background or correct deficiencies. Such an elective might be in educational foundations, methodology, or in a subject-matter field.

The spring semester will be devoted primarily to an intensive practice teaching experience. Each student will be assigned to a school in the field three full days and two half days per week. He will be guided by a cooperating teacher at the school and a visiting supervising teacher from the University. Regular conferences among the student and his supervisor and cooperating teacher will take place. A seminar related to practice teaching will be held once a week to help the student analyze, evaluate, and improve his teaching experience.

Concurrently with practice teaching, the student will continue to pursue the special methods study appropriate to his particular subject area.

The Schedule of Courses

	Summer Sessions	*Credits*
Educational Psychology		3
Philosophical Foundations of Education		3
Child Development and the Program of Childhood Education		2
Introduction to Elementary Education: Aims, Organization, Practices		2
		10

Fall Semester	*Credits*
General Elementary Curriculum, Methods, and Materials . . .	6
Field Experience in Elementary Education	3
Language Arts in Childhood Education (first half of course) . .	2

The Teaching of Science in the Elementary School . . . . ⎫
  or
The Teaching of Arithmetic . . . .
  or ⎬ 2–3
Teaching Reading and Literature in the Elementary School .
  or
Reading: Prevention, Detection, and Correction of Disabilities I ⎭

Elective under advisement to correct deficiency	2–3
	——
	16

Spring Semester

Supervised Student Teaching	8
Problems of Elementary Teaching	2
Social Studies in Childhood Education	2

The Teaching of Science in the Elementary School . . . . ⎫
  or
The Teaching of Arithmetic . . . . ⎬ 2
  or
Language Arts in Childhood Education . . . . ⎭

	——
	14
TOTAL CREDITS	40

NEW YORK STATE REQUIREMENTS

The 1959 requirements of the University of the State of New York for a certificate for teaching "common branch subjects" are as follows:

The candidate shall have completed a four-year curriculum approved for the preparation of elementary school teachers leading to the baccalaureate degree (or approved equivalent preparation) including 36 semester hours in appropriate professional courses, 12 of which shall have been in observation and supervised student practice teaching in elementary schools.

The schedule which follows will be used to appraise the said 36 semester hour program:

Fields	Semester-Hour Range
1. Observation and supervised student practice teaching in elementary schools including conferences on teaching problems	12 to 15
2. Elementary school methods and materials	8 to 12
3. Psychology for teachers and child development or child psychology	6 to 10
4. History, principles, problems and/or philosophy of education	2 to 6

It is clear that graduates of "888" will meet the requirements of the New York State Department of Education for teaching the "common branches"—and exceed them in significant ways. In fact, the new curriculum lends an old-fashioned air to the present state requirements, for the state does not as yet certify specialists in mathematics, science, and the language arts for the elementary schools. In any case, the graduates seeking placement may find themselves in a unitary grade system with an opportunity eventually to become a specialized supervisor. (This condition does not apply to teachers of art, music, and physical education, long recognized as specialties.) In the Dual Progress Plan specialized supervisors will be supervising other specialists; they will no longer be in the position of dominating general teachers who, except in the "core," scarcely speak the same language as the subject-matter experts. Another transitional outlet for the graduates of programs like "888" may be to teach in junior or senior high school; what extra preparation this will call for can be ascertained, state by state.

FIRST RESPONSES TO "888"

Doubtless "888" will be revised after the trial run in 1961–1962. Thus the course, "The Teaching of Arithmetic," appears anachronistic in a dual progress system. Also a place will need to be made for methods in the teaching of music and art. These, and other matters will be investigated by the Experimental Teaching Center. The proposed evaluation, as set forth by Kleinman and Heathers, will cover four main areas:

1. Appraisal of student's characteristics at the beginning of the program:
   a. Intellectual abilities
   b. Background knowledge in the elementary curricular areas
   c. Personality characteristics relevant to teaching young children
   d. Educational values
   e. Attitudes and views concerning the aims and methods of elementary education
   f. Career goals
2. Appraisal of student's characteristics as in (1) above, where appropriate, at the end of the program
3. Appraisal of student's occupational status following graduation from the program (especially during first year or two)
4. Appraisal of teaching competencies during the first year following the program in relation to accepted learning goals
   a. By supervisory personnel in his school system
   b. By ETC observational study of teacher behavior
   c. (Possibly) By measures of pupils' achievement and of pupils' personal social behavior

If practicable, a suitable control group will be selected and evaluated on the items listed above.

In the meantime the center has mailed a questionnaire to the superintendents of 167 public school systems in the metropolitan area of New York City, to ascertain their readiness to accept qualified graduates of program "888." The 83 returns have been analyzed by Heathers and Kleinman. Two thirds of the superintendents indicated that they would prefer elementary teachers with a specialty for most or for some positions in their school systems, while only one in nine would prefer candidates without a specialty for all positions (see Table XIII). While the majority of the superintendents would wish to use "elementary teachers with a specialty" as teachers in the self-contained classroom, one in four would prefer to use them as teachers of a specialty in a "teacher-team" pattern and one in ten would wish to employ them as specialist teachers in a departmental-ized, or semidepartmentalized, pattern.

TABLE XIII

ATTITUDES OF EIGHTY-THREE PUBLIC SCHOOL SUPERINTENDENTS
TOWARD EMPLOYING ELEMENTARY TEACHERS
WITH A SPECIALTY

Alternative	Number Checking	Per Cent Checking
a. Would prefer such candidates for most positions	16	20
b. Would prefer such candidates for some positions	37	46
c. Would evaluate candidates without regard to specialist preparation	19	23
d. For all positions, would prefer candidates *without* a specialty	9	11

THE LIBERAL ARTS AND TEACHER EDUCATION

In some places, as we have seen, there is an awakening to the need for school systems to tap the sources of teacher recruitment that exist in liberal arts colleges. The concern is mutual, for many graduates in liberal arts find themselves scarcely prepared to enter any vocation or profession: beyond the reach of the unskilled labor force, they have not as yet acquired career proficiencies. A statement from the *Yale-Fairfield Study of Elementary Teaching*[7] is relevant:

Recently liberal arts colleges have manifested a growing interest in the preparation of teachers, especially for the elementary schools. Most of them, usually the smaller colleges of the community or regional type, have always trained teachers for the secondary schools. Many respondents to our questionnaires said they would have considered teaching if their colleges had provided good opportunities for teacher training. Colleges desiring to develop programs for the preparation of elementary teachers should take the assignment very seriously, recogniz-

[7] Clyde M. Hill (ed.), (abridged ed., New York, 1956), p. 136.

ing that it is a highly professional task requiring specialized resources both in personnel and equipment. It is probably safe to say that our elementary teachers are the real professionals among all groups of teachers. Liberal arts colleges can be a great source of well-qualified elementary teachers if in their planning they approach the problems without prejudice and take advantage of what very competent scholars have learned about teaching and learning. Too often the attitude of liberal arts colleges toward elementary teaching as a profession tempts them to engage in practices on even a lower professional level than those they have so frequently decried in the teachers colleges.

The five-year success of the Cornell Experimental Program for the Preparation of Elementary Teachers, as reported in *An Exciting Adventure in Education*[8] bears witness to the potentiality of the liberal arts colleges in meeting teacher shortages. There are, it seems, in all such programs, three underlying factors:

1. A high selection of students, in terms of both academic status and personality
2. A desire on the part of the students to teach
3. Sponsorship and supervision in an experienced institution of teacher education.

The unique feature of the Cornell plan is its substitution of discussions, seminars, and supervised experiences for conventional courses. Perhaps to the liberal arts graduate this opportunity to get free from standard class meetings and assignments is an "extra added attraction." In any event, the directors report these findings and conclusions, among others:

Liberal arts college graduates with the personal qualities essential for elementary school teaching are good candidates for a fifth-year professional preparation program and a teaching career. Liberal arts college graduates possess much professional knowledge, *before* formal professional preparation. Following one year of seminar-internship experience, they teach as well as those with conventional preparation. School administrators have welcomed teachers with this type of preparation and are interested in those who have first secured the liberal arts degree. School systems employing Program graduates generally have continued to ask for more candidates with the same preparation. Program gradu-

8 Cornell University Press, Ithaca, 1957.

ates have been certified in many states. More than two-thirds of the graduates have taught beyond the first year.

Upon the basis of evidence presented in this Report, the staff is convinced that the Cornell Program, devoid of conventional courses in education, and made up of seminars based in part upon the *real* problems of student teachers, together with student teaching and observation in public school classrooms, was a highly successful method of preparing liberal arts college graduates *without prior professional work,* for elementary school teaching.

In brief, while teacher education may now be regarded as an abiding interest of every comprehensive college or university, the specialized school or college of education should not abrogate its professional responsibility; its function is to lead. One great test of leadership will be found in a new integration of the four basic factors that contribute to teacher effectiveness: general education (the liberal arts); specialized education (a concentration); supporting education (psychology and the social studies); and supervised practice in the art of teaching. It is not beyond reason to hope that the Dual Progress Plan, which incorporates all four factors, will contribute to the advancement of teacher education.

IO

THE DEMONSTRATION-TEST: REVIEW AND PREVIEW

My purpose in this chapter is limited; it is to recapitulate the means by which there will emerge eventually, in both Long Beach and Ossining, objective data and analyses of student progress under the Dual Progress Plan. The findings from pretest and process-test data, like the opinions reported in Chapters 6 and 7 are tentative; they are cumulative and subject to refinement year by year. Presently we are confronted with a paucity of objective evidence applicable to *any* plan of school organization.

With the abandonment of the idea of setting up matched groups, comparing the unitary grade plan and the Dual Progress Plan at various check points, it was necessary to establish an objective system for measuring student progress, student grouping, and, finally, differences in outcome between the old and new plans.

Accordingly "pretest" data were obtained at the start of the project, the "posttest" data to be presented by way of comparison at the end of three years (subsequently five years). Each year "process data" are obtained for the same variables, one set applying to pupils, and another to teachers. The pupil measurements are regarded as more reliable and significant, for teacher variables are not easily encompassed in any compact testing program. Merit ratings of teachers are acceptable only if they are based on a composite of measures and judgments that pay homage to teaching as a profession; teaching is no clock-punching, time-and-motion job.

HYPOTHESES AND TESTS

Certain items in student advancement proposed by the working party (see Chapter 5) are the ones being used, each set up and examined *as a hypothesis*. They form the basis of a series of studies by Dr. Glen Heathers, Dr. Esin Kaya, and others in the Experimental Teaching Center. These hypotheses stand out:

1. *General achievement.* The general achievement level of the pupils in language arts, social studies, science, and mathematics will be higher after the Dual Progress Plan has been in effect than otherwise.
2. *Analytic thinking.* Pupils will show more evidence of analytic thinking and problem solving in all subject-matter areas after the Dual Progress Plan has been in effect than otherwise.
3. *Intelligence.* There will be no change in I.Q. of the child due to the Dual Progress Plan.
4. *Pupils' personal-social adjustment.* The Dual Progress Plan will not produce any changes in the number and intensity of social and emotional problems reported by pupils.
5. *Interest.* Instruction under the Dual Progress Plan will produce an increase of interest in subject-matter areas on the part of the pupils.

Both the Long Beach and Ossining systems had testing programs in the "core" areas of language and the social studies. Scores on the Stanford Achievement Tests were, therefore, to be used for the graded portion of the plan. For the ungraded section, it was decided to use the STEP (Sequential Tests of Educational Progress) series in mathematics and science. These tests, standardized by the Educational Testing Service, emphasize problem solving. Both systems also used the arithmetic section of the Stanford Achievement Test and, later, the science section.

The two school systems had I.Q. data for most of the children, based on the *California Mental Maturity Test*. There were also some individual *Stanford-Binet* I.Q. records. These tests are retained.

As one measure of the status and growth of personality it was decided to use the *Junior Inventory* of the Science Research Associates; other measures have been added.

Interests are being surveyed through the test, *What I Like To Do*, published by the Science Research Associates. It covers seven areas of children's interests.

Dr. Kaya has developed a test of creativity, which is being used in the study. It is called the *Solving Puzzles Test*. The analytic support for it is found in J. P. Guilford's factor analyses. These factors that were found at the adult level are used in the children's tests: flexibility, originality, perceptual sensitivity, analysis, synthesis, critical conceptualization. Words familiar to the elementary school child were used, as determined by a questionnaire tried out with pupils in Grades II to VI in Long Beach and Ossining.

In the fall of 1958 all the tests were given to pupils in Grades IV–VII, that is, to pupils in Grades III–VI the previous year for the most part.

These tests, involving twenty-seven hundred pupils, were administered by the teachers and sent to the center for processing and analysis. The center established age norms on each test, with the exception of the *Junior Inventory* and *What I Like To Do*. (The scores on these latter two will be reserved for research purposes.) Grades VII and VIII were included in the test programs, starting with the second year of the project.

Thus far the main application of test results has been as an aid to sectioning. For the long-range comparisons, there are not, as yet, results that can be regarded as stable. The research staff of the Experimental Teaching Center is still engrossed with test validation and the analysis of yearly "process data." There follows Dr. Kaya's recapitulation of the tests administered during this period.

April, 1959 (Kaya)

STEP Mathematics 4A and Science 4A were given to all pupils in Grades III–VI. STEP Mathematics 3A and Science 3A were given to high-ability groups in Grades IV–VI. STEP Social Studies 4A and 3A were added to the testing program, since the Stanford Achievement Battery did not provide a test in this subject for Grades III–IV. The higher level of this test was administered to high-ability groups in Grades IV–VI. *Solving Puzzles I* was administered to all pupils in Grade III, and to low-ability groups in Grades IV–VI in both school systems. Long Beach decided to give it to pupils in Grade II as well. *Solving Puzzles*

II was given to high-ability groups in Grades IV–VI in both school systems. The *Stanford Achievement Test* battery was repeated in both school systems.

The Stanford Achievement scores for the Ossining pupils (after two years of DPP) showed no definite gains or losses over the scores for 1956 to 1960, inclusive, in reading, spelling, arithmetic, science, or social studies. The comparisons are for *grade* scores, since the raw scores from form to form are not comparable. These grade scores are really monotonous. Time after time the pupils score a grade above their school placement (occasionally nearly two grades above). It occurs to me that the subtests of the *Stanford Achievement Test* are not indicative of the kind of progress we are trying to encourage in the Dual Progress Plan—a progress in which a growing sense of structure, meaning, and application is paramount. New teaching and testing henceforth must go hand in hand.

April, 1960 (Kaya)

The same achievement, interest and personality tests were administered to the same grade and ability groups as in April, 1959. The *Solving Puzzles Test* was dropped from the program for 1960 in both school systems with the exception of Second Grade in Long Beach; it will be given again in September, 1963 by way of a pretest-posttest comparison. Like the I.Q., the scores from this test are treated as indicators of relative ability in an age group.

A section on mathematics was developed and added to the *What I Like To Do* interest test, with the permission of Mr. L. Brown, Executive Vice President of the SRA.

The testing program for the Junior High Schools in both systems was added in spring 1960. STEP Mathematics 3A, Science 3A, and Social Studies 3A were administered to all pupils in Grades VII–VIII. Level 2A of the same tests, which is geared for high school level, was administered to the top half of each grade.

Dr. Kaya adds a technical note:

A question was raised by the school systems in the spring of 1960 as to whether the STEP tests were suitable for determining level of advancement. The possibility of using Stanford Achievement test scores was offered as a solution. Bivariate frequency distributions of STEP and Stanford Achievement scores in mathematics indicated that STEP differentiated better than Stanford Achievement. Furthermore, the Stanford battery does not have a science section for all grades concerned. As a result, it was decided to continue using the STEP scores.

The STEP (Mathematics 4A) results based on the interval from September, 1958, to April, 1959, for the same pupils, indicate an upward trend, in each of the grades IV, V, and VI, for both Long Beach and Ossining. The same can be said for STEP, Science 4A. The change over the same period in scores on the *What I Like To Do* interest test did not appear significant. For the *Junior Inventory* (disturbances) a substantial reduction of incidents occurred in schools that were initially high in this respect. Problem situations were usually at a peak at the beginning of the fourth grade; the decline thereafter could be attributed to maturation. With respect to the item *Getting Along With Other People*, the only noticeable change for the period was a reduction in the number of problem situations in grades that had shown unusually large amounts. On the whole, crosssection comparisons based on STEP mathematics, science, and social studies indicate that the pupils did as well in 1960 as in 1959.

All the comparisons above are to be regarded as straws in the wind and nothing more. In most cases, a shift of a few points in tests that are themselves not very responsive to the goals of instruction under the new plan would change the tentative findings. So we must wait and see. Clearly, we need tests in every elementary school subject that parallel new teaching aims—tests with a higher ingredient of problem solving, intellectual maturation, and originality than is common to "old-line" standardized instruments.

I have already referred to the first results on the personal-social adjustments of students. Further materials along the same lines should be reported in research journals, with a final summary on behalf of the two co-operating school systems about 1964. In the meantime, largely through samplings, the following studies are being carried on:

1. An exploratory analysis of the child's day in the Dual Progress Plan and the self-contained classroom.
2. An exploratory study of the frequency of discipline infractions under the Dual Progress Plan.

3. Test anxiety, achievement self-concept, and affiliation self-concept as a function of the type of elementary organization.
4. A study of children's friendship patterns as a function of type of elementary school organization.
5. An observational study of the classroom behavior of third graders.

It goes without saying that such inquiries are loaded with statistical pitfalls; it is unlikely that anything more than trend lines can be discerned in the samplings to be utilized. However, so many fears have been aroused by teachers and theorists on the possible deleterious effect on pupils of having several teachers each day that some objective measures are in order. For the present, we are reassured by the statements of the pupils themselves, but there again the sampling is tiny (if we consider the American elementary school population) and hence subject to unreliability. To track down the *sources* or the *causative* events in child misbehavior—at home, at school, or on the street—has always proved difficult. Doubtless we shall again buttress semi-objective measures with subjective reports and observations.

With respect to teacher ratings, the Working Party proposed two main categories: (1) teacher satisfaction and (2) efficiency of instruction. (It may be said, in passing, that the first is subject to fluctuation and the second is notoriously hard to measure.) The staff of the Experimental Teaching Center, finding no suitable tests in either category, proceeded to develop a "Q-sort" to measure the teachers' instructional goals, with cells that included: *facts and terms; tool skills; understanding concept formation; self-directed learning; applications.*

Inevitably *implementation* and *evaluation* are tied together, and in no other facet of the demonstration study is such close co-ordination required between the Experimental Teaching Center and the co-operating school systems. Self-evaluation will not suffice in such projects and neither will a testing program so alien as to lose sight of the schools' chief aims. Objectivity is one thing, relevance quite another—so much so that I am loath to accept any battery of existing tests as the sole criterion for judging either the old plan or the new. In recent years, the disjunction between objective test programs and educational aims (due in part to the fragmentary, machine-item character of the former and the vagueness of the latter) has reached alarming proportions. For the most part, the tests are *predictors* of scholastic success along conventional lines; they score only what machines can score, and that is not enough. Nevertheless, *some* criteria must be set up and examined with increasing reliability.

A LOOK TO THE FUTURE

In the present demonstration, what should we expect as to the *character* of the successive reports that can be made in 1961, 1963, and 1965? Let us consider, first, the requirements that have been met in setting up the plan in Long Beach and Ossining and, second, the ways of testing the outcomes there and in other school systems affiliated with the Experimental Teaching Center (these items are from Dr. Glen Heathers, director of the center).

The Dual Progress Plan requirements:

1. Setting up a schedule for the school day that provides for semi-departmentalized instruction.
2. Grouping students for grade-level advancement in the cultural imperatives, and for nongrade-level advancement in the cultural electives.
3. Assigning teachers of Grades III–VI (subsequently of VII and VIII also) to their roles as full-time specialists of one curricular area.
4. Adapting the curricula in mathematics, science, art, and music to non-graded grouping and advancement.
5. Setting up classrooms as laboratories for one curricular area.
6. Conducting in-service courses to prepare teachers for their roles as specialist teachers in the plan.
7. Developing new procedures of marking and reporting.
8. Providing for assemblies, field trips, chorus, band, and other cocurricular activities within the semidepartmentalized plan.

The tests previously mentioned (and recapitulated in this chapter) will be systematically utilized and the results analyzed. In the aggregate, they will afford a general measure of the comparative status of the students and of their rates of progress. Dr. Heathers' view of the over-all situation is as follows:

The evaluation of the Dual Progress Plan in the Co-operative Study employs a pretest-posttest design, instead of a direct comparison of the Dual Progress Plan with the unitary grade plan. While a controlled study of the plan would have had certain advantages over a demonstration test, there were important reasons for the decision to employ the latter in the Co-operative Study. The Dual Progress Plan is new and untried. Because of this fact, it was necessary, first of all, to transfer it from the drawing board to the actual school setting. In the process, ways of implementing its essential features can be devised, tried out, and modified on the basis of the initial trial. Once this essential "tooling-in" process has been completed, a controlled comparison with the unitary grade plan would be in order. The purposes of the evaluation in the demonstration test are to determine whether the plan can be made to work, whether it wins the approval of teachers, students, and parents, and (most importantly) whether it appears to offer advantages in students' achievements and in teacher utilization without detriment to students' personal-social adjustment and their personality growth. These are the purposes that are incorporated in the evaluation program.

It should be recognized that the unitary grade plan was installed in elementary schools throughout the country without any research evidence that it was superior to the plans it replaced. Also, it should be noted that elementary educators today who defend the unitary grade plan do so without research evidence to support their allegiance to that plan.

A final point is this: an adequate, controlled study comparing the Dual Progress Plan and the unitary grade plan would require a large number of school systems under the Dual Progress Plan and under the unitary grade plan, since many differences among school systems would need to be controlled as between the two plans being compared. Such differences include the socioeconomic levels represented in the community, cost per pupil, the training and experience of teachers, school leadership, and many intangibles that affect the caliber of education offered in a school system. An inadequately designed controlled study would be worse than none at all, since it would lead to erroneous conclusions.

. . . We have some early indications of outcomes of the Dual Progress Plan in Long Beach and Ossining. In particular, attitudes of teachers, students, and parents are reported since these reflect the initial reception of the plan by the participants who are most directly concerned. Data on subject-matter learning during the first two years of the Study do not show any distinct advantages of the Dual Progress Plan over the unitary grade plan. This should surprise no one, since two years is too short a time for teachers whose training and experience have been in the unitary grade plan to become proficient as specialist teachers in the new plan. Another point to note is that the achievement tests currently available are ill-suited for measuring the sorts of learning that the Plan is intended to foster: problem-solving thinking and self-direction in acquiring and using knowledge. The important question is whether, as the potential of the plan is realized in the classroom, and as what is taught is measured by appropriate tests, the Dual Progress Plan shows advantages over the unitary grade plan.

Heathers' observations apply to *all* new departures in content, method, or school organization. Especially in the elementary grades, the existing pattern has been thoroughly entrenched and almost immune to a need for massive measures of accomplishment. To know comparatively how good (or bad) the Dual Progress Plan is (or will be), we need to know much more about the development of children in the self-contained classroom—and not in terms of little memoriter exercises in arithmetic, science, or the social studies. Very likely, the existence of the Dual Progress Plan in a few school systems will serve to get the long avoided questions asked.

I I

RELATED STUDIES AND
DEMONSTRATIONS; AFFILIATES

Any new plan or program in elementary education is only partially new. Everything is dependent on a few variables that have been intensively explored for years, or perhaps centuries. We have the child and the curriculum. We have the special methods employed by teachers who, in turn, learned them in a teacher education program. We have the vastly complex social structure in which all plans are embedded. The child grows; he is at once similar to and different from himself at an earlier chronological age. Nevertheless, thanks to a modest development of the art of measurement, the child is the most predictable factor in the school system. It is not strange that so much effort is devoted to understanding the characteristics of learning and behavior in the child: his defects and abilities—his resistances, too—set the limits to progress in any school system.

Still, we cannot afford to regard other factors as inconsequential. When a Nazi political system penetrates the schools, it makes nasty little Nazis of the pupils. So it is under any form of government that sets out to conquer by corrupting the minds of men. To ruin the man—that is, to use him for obscurantist or tyrannical purposes—it is best to catch him young, applying a full knowledge of instructional technique, and, above all, *not* permitting him the freedom to criticize, to ask hard questions, to expect the "straight goods." Any form of unexamined orthodoxy, any subservience in the realm of the intellect, will serve to close the mind to alternatives.

Hence, as we examine the numerous proposals to improve, and perhaps reform, elementary education, we should closely examine the outcomes envisaged as desirable. Some plans are little more than a dressing up of old practices. Some are only administrative; they leave untouched the essential pattern of instruction. My purpose in referring to them at all is to present something of a background for the emergence of the Dual Progress Plan, which, as far as I know, is not quite the same as any other.

THE PAST AS PRELUDE

The early American elementary school was frequently "self-contained" *as a school*. In fact, the one-room school has not as yet passed out of the picture. When one teacher taught all subjects and all the children, the content was presented in simplest terms. The textbook or "reader" took hold (it is still an important element in school practice). The "3R's" of reading, writing, and arithmetic were considered adequate for the basic preparation of America's future citizens, but "citizenship" itself, both as subject matter and as a permeating influence, was soon given a prominent place. The twin social phenomena of fast growth in industrialization and immigration rendered obsolete schools that were designed for a rural population. (That they were inadequate for rural children, too, later became apparent.) Belatedly, child labor laws highlighted the need to protect children against exploitation. All these forces converged to provide both a longer school day and a longer school year. Students moved up to Grades VII and VIII (or even IX) and then, in increasing numbers, to the first two years of high school. Compulsory attendance laws followed the general trend and were, in turn, a causative factor.

The plain truth is that, except on the farm, the children had become an economic liability. The new families coming to the United States, especially from Europe, ran to large families and they usually stayed in the city. Lengthened schooling, at first accepted as part of the new life in the United States, gradually won its way as a tremendous contribution to economic, industrial, and civic health. After all, simple literacy had long been considered a luxury over the world. Although the high school movement was slow to develop (the first public high school in the United States was opened during the Civil

War), it had an immediate effect on the grade schools. There was then more attention to individual abilities (who should go to high school, who should stay in high school beyond the compulsory minimum school-leaving age, who should go to college *from the public schools*). As the subject matter became "harder," specialists were introduced, and this practice, typical of secondary education, seeped down somewhat into the elementary years. Art, music, shopwork, and physical education were the first to break through the self-containment of the classroom.

Throughout this whole period, and, in fact, up to the 1940's, it was commonly held that a child grew in mentality by some fixed rate, both the rate and final level being determined by inborn, genetic characteristics. Oddly, this belief in intellectual predestination was often accompanied by drastic punishment for a lack of effort or achievement on the child's part. Since the teachers, like the parents themselves, had no reliable data on the intelligence of a given child, either at birth or any other time, some confusion in assigning the responsibility for failure to learn was understandable. It cannot be said that this particular ethical problem is resolved to this day.

The Dual Progress Plan, while demanding full attention to individual differences in general ability and special aptitude, as do most other plans, does have a further "ethical" dimension: it holds that we can, in good conscience, ease the burden for the faltering child; we can help children to be selective in what they learn. Now this is no mean privilege! Millions of children have plodded through dry memoriter material on the mistaken notion of teachers that it was good for the mind. The brain was likened to a muscle that would thrive under repeated exercise, the more useless the better. Even now in the 1960's this fallacy of mental discipline is disseminated as a fact by magazines of national circulation whose editors should know better. In any event, informed educators and teachers know better. They do not equate one subject matter with another and they give a high place to process, to problem-solving, to creativity. The chief learning in the alert school of today is to learn how to learn and to indulge deeply in the habit. The child is expected to use some of his learning at once, but also to sense the reason, not for the postponement of applications to some vague future, but for building structures that will survive and be available. The future itself is thus made clearer to the learner; no hard line has to be drawn.

EARLY PLANS

Of course, in early days, even a small attention to educational theory led to questions. Could a school have larger classes without loss of quality? Could costs be held down? Could the school plant be more efficiently utilized? Some "reforms" were primarily attempts to get answers for practical problems in school administration. (This need not detract from validity, provided validity is determined on the basis of the fundamental aims of education.)

Thus the "platoon" school or Gary plan, devised by William A. Wirt in 1900, divided the pupils into two groups or platoons, one working in a homeroom and the other repairing to special rooms or recreational facilities. The school plant was more fully utilized than previously and a certain amount of specialization in subject matter or activity was predicated. With the advent of specialist teachers and a freer use of gymnasium, auditorium, and outdoor facilities, many schools incorporated into a general plan various features of the platoon system. However, the teaching of mathematics was left to the general classroom teacher, and there was little evidence of effective integration as between "academic" studies and "activities."

The Dalton Plan, still in use in a few schools, emphasized individual progress in academic subjects, each pupil taking on "work contracts." The pupil has to finish one job before starting another, and there is a built-in system for attaining a spread of academic interest. The class convenes as a whole for social and physical activities.

The Winnetka Plan also stresses individualized progress, but the classroom is kept intact for the academic subject matter. Its "common essentials" segment resembles the cultural imperatives in the Dual Progress Plan, but it does not stress growth in a structure of knowledge. There is a heavy dependence on especially prepared learning materials, which may, or may not, conform to contemporary thought in regard to such materials. The Winnetka group activities lump music, art, projects, discussions, and the like into an aggregation of events that occupy about one half the school day. It can be said that both the Dalton and Winnetka plans place a burden of proof on the "homeroom" concept. Over the years, so many activities—welfare drives and special projects—have been shoved into the homeroom, as to make of it, as I have indicated previously, a hodgepodge.

NEW DEMONSTRATIONS

Almost all new plans are designed to restore a larger measure of systematic learning to the schools. This can be seen by listing, devoid of identification with a particular school system or plan, some of the features, old and new, now under study:

1. measurement—intelligence, special aptitudes, personality, attitudes;
2. provision for the individual differences *always* revealed by test programs—by grouping (in many forms), freedom from grades, tutorial instruction, curricular options;
3. team teaching; specialist teaching; a division of labor in the classroom (to reduce the "housekeeping" duties of the regular teacher);
4. provision of various graded or ungraded "tracks" for pupil progress;
5. a new clustering or merging of grades, to break up the one-year—one-grade plan from kindergarten through high school;
6. the use of slides, films, film strips, radio, recordings, and television, by way of teacher reinforcement or substitution.

Perhaps a quick swing around the circle of U. S. education will indicate how various devices and plans are incorporated in existing programs of the elementary school.

Supported by the Carnegie Corporation, four school systems (Cedar Rapids, Iowa; Lansing, Michigan; Washington, D.C.; Versailles, Kentucky) are engaged in a study of the use of special teachers of science and mathematics in Grades V and VI. In a bulletin (undated) of the American Association for the Advancement of Science, the study directors state:

There are very few teachers who can teach all subject areas in the modern elementary school equally well. Furthermore, teachers may even tend to slight those areas of instruction in which they have less interest or professional preparation. It we expect more than skills of techniques and computation to be taught in arithmetic, and if we expect to begin the development of science concepts in the elementary school, then we need teachers who not only know how to teach but also know what to teach. They must have an understanding of the mathematical and scientific ideas if they are to select intelligently experiences suitable for initiating the idea for continuing development.

The study is being oriented in the direction of two major questions:

a. Can science and mathematics each be more effectively taught by special science teachers than by the regular teacher?

b. Are the effects the same for all children regardless of the ability of the child?

In the Madison project, supervised by Dr. Robert B. Davis of Syracuse University, seventh-graders study algebra; indeed, algebra, in unconventional form, replaces the further study of arithmetic. The students take to the instruction, but it is too early to tell whether the zest indicates a relief from the boredom of further arithmetic, interest in playing "games that may be unrelated to further mathematic progress," or a true deepening of understanding of mathematical principles and problem-solving approaches. The same "wait-and-see" attitude applies to the related projects of Dr. Max Beberman, Dr. Howard Page, and their associates in Illinois. Regardless of the outcome, it is good to have such experiments in content and methodology. Davis[1] states that the Madison project began with low I.Q. seventh-graders but has shifted to average and above-average pupils. This, in principle, is defensible for we may well ask what possible gain there is in the study of algebra by dull pupils; such pupils will almost never be judged by their deficiencies in algebra, but will almost never be free from criticism in the domain of reading, writing, speaking, and deciding. Now that bright children are free to study algebra early, we need a definitive test of what kind of algebra, for this population includes mathematicians, scientists, and engineers in the making.

[1] Robert B. Davis, "Seventh Grade Algebra: The Madison Project," *New York State Mathematics Teacher*, 9, No. 2 (April, 1959), 5–8.

NEW ENGLAND PLANS

I am indebted to Glen Heathers and Esin Kaya for reports of visits to various New England centers in the spring of 1959. The programs at Newton and Lexington are a part of the general University Program for Research and Development which centers in the Graduate School of Education of Harvard University; the Dedham project is under the general supervision of Dr. Donald D. Durrell of Boston University.

In the Newton Junior High School Grouping project, two schools are utilizing both homogeneous and heterogeneous groups, the latter in a "core" consisting of English, social studies, and guidance. For English, there is a twice-a-week regrouping on a homogeneous basis, the range of content being from remedial work to literature. In mathematics and science, homogeneous groups prevail, but the top 20 per cent is given "advanced" instruction. It is of interest to note that the Newton schools in the project have lengthened the school week by 330 minutes and, further, that over half this extra time is devoted to "activities"—"clubs, student government, orchestra, band, etc.—or for extra help from teachers." This is indeed a hopeful sign. As to comparison with the Dual Progress Plan, it appears that only in mathematics does acceleration carry a pupil beyond his regular grade level. "Enrichment" is the key concept in the Newton program.

The project being carried on at the Franklin Elementary School of Lexington is chiefly concerned with team teaching; "team members share the instruction of all pupils in one or more grades." Harvard specialists assist at all points in the research, and there is a control school. In 1958–1959, four teachers had 104 pupils in Grade I; six teachers had 144 pupils in Grades II and III; and eight teachers had 217 pupils in Grades IV–VI. Heathers and Kaya in a report to the Experimental Teaching Center (April 3, 1959) succinctly describe this cluster of experiments which is being financially aided by the Fund for the Advancement of Education:

The plan provides the following hierarchy of positions for teachers and teacher aides:

Team leader—a superior teacher with the M.A. and 10 years' experience

Senior teacher—a superior, experienced teacher

Teacher—a regularly qualified teacher

Part-time teacher—a regularly qualified teacher not available full time

Intern—a student teacher who works for a semester under supervision

Clerical aide—for routine, nontechnical work—attendance, grading, etc.

A differential salary schedule provides increased economic incentives for team leaders and senior teachers. Because of these salary increments and the provision of clerical aides, the teaching teams plan is somewhat more expensive than the usual plans for staffing the elementary school. The plan allows great flexibility in grouping pupils for instruction in different curricular areas. All the pupils in one grade may meet in a large group session. Large group sessions may also cross grade lines. The pupils under a teaching team may be divided into several groups on the basis of abilities or progress. Pupils with special learning needs may be taught in groups of any desired size, or individually. The purpose of these provisions is to permit the best use of the competencies of members of the teaching team in serving the learning needs of all pupils. The flexibility in teacher deployment also gives teachers considerable time for team planning of instruction and for consultation with one another in regard to the learning needs and progress of individual pupils.

Teacher specialization is emphasized in the plan. This applies to specialization in broad subject-matter areas (music, social studies, reading, etc.), or to specialization in particular learning units within those areas. Early indications are that, at all grade levels, pupils accommodate well to changing class groupings and to learning with different teachers. Also it appears that teachers are responding well to the plan. Obviously, it is too early to appraise the potential benefits of the plan for teachers and pupils; as is true with the Dual Progress Plan, several years are needed to establish the plan fully and to achieve the outcomes of its full operation.

A question of particular importance is the extent to which self-direction and analytic thinking may be taught in large classes. A related question is whether, if large-class teaching is now well suited to these emphases, sufficient provision can be made for these critical objectives of instruction in small-group and individual instruction under the teaching teams plan.

Compared to the Dual Progress Plan, it should be noted that the teaching teams plan involves less teacher specialization. Also the latter plan does not make specific provisions for non-graded advancement, though cross-graded instruction occurs frequently. A significant feature of the teaching teams plan is the development of the role of the team leader. This calls for clarifying, perhaps modifying, the principal's role as educational leader in relation to the role of the team leader.

Thus far the Dedham Plan is confined to Grades IV–VI in the Dedham school system. Its emphasis is on the individualization of instruction, self-directed learning, and curricular enrichment. Here *pupils* are teamed, in small numbers per team, and each member in rotation plays a role—discussion leader, reciter, etc. Heathers and Kaya report:

Observation of small pupil teams in several classes in grades 4, 5, and 6 indicated that pupils respond with great enthusiasm and success to self-directed learning in the skill areas. Each pupil appeared to be hard at work, either with his team mates, or by himself. For each subject, a progress chart on the wall indicated each pupil's advancement in terms of units mastered. In spelling and arithmetic, many pupils had already (as of March) completed the year's assigned work. All grades entered on the charts for unit qualifying tests were 90 or above since no pupil is permitted to advance to the next unit until he has achieved this criterion of mastery of the unit. The few teachers who were interviewed indicated that they liked the Dedham Plan and had been successful in adapting themselves to it quickly. It was reported that many pupils carry their new enthusiasm for learning home with them and that some do more homework than seems good for them. Also it was reported that project work stimulated by the plan has doubled the circulation of the Dedham Public Library.

An important question is whether the self-directed learning can be effective for other than fact or tool-skill learning. Pupils questioned about *why* they were studying a particular unit had difficulty answering the question. It seems that the program, to date, does not sufficiently emphasize pupil planning, analytic thinking, and acquiring the sorts of understandings that permit applying what is learned to *new* problem situations.

Another question concerns whether the Dedham Plan can break free of the grade-level course of study so that able pupils can *advance* in a subject each year as far as their abilities would permit. To date, it appears that horizontal enrichment rather than vertical progression is employed to keep able pupils busy.

Running through these Massachusetts studies is a common element of close co-operation between a university and various schools and school systems. No one factor is all-powerful, but if we are to select the dominant ones on which success will chiefly depend, they appear to be these: (1) new curricular materials; (2) new programs in teacher education; (3) attention to the abilities and needs of individual pupils, through grouping and other devices, and (4) a division of labor among the teachers. These factors also bear upon the effectiveness of the Dual Progress Plan but, taken in the aggregate in their present stage of development, they do not strike me as sufficiently attentive to the development of structures of knowledge, to a differentiation between *cultural imperatives* and *cultural electives*, or to the need for true specialization in response to the demands of contemporary society. Specialization, if it does not lead to a new and higher level of integration, is in itself vulnerable. Hence the Dual Progress Plan, like the promising ventures mentioned above, cannot succeed unless *its* curricula, teaching methods, and incentives are superior to any ameliorative measures, however praiseworthy, that carry the inherent burden of the self-contained classroom.

OTHER PLANS

The permutations possible with varying degrees of grouping, nongrouping, grade classification, and nongrade classification are, of course, numerous. At one extreme is the ungraded elementary school which abandons, or makes light use of, standard grades, marks, promotions, and the like. Thus in Appleton, Wisconsin, a one-year kindergarten is followed by a three-year "intermediate school" and this in turn by a third unit which qualifies practically all the pupils for Grade VII, the first year of junior high school. The teaching is of a type characteristic of the self-contained classroom; for this reason the device of reporting a child's achievement, from time to time, without benefit of the generalization afforded by a grade status, does not appear to constitute a gain.

The full impact of teaching by television on the promulgation and success of the Dual Progress Plan cannot be assessed at this time.

In principle, the plan lends itself well to the use of motion pictures and television, since teaching by these devices relies heavily on the specialist or the "gifted teacher." (Except experimentally, there is no point in filming or telecasting an ineffective lesson or in choosing demonstrably poor teachers.) Also, where expert teachers are in short supply—a common situation in every elementary field except English and the social studies—the closed circuit TV program may prove to be a boon. This is the experience reported at all grade levels in Hagerstown, Maryland. Perhaps the chief question raised by the Dual Progress Plan in this context is the necessity of comparing the results of TV teaching by experts, not with the progress of shortchanged pupils, say in art or music, but with the progress of pupils who receive their art and music instruction from teachers all of whom are experts. Hence a follow-through research program is in order.

Similar observations apply to the experience with teacher aides, as pioneered in Bay City, Michigan. This is a special case of the team teaching plan. A second teacher or assistant in the classroom permits a division of labor, such that selected housewives may effectively play this role. The self-contained classroom has been weighed down with chores and "fringe" activities; the Bay City plan spreads these to the aides, thus permitting larger classes and possibly some further economy in salaries paid. It does seem a pity that some of these marginal activities, as I have indicated, cannot be pushed to the end of the day, to the weekend, and the summer season. In that case, homemakers might be even more ready to become assistant teachers and to undertake appropriate training for these assignments. Thus far, the basic curriculum on which this promising idea of a division of labor has been imposed is that of the self-contained classroom. In the Dual Progress Plan there is probably less opportunity for the employment of such aides until such time as the schools under this plan *cluster* the activities and recreational events. (I am not referring to activities that are prescribed as an integral part of a curricular sequence.)

Of course there are promising linkages. Dr. Glen Heathers, for example, has worked out an intriguing combination of a nongraded primary (Grades I and II), the Dual Progress Plan (Grades III–VI), and the use of teams, as in Dedham. The scheme merits a controlled testing.

AFFILIATES: PENNSBURY

It has been noted that the Ford grant of 1959, in addition to strengthening and extending the demonstrations in Long Beach and Ossining, called upon the staff of the Experimental Teaching Center to aid school systems that desired to be affiliated with the Dual Progress Plan. Such affiliation might involve all the essentials of the plan or only certain features of it. The closest affiliate to date is the Pennsbury Schools of Fallsington, Pennsylvania, which in 1960–1961 introduced the Dual Progress Plan in Grades IV–VI of the Fairless View School. The staff was drawn from the entire school system. The director of the demonstration is Dr. Charles Muschell, superintendent of schools. The Experimental Teaching Center is actively engaged in assisting the Pennsbury Schools in all aspects of the project.

I am indebted to Dr. Lou Kleinman for the following paragraphs that describe the initial stages of the Dual Progress Plan in the Pennsbury system.

All the DPP teachers are volunteers. They were selected on the basis of a meticulous screening process from among many applicants *throughout* the school system. Special attention was given in the selection procedure to special interests and competences as evidenced by experiential background. Because the theory, themes, and features of DPP were fully explained to all interested teachers, the decision to apply was an informed one. The status of DPP teachers has been upgraded in the eyes of their colleagues because they constitute a select group. All of these factors have yielded a dedication based on self-commitment.

The schedule devised for Fairless View, consisting of eight forty-minute periods of instruction plus one hour for lunch and two ten-minute homeroom periods, provides an invaluable administrative and instructional flexibility which may prove to be indispensable to the success of the plan in Pennsbury. The eight-period day makes room for foreign language instruction, a library period which might be used among other purposes to encourage self-directed learning, and special reading instruction for all students in addition to the usual work in language arts. Furthermore, two "free" periods are provided for each teacher, one in the morning and one in the afternoon. The proper utilization of the free period promotes the team approach to teaching, the sharing of problems and their solutions, and the possibility of adequate preparation by teachers. It serves also to compensate teachers for the heavier load under DPP in terms of the increased number of students to whom they must relate, and has, therefore, a salutary effect on teacher morale. The free periods likewise make it possible for teachers to "cover" for one another in relation to full-day field trips, preparation for assemblies, and other instructional assignments outside the classroom.

The teaching staff expressed concern over the problem of assembly programs under DPP. It has been traditional at Fairless View that each self-contained classroom unit take responsibility for one assembly during the school year. The staff felt that the assembly programs have been educationally valuable and should not be discounted. The solution evolved was that each "subject area," rather than each self-contained unit, should be held responsible for an assembly program appropriate to the nature of the subject. For example, the science teachers and their classes would be expected to present a science assembly. The staff felt that this would be fitting to the themes of DPP. Such an arrangement, moreover, should encourage interclass co-operation on a cross-graded basis.

The staff was concerned similarly about the feasibility of extended field trips under DPP. Trips might be difficult to arrange under the new plan because each teacher is responsible for more than one class and because of cross-graded grouping. An exchange of views revealed that extended trips would be possible because of the flexibility of the eight-period day, and the willingness of the teachers to cover each other's classes during "free" periods and to plan occasional Saturday trips.

If I were to indulge in an optimistic prediction regarding the acceptance of the Dual Progress Plan in future it would be this: *Given more time for preparedness with respect to theory, lesson plans, and school organization, the teaching and administrative staffs are able to overcome all obstacles.* Rather fast, it seems to me, school people manage to separate "bugbears" and prejudices from real problems and to move toward acceptable solutions. There will come a time when the pioneering stages will give way to controlled studies and massive demonstrations. The greatest debt will always be owed to the two school systems, Long Beach and Ossining, which "took the plunge" when tradition might easily have held them back.

The experience in Long Beach, Ossining, and Pennsbury confirms the view that the Dual Progress Plan eventually will be extended beyond Grade VIII. While the experimental reorganization of the elementary grades has borrowed from the typical American high school plan, the Dual Progress Plan and the high school of today differ in certain important respects. Frequently high school teachers, like their counterparts in the elementary schools, are not prepared to teach the curriculum at the highest levels for the gifted students. Also, there is not at present a real academic core in the high school upon which student advancement depends. The introduction of such a core on a systematic basis in either a three-year or four-year high school is defensible on the same theoretical grounds that obtain in the elementary grades, namely, that school progress, grade by grade, should be based upon the cultural imperatives. As students are graduated from the Dual Progress Plan into the higher grades, the need for a new curricular articulation will be apparent. It is proposed to study the situation as a follow-through of the Dual Progress Plan and, if feasible, to establish demonstrations of a plan covering the range from Grade I through high school.

I 2

EDUCATION FOR ALL
THE PEOPLE

STATISTICS OF GROWTH

The distinguishing features of the American educational system are *size*, *complexity*, and *evolutionary change*. Any new plan, regardless of its theoretical validity or effectiveness, is confronted with a composite of these three forces. Hence, to place the Dual Progress Plan in a realistic setting, it is necessary to look below the surface of statistics and educational reports. Above all, we need to examine the aims of education in order to get a better sense of future developments. While quoting others in all these respects, in this final chapter, I am presenting views that reveal my own philosophy. Since we are concerned with the whole range of school and society, these observations are not restricted to the elementary grades.

Many persons underestimate the size of the American school population. As a curtain against which to present some current trends in education, certain statistical items are presented.

First, we have the following report from the Office of Education.[1]

Well might Paul Woodring entitle his recent stimulating book *A Fourth of a Nation*,[2] for that is exactly what the school population is today.

[1] U.S. Department of Health, Education, and Welfare, Office of Education, *Progress of Public Education* (Washington: U.S. Government Printing Office, 1958), p. 26; (1959), p. 10.

[2] Paul Woodring, *A Fourth of a Nation* (New York: McGraw-Hill Book Co., 1957).

TABLE XIV

ENROLLMENT IN THE CONTINENTAL UNITED STATES IN 1956–1957, 1957–
1958 AND 1958–1959, U.S. OFFICE OF EDUCATION ESTIMATES

| | In Thousands | | |
School	1958–59	1957–58	1956–57
Kindergarten through Grade VIII			
Public school system (regular full time)	26,927	26,037	25,283
Nonpublic schools (regular full time)	4,693	4,466	4,267
Federal schools for Indians	25	26	26
Federal schools on military posts	20	20	19
Other	128	121	116
Total	31,793	30,670	29,711
Grades IX–XII			
Public school system (regular full time)	7,790	7,399	6,876
Nonpublic schools (regular full time)	1,002	942	866
Federal schools for Indians	11	11	11
Federal schools on military posts	1	1	1
Other	76	71	66
Total	8,880	8,424	7,820
Higher education			
Universities, colleges, professional schools, including junior colleges and normal schools	3,623	3,450	3,244
Other schools			
Private commercial schools (day and evening)	560	500	500
Nurse training schools (not affiliated with colleges and universities)	89	91	91
Total	649	591	591
Grand total	44,945	43,135	41,366

The dollar sign is equally impressive: the total cost for 1957–1958
was $20 billion or an average cost of $431 per pupil in average daily
attendance. Of this sum, $320 was for current operating costs and
$111 for debt service and capital outlay. The comparative 1958–
1959 estimates for total costs were $22 billion and $456.

In view of my critical approach to the whole structure of elementary education, which to some readers may seem unwarranted, it is enlightening—in a perverse sense—to read an official statement by Dr. Lawrence G. Derthick, then United States Commissioner of Education (in the report of progress referred to above):

Elementary schools seek to provide the basic education needed by all people. Though they may differ in philosophy, all schools stress the development of skills in reading, writing, and arithmetic.

Curriculum development—No major changes were made in the elementary school program, but there was a new emphasis on conservation, safety, physical education, understanding other peoples of the world, and foreign languages.

Science was taught in most elementary schools and mathematics in all. Science was taught both as a separate subject and in connection with other subjects. Lessons were organized around such topics as living things, weather, machines, earth's surface, and forms of energy. Mathematics, largely arithmetic, was usually taught as a separate subject, but teachers were encouraged to develop mathematics concepts whenever possible.

As to textbooks, the commissioner was content to make a single laconic statement: "Textbooks continued to come from the printing presses in increasing numbers."

As yet, no sense of urgency!

Comparable figures for 1958–1959 and 1959–1960 are also available, on a slightly modified basis, as follows:

TABLE XV

OFFICE OF EDUCATION ENROLLMENT ESTIMATES: CONTINENTAL UNITED STATES (EXCLUDING ALASKA), 1959–1960 AND 1958–1959

(Estimates are for total enrollment during the school year. These figures are larger than figures for fall enrollment.)

Grade Level and Type of School	1959–1960	1958–1959
Kindergarten through Grade VIII		
Public school system (regular full time)	27,890,000	26,780,000
Nonpublic schools (regular full time)	5,400,000	5,060,000
Other schools*	170,000	170,000
Total	33,460,000	32,010,000

TABLE XV (Continued)

Grade Level and Type of School	1959–1960	1958–1959
Grades IX–XII		
Public school system (regular full time)	8,100,000	7,840,000
Nonpublic schools (regular full time)	1,050,000	1,010,000
Other schools*	90,000	90,000
Total	9,240,000	8,940,000
Kindergarten through Grade XII		
Public school system (regular full time)	35,990,000	34,620,000
Nonpublic schools (regular full time)	6,450,000	6,070,000
Other schools*	260,000	260,000
Total	42,700,000	40,950,000
Higher education		
Universities, colleges, professional schools, junior colleges, normal schools, and teachers colleges (degree credit enrollment)	3,780,000	3,590,000
Total elementary, secondary, and higher education	46,480,000	44,540,000

* Includes federal schools for Indians, federally-operated elementary-secondary schools on posts, model and practice schools in teacher training institutions, subcollegiate departments of colleges, and residential schools for exceptional children.

The U.S. Commissioner of Education, in his press release of August 30, 1959, estimated that 1,563,000 teachers would be needed at all levels in public and private schools and that the number qualified (i.e., certified) was only, 1,368,000. Apparently about 11 per cent of the teaching staff leaves the profession each year. The indicated percentage increase in number of students is likely to continue for some years, in view of certain predictable trend lines:

1. The increasing population of the United States.
2. The increasing provision of education at the middle and higher levels for nonwhite children.
3. The availability of new high schools and community colleges; this tends to raise the school-leaving age beyond the legal minimum; the raising of the minimum age in various states.

4. The increasing vocational, social and military demand for higher education.
5. The prosperity of persons, corporations, government agencies, and churches interested in furthering education.

The shortage of properly qualified teachers at many grade levels will also continue. This statement, of course, refers to qualifications for *standard* teaching services, as in the self-contained classrooms of the elementary grades. Real educational reforms are slow to propagate: like the iceberg, most of the weight of resistance lies below the surface.

EDUCATION IN AMERICA IS OLD

American education, both public and private, is much older than the United States. By coincidence the first public school in North America and the first private university were both established in the late 1630's. One was a Dutch school in Manhattan and the other, of course, was Harvard University. For two centuries education was almost entirely under private auspices. As for higher education in the colonial days, it was considered important only for the selected few who desired to go into law, medicine, or the ministry.

A report of the University of the State of New York, covering its then 170-year-old history, states that "the first official declaration relating to common school education in the Colony of New York appeared in the so-called 'Freedoms and Exemptions' granted by the Dutch West India Company to settlers in the New Netherlands on June 7, 1629. Patrons and colonists were required to provide for a minister and schoolmaster 'that thus the service of God and zeal for religion may not grow cool and be neglected among them.'" The first official schoolmaster took office there in 1638. The school was supported by both public and private funds for many years. It exists to this day. In the State of New York, however, free public education was to lead a checkered life. Even as late as the 1840's there was substantial opposition.

Although general state funds had been available since 1805, what has emerged, particularly in the eastern part of the country, is a dual system of public and private education. As indicated in the statistical tables, most children are now in public schools. After the Civil War there was a vast increase in pupil enrollment in the elementary school, and it was then that the American public high school was established.

SEVEN STEPS FORWARD

It is convenient to distinguish seven great landmarks in the advancement of education in the United States, namely:

1. The development in the first half of the nineteenth century, at first gradual and then rapidly accelerated, of free public education for a school term of six to eight years. The great leader in this movement, the true founder of the American public school system, was Horace Mann.
2. The development, after the Civil War, of public high schools in the various states and territories.
3. The signing by President Abraham Lincoln of the Land Grant Act to establish public higher education in the states and territories of the Union, using funds from the sale of public lands as a starting capital. These great institutions, in some instances combined with the state university (as in Ohio, Illinois, Minnesota, Wisconsin, and California), at first grew slowly. Eventually they developed elaborate programs in many technical, humane, and professional branches. Where there is a separated state university (as in Michigan, Indiana, and Iowa), the professional colleges of law and medicine are found in the state university. Even in these states, there may be found many academic areas in common as between the land-grant college and the separate state university. This is particularly true in the natural sciences and technologies. Agriculture remains essentially a land-grant enterprise, but this does not preclude extensive programs in botany, entomology, and genetics in other publicly supported institutions. In fact, there is no longer any legal reason why most states should not develop as many colleges and universities as they are willing to support and with such academic duplication as appears desirable.

4. The federal aid to veterans in public and private institutions of higher learning—the so-called G.I. bills. This legislation has had an immense impact upon both the student body and the institutions themselves. This financial aid is more than the mark of a grateful nation to young men who gave up time, energy, and safety for the defense of their country. It also marks a positive attitude on the part of the American government toward discovering and encouraging talent at the college level.

5. The activities of the United States and of persons and corporations in support of higher education across national borders. There are thousands of American students and scholars abroad, especially under the aegis of the Fulbright grants; there are thousands of foreign students in American colleges and universities. Such organizations as the Carnegie Corporation, the Rockefeller Foundation, the Ford Foundation and its auxiliary units, and the Institute of International Education add great impetus to this academic exchange among the free nations of the world. The United States Government, by its support of UNESCO, similarly is a party to many enterprises and to exchanges of persons among the more than eighty member states. The United States National Commission for UNESCO, a body created by Congressional action, serves as a clearing house in the United States for all UNESCO activities. In its membership will be found leaders from science, education, commerce, art, and religion. It is a strong force for intercultural exchange.

6. The Supreme Court decision of May 17, 1954, is, at once, a landmark in law, education, and human rights. A program of true equality (not just "equal but separate") is moving from the abstract to the concrete, but the impact cannot as yet be fully measured. This decision in effect grants a new franchise to millions of American citizens who, thus far, have been deprived of their full rights.

7. The sudden, post-Sputnik interest of the federal government in assisting the schools to strengthen their offerings in science, foreign languages, and educational guidance. While this is a matter of "piecemeal" aid, it is one more step—if a belated one —toward a full partnership of federal, state, and local agencies in support of public education.

THE CURRENT SCENE

With the gross national product hovering around 500 billion dollars, it seems irrational to express concern about meeting the costs of education in the United States. Yet those of us who have worked in various parts of the American educational system know of many impoverishing conditions. There are hundreds of rural counties in which few of the accepted standards in education are met, and this can be said also of substantial areas in rich cities like New York, Chicago, and Philadelphia. Many classrooms and school buildings would get a low rating, whatever the standard. By any reasonable criterion, most teachers are underpaid; they do not receive enough money to do the things a teacher is expected to do in our society.

These indefensible situations arise in part from the obsolete financial basis of the schools. Education may be a national *interest* of the United States, but it is not by law a national *responsibility*. It is essentially a combined local and state responsibility. In the eastern part of the United States, communities build their schools, pay their teachers, and meet other expenses of the school system with modest help from the state. However, the state aid for such purposes is generally increasing. Moving westward across the country, we find that the percentage of expense assumed by the state markedly increases. In the Far West, some states carry almost the full cost of education from the first grade through the state college.

There is good reason for this assumption of expense by the state. It lies in the fact that the state, through general sales, corporation, and income taxes, has financial resources that have grown immensely in the past few decades. Local municipalities, on the other hand, have had to depend heavily on a single real estate tax; moreover, they are subject to wide variations in their financial ability to support education, variations which, at the state level, are somewhat smoothed out. Thus a poor community in Oregon, Texas, or Illinois gains from access to large state funds. In fact, everybody gains, since Americans move easily from one community to another, carrying with them their education or lack of it—their social currency, as it were. If they are products of a good school system, they benefit not only that locality but also any locality to which they may move or with which they may establish some external relation.

Northern cities that have long remained indifferent to poor education in the South think further about the problem as they receive the influx of hundreds of thousands of Negroes unable to meet, grade for grade, the standards of the Northern schools. At the present time, New York City is facing such a problem in regard to a huge Puerto Rican population whose standards of health, education, and social responsibility are, on first arrival, below that of the city where they now make their home. Educational authorities know that, given a generation of economic and educational prosperity, these new families will catch up. From such sources, as in the past, our cities will recruit enormous numbers of its best citizens. These persons will tell the story, as it has been told before, of the essential equality of basic intelligence among all races and nationalities. The differences are rarely genetic for a whole population; rather they are economic and cultural. As these differences are wiped out—and they get wiped out fast in our best schools and communities—we see the emergence of the new American citizen, wonderfully in accord with the audacious predictions of Thomas Jefferson.

So much by way of statistical and historical background.

WHAT TO TEACH

Let us consider now the dilemma met at every level from grade school to the university in choosing what to teach from a geometrically increasing body of knowledge and, moreover, in teaching it with a newly found awareness of a need for understanding and personal growth. How can we extend education in depth and breadth in a school day that is unlengthened?

Few persons realize what a small percentage of a child's time is really spent in school. In the United States the average school year is about one hundred eighty days or one half a calendar year. During these one hundred eighty days, the instructional day is not, on the average, over six hours, or approximately one-half the waking time of the school-age child. This leaves to the classroom and to auxiliary enterprises that fall within the regular school day only ninety full days of a child's time and energy. The rest of his time is not neutral. In good homes and good neighborhoods, what happens outside of school reinforces what happens inside. This is illustrated by good reading, conversation, and constructive experience. On the other hand, for millions of children and adolescents the out-of-school experience is an eraser of intellectual events. Frequently the school cannot keep pace with these conflicting outside experiences. If the school does not gain over all negative outside experiences, the growing child becomes relatively less intelligent, less informed, and less able to meet the practical problems of life. Dismal records in the registrar's or counselor's office in any high school or college will show that this outcome is not confined to those who leave school when it is legally permissible to do so.

We are faced not only with a selection of curricular content but also with a choice of teaching methods that will place the student on a good learning track and keep him there against all distractions. It is not enough to map out an elegant program of studies without giving thought to the problem of interest, involvement, and achievement on the part of the participant. In fact it may be fatal to motivation and therefore meaningless with respect to the higher aims of education to permit fragmented subject matter to obscure the larger learnings.

It is on the basis of such choices, whose variance is exaggerated for the sake of argument, that we sometimes find educationists and advocates of the liberal arts squared off in mutual hostility. On the surface it seems like a silly contest, but down underneath there is a conviction on the part of the subject-matter specialist that students are being deprived of their scientific and humane birthright, and, on the part of the educationist, that specialists in the liberal arts are indifferent to the all-round need for personal growth and pleasure. The most fought over academic battlefield is the American comprehensive high school.

Subject matters, or even the "disciplines," may be so desiccated as to lose their organic wholeness and their appeal to the inquiring mind. This outcome is not the result of dirty work by professors of education: they have no monopoly of meaningless proliferation. If this seems unfair to specialists in liberal disciplines, I suggest that they examine textbooks, tests, and examinations prepared by teachers in the liberal arts who have not studied the art of teaching. I know very well that bad examples can be found in the textbooks of teachers of teachers. For example, like many other observers, I have been struck by the ability of pupils to produce better drawings and more exciting sentences than are commonly found in readers and reading manuals. No one is immune. The professor of education may be twice removed from the subject matter in which he is "an expert in the teaching of," but the teacher of science is not much better off, for he, too, is often once or twice removed from the crucial experiments which he proposes to repeat and exemplify, or from the great demonstrations. Scholars who reluctantly teach have been known to depend on a compendium of criticisms, revisions, and interpretations. The scholastic who proceeds from footnote to footnote is an easy target for the educationist who looks into the child's eye to see what might prove acceptable in the way of personal adjustment.

MIND, MATTER, AND THE ENVIRONMENT

It comes down to a defensible concept of what is meant by integration between the child and his environment. There is no sense in playing off the organism (in this case, the mind of the child) *against* the environment. Mind is a function of matter, and matter, although it existed long before man, means nothing to him except as it relates to his sense organs or his power of abstraction. Of course, any breathing animal, second by second, is in the closest contact with the physical world. If man took in air like water, through little tubes running out of great tanks containing all the earthly oxygen, the interdependence of all mankind would be seen as the first rule of life.

It would be hard to improve on Dewey's clarity here.[3]

Whatever else organic life is or is not, it is a process of activity that involves an environment. It is a transaction extending beyond the spatial limits of the organism. An organism does not live *in* an environment; it lives by means of an environment. Breathing, the ingestion of food, the ejection of waste products, are cases of *direct* integration; the

[3] John Dewey, *Logic, The Theory of Inquiry* (New York: Henry Holt & Company, 1938), p. 25.

circulation of the blood and the energizing of the nervous system are relatively *indirect*. But every organic function is an interaction of intra-organic and extra-organic energies, either directly or indirectly. For life involves expenditure of energy and the energy expended can be replenished only as the activities performed succeed in making return drafts upon the environment—the only source of restoration of energy. Not even a hibernating animal can live indefinitely upon itself. The energy that is drawn is not forced in from without; it is a consequence of energy expended. If there is a surplus balance, growth occurs. If there is a deficit balance, degeneration commences. There are things in the world that are indifferent to the life-activities of an organism. But they are not parts of *its* environment, save potentially. The processes of living are enacted by the environment as truly as by the organism; for they *are* an integration.

It follows that with every differentiation of structure the environment expands. For a new organ provides a new way of interacting in which things in the world that were previously indifferent enter into life-functions.

Let us get clear, if we may, on what is meant by *mind*.

To use a common example, what one person sees in another is in neither one exclusively, nor in both together. Our senses respond to the data of the physical world. We see only in a world of light. We hear only in a world of vibrations. Still, the whole physical and chemical world taken together, while underwriting all that happens, is not exhaustive: it is certainly not very helpful as a measure of thought or feeling. Two test tubes may look exactly alike, but if I state (in such a manner as to induce belief) that one contains distilled water and the other a colorless deadly poison, human reactions will differ accordingly. Thus, *words*, just as surely as the sight of a charging animal or the sound of thunder, carry a warning. Long before words came to any species, cries and gestures served the same purpose. It is a fair guess that the lateral shaking of the head to express *no* goes back to moving the mouth away from anything hot, bitter, or unwanted.

However, the mind does have a locus; even as function it is not just any function; it is the nervous system and especially the brain and more especially the cerebral cortex, in action. You may lose a leg and keep your intelligence intact, but if you lose a spoonful of gray matter from your frontal lobes you will think less effectively; if you lose a few ounces of it you will score below par in all tests that involve new solutions or the exercise of imagination. But the point is this: you may keep not only your arms and legs but your brain intact and still begin to lose your mind. (No mysticism is implied, for electrochemical actions intervene.)

Since the days of Alfred Binet, we have known that to remain at rest or to slow down intellectually, while adding the inexorable months and years chronologically, is to suffer mental retardation. After all, this is inherent in the overworked expression, "Intelligence Quotient." The I.Q. is simply a rather inadequate measure of the relation between mental and chronological age, the former derived from normative tests and the latter from the calendar. If a child learns faster, or rather, sooner than other children, he is bright; if slower or later, dull.

Once I saw a patient in an Iowa hospital whose I.Q. approached zero in any calculus of measurement. In thirty bedridden years as a congenital idiot she had learned only one thing and that fell below the threshold of any mental test I know of: she could manage a fleeting, foolish smile when the physician on his rounds stuck his head in the door.

At the other extreme lies genius. In between the helpless, hopeless ones and men like Da Vinci, Shakespeare, and Einstein, will be found the whole human race. We may leave it to the statistician to measure the differences and to the philosopher to speculate upon them.

In our present state of science, we do not know how most feebleminded children got that way, although we have some clues; still less do we comprehend the stuff of genius. Nevertheless, our whole educational system is based on the theory, backed by three thousand years of experience, that what happens to a person makes a difference. On the positive side we have the exquisite training of the violinist, without which nothing will produce the marvelous results, and we add the contribution of a Beethoven and a Stradivari. On the negative side, we have long had, but not fully recognized, destructive forces—antilearning, if you will—exemplified by recent attempts at "brainwashing." Is not every adult illiterate already brainwashed by a society that permits a healthy nervous system to be deprived of the art of reading and writing? Until recent years this appalling condition applied to 50 per cent of the population of Latin America and to 80 per cent of the population of India and China.

In short, we are considering a fundamental concept. The healthy mind is a growing mind and the growth, unlike that of an insect first unfolding its wings, is no instinctive outcome of patterns genetically laid down. (Of course, things have to be right for the insect, too.) Some infants lack the essentials of a workable pattern and no two infants are exactly alike. To be born at all is to demonstrate a reasonably effective chain linkage in past generations, but to some embryonic nervous systems—through physical or chemical means —damage was done. The newest and most deadly carrier of harmful effects may turn out to be certain by-products of atomic explosions; thousands of scientists are convinced of this.

In any event, the healthy mind *must grow*. Mental testers used to report what they felt to be untrue; namely, that the curve of intelligence flattened out at chronological age fourteen or sixteen; actually all that happened was that the little games, puzzles, and memory schemes of standard tests failed to elicit responses that involved intellectual integration and, when called for, truly original solutions. Even so, intelligence as measured today does reach a plateau, perhaps at forty or fifty on the average, but it is so variable as to bolster the ego of any particular old man. Would an age-dulled Churchill feel outdistanced in a gathering of fresh young talent? Yes, to be sure, if he were called upon to tackle mathematical or scientific assignments. In broad human affairs, however, the growth pattern is revealed not in details but in the sense of structure and wholeness given to problems that cannot be compartmentalized— to problems whose solutions depend upon the whole mind—and upon character, if you will. That is why two young persons of equal starting ability may be found poles apart only ten years later, the one facing, analyzing, solving problems, and the other falling back upon easy ways of half solutions and slogans, conforming rather than creating.

This observation leads to the question of balance and maturity. More dangerous than any form of languor is that corruption of thought and personality that has its roots in personal and social conflict. When unchecked, the infection acquires various psychological names that need not concern us here, but always there is retreat and escape, a covering up, a deep-lying fear of failure. In the words of W. Grey Walter:[4]

You may learn nothing and get away with it; but you cannot in sanity learn not to learn. The mechanism breaks down, sooner or later, when these natural functions are tampered with; the mind is flattened into a shallow mould; anything can mean anything and untruth be truth.

The important two words in this quotation are "in sanity." After all, our sanitariums are filled with persons who, with some degree of self-satisfaction, have abandoned the life of reason. They may go back to the cozy life of the infant, refusing to walk or talk; they may even lie curled up for weeks at a time pretending they have never been born or wishing deeply they had not been. Others need not go back quite so far to get away from an intolerable present; they call up happy days, a high school dance, a trip to the zoo—and dwell endlessly in comforting thoughts.

Unhappily, such queer persons, like the feeble-minded, are not rare. Many frightened, tragically confused persons were once bright as measured by school or job success. Their trouble is not revealed by low scores in most tests but by a deep-seated inability to accept reality, the reality, that is, of the world as conceived by others. They are out of touch. The failure is in communication. Their world is private and, doubtless, up to a point, satisfying. To the person whose inner conflicts have split his personality and corroded his intellect, nothing is impossible, nothing denied. Self-contempt is magically transformed into pity for others. He gets to be an honored scientist, a popular writer, or a great lover, simply by staking out the claim. Nobody can dispute him; those who try are written off as stupid, envious, or malicious. What counts is the self-accepted *image*. I have known men to polish this image to such perfection as to sway others in hypnotic fashion. This is the power that drives the fanatic; perhaps a touch of it is needed to produce the swindler, the impersonator, the medicine man. Above all, a neurotic

[4] W. Grey Walter, *The Living Brain* (New York: W. W. Norton & Company, Inc., 1953), pp. 265–266.

or psychotic condition *hides the truth from the person himself.* In advanced stages the outward personality loses all meaning; conversation is not with you—an outsider not to be trusted—but with voices or spirits that seem to represent others but are, alas, merely splinters of the shattered self.

Now, what has all this got to do with mind? The answer is that I have been describing a potentially good mind, a potentially stable and likable person who has beat a retreat. However high the I.Q., a failure here will deprive the person of all sense of fulfillment. Illogically we refer to such a person as "a lost soul," even though it is the mind that has gone astray.

EDUCATIONAL IMPLICATIONS

Let us look for a moment at the related pedagogical problems.

We have used the term *mental content* in American education since the days of G. Stanley Hall, who published a study entitled *The Contents of Children's Minds on First Entering School.* Still, we have learned to be wary of the word *contents.* It is too much like canned goods on the shelf. It reminds us of the columns of courses taken, as reported in the placement materials of teacher candidates. Such data do not show what the person is but only what he was once subjected to. A much harder test is to discover in what way skills, information, and methods have been woven into a dynamic pattern that will serve the person at all times. The test of the adequacy of knowledge is inevitably pragmatic. A student is not a blank sheet of paper to be printed on, and a curriculum is, or should be, different from a dictionary.

Confusion along these lines has led many persons to cling to traditional methods of teaching and to ignore the dynamic aspects. We may practice a golf shot one hundred times without improving it. Personally, having written hundreds of pages on the typewriter, I still tend to spell *the* "hte." How can this come about? Does not practice make perfect? In the case of the golf shot, unless you analyze—or somebody analyzes for you—the difference between good and bad form, your practice will hammer in your mistakes. In the humble case of typing errors, a failure to analyze the sequence of motor acts will leave you unimproved. The late Knight Dunlap was once so enamored of this problem that he practiced wrong ways of typing in the hope that some right ones would emerge!

As we get into the more complex areas, the same principles apply, but they are now much harder to deduce. Thus, the stutterer gets as much practice in stuttering as the average speaker does in smooth speech. If it can be demonstrated that under certain circumstances, as in singing or a relaxed atmosphere, there is less stuttering or perhaps none at all, the person has received the wonderful assurance that there is nothing basically wrong with his physical and physiological mechanisms. What can be done under the best of conditions can be done under the worst, provided we discover what "the worst" is for a given individual and how to restructure it so as to remove the sting.

We *learn* to escape just as we learn to face reality. We learn to deny as well as to accept values. If we seek a simple snobbishness from knowing more Latin, French, or algebra than somebody else (who has elected to know less), then the *practice* of this "show-off" trait will harden our character in unpleasant ways. Giving discomfort to others is not a normal source of enlightenment. If a person's sense of security depends upon such factors, he will lead a life of inner fear and of outward cynicism; he will face the danger of meeting somebody who knows more than he does and the discovery may be intolerable.

THE PURSUIT OF EXCELLENCE

The good teacher allows a margin for failure, trying to overcome the pupil's frustration by giving him repeated chances for success and, basically, by overcoming the temptation to regard every little school deficiency as a mark of personal unfitness. The desire for excellence, which should be kept strong in every classroom and in every learning situation, will be diminished if it is overcharged with moral principles. The good teacher knows what the good student has already discovered, namely, that, while excellence is important and admittedly decisive in many situations, every departure from it does not make one a fool, an outcast, or a delinquent. There is a vast difference between *perfection* and *perfectionism;* in the former, a final goal transcends any of the immediate steps, and the steps have no divorced meaning. When Michelangelo was asked why he was willing to spend so many painful hours to get certain brush strokes just right, he replied, "These trifles make perfection, and perfection is no trifle."

We should again call on some traits that are typically American. Since colonial days, Americans have stressed two great attributes that some other national cultures have regarded as incompatible: (1) a dependence on tools, machines, and inventions and (2) an insistence on the rights and pleasures of individualism. In the last century, much of our humor has arisen from the presumed disjunction between the confirmed individualist and a machine-dominated industrialism. Even today, responding to something several Freudian layers down, cartoonists portray "the little woman" as sitting at the wheel of a car, delightfully confused. Why? Let us face it—when it comes to technical matters, we are all confused. Puzzlement did not wait upon the machinery of rockets or nuclear reactors; long ago, the intricacies of a printing press or an adding machine sufficed.

As an essential part of freedom, we need a new opportunity for youth. As a nation, we cannot afford to waste that great store of intellectual power which for generations has been allowed to languish short of college and, not infrequently, short of high school graduation. Of the *upper 5 per cent* of high school graduates in the United States, three out of ten do not graduate from college. Of all the teenagers entering the junior high school, only one-half ever receive senior high school diplomas, and of this fraction only about one-fourth go to college. While there are other roads to achievement, the fact remains that in the United States of the mid-century, to deny the college experience to any bright and willing young person is to set up a heavy handicap. The call is neither for compulsory college nor compulsory occupational choice. What we seek is the sheer allurement of learning that is engendered when youth is brought into contact with the good teacher in a good environment. Intuitively the American people are sound in this respect. We do not measure ability in order to restrict it, but to bring it to fulfillment and, characteristically, to play the long chance where human aspirations are concerned.

We do not need doctoral dissertations or jeremiads to tell us that in a time of prosperity unmatched in the history of the United States, we are again rationing education. Education is the one corporate agency that stands aghast before the prospect of more clients who want more of its product for a longer period of time and at a higher level of quality. In so doing, education is out of character.

INTELLIGENCE

The one great complex factor that conditions all learning to some extent and is decisive in reading comprehension, problem solving, and the ability to do abstract thinking is *intelligence;* it is, of course, not a thing, but a power. There are many short definitions of intelligence, but they serve their shorthand purpose best after a more comprehensive statement has been studied. One I submitted nearly twenty years ago appears to hold up:[5]

Intelligence is the ability to undertake activities that are characterized by (1) difficulty, (2) complexity, (3) abstractness, (4) economy, (5) adaptiveness to a goal, (6) social value, and (7) the emergence of originals, and to maintain such activities under conditions that demand a concentration of energy and a resistance to emotional forces.

Through observation and experience, counselors and teachers may themselves elaborate the educational implications of the parts of this definition. As a start, it is to be noted that the concern is not directly with some internal mechanism. Not *intelligence,* but the *intelligent behavior pattern*—the effective acts and choices—is what the teacher can appraise. In a large school, the range of talent for such behavior will prove enormous—at one extreme well into feeble-mindedness, however defined, and at the other, an approach to genius.

Knowing that the parts, if separated, must be recombined into a functional whole, and that only the dynamic aspects are meaningful in the art of teaching, I shall attempt a breakdown of the definition above.

Difficulty refers to the percentage passing, provided this per-

---

[5] George D. Stoddard, *The Meaning of Intelligence* (New York: The Macmillan Company, 1943), p. 4.

centage increases with chronological age and is progressively related to the requirements of the other attributes. For example, success at difficult levels that involve abstraction outweighs accomplishment in repeating digits.

Complexity refers to the multiple-track nature of abilities that combine to form general intelligence. The base is to be kept broad, so that intelligence, while entering into a specialization (scientific, musical, artistic, or literary) is not identified with it.

Abstractness is close to the core of intelligence; it is not the all-in-all of the concept, but a necessary ingredient. In mental activity we deal with symbols, speech being the prime example. There are levels of abstraction and different media are employed. The teacher, testing for language, problem solving, and art forms, finally gets a crude measure of this ability in each pupil. The child inclined to mental accretion should not meet standards of grade performance by more accretion. Unhappily he is often allowed to do so, as in substituting computational skill for mathematical insight. If the teacher himself avoids the abstract, the spiraling process of learning is held back; inevitably his pupils will suffer.

For present purposes, it will suffice to say that *economy* is the same as speed. If insight is reached fast and not seen as immediately related to the task at hand (the problem may have been "put on the shelf"), we call it *intuition*. Even so, the logical steps appear to have been taken, though unconsciously. While, in education, we may question the appropriateness of *economy* as an attribute of intelligence, I believe it is better to retain it. Other things being equal, a fast mental solution is better than a slow one, if only because it permits the learner to keep more of the relevant variables in mind, and to move on to other examples or problems. Also there is a positive correlation between speed and comprehension. The term "slow learner" is often misunderstood. It is true that a slow learner, given a few more years of growth, will solve some of the problems solved earlier by bright children. If he keeps to his pace as a slow learner, he will not catch up at all. The habitually slow learner is defective in mental power as well as in his rate of getting the right answers. That many outstanding persons were considered dull in school should not deceive us. Perhaps they were only dull as measured by incompetent observers or prosaic teachers in an atmosphere of orthodoxy. Perhaps their greatness, like that of saints or military leaders, did not demand unusual intellectual gifts. We know, too, that neurotic involvements that cover up scholastic intelligence may be later overcome; they may even be transformed into a driving force.

Adaptiveness to a goal is a common factor in measures of intelligence, if not in its definition. Aimlessness results in a low score. Thus if you try to solve the ball-and-field item in the Stanford Revision of the Binet-Simon Scale the way golfers actually hunt for a lost ball, you will fail. (The goal is not really the same in the two situations. The child attacks this little geometric problem without clues, and the empty field is enclosed. The golfer thinks he knows where the ball is, resisting the idea of its being lost at all; the systematic approach, usually instigated by other players, is saved for last. In any case, a departure of the "theoretical" from the "actual" does not invalidate a test item.)

Social value reflects the importance of the culture pattern in the tests chosen to measure mental ability. Vocabulary, reading comprehension, the following of verbal directions, and general information get a high place in modern testing, as they generally do in life. For adult illiterates, special tests, such as Army Beta, have been devised, but few teachers will have occasion to use them. After all, an important function of the early elementary grades is to change little "illiterates" into literates. The measures of intelligence based on the abilities of preschool children in speech and performance do, however, give some indication of readiness to do standard school work. Excellence in the spoken language is one indicator of general ability. On the other hand, speech defects spring from so many physical and social causes as to be unreliable in prognosis. Defective speech due to mechanical or emotional blocking has no bearing on mentality.

It would be repetitious at this point to enlarge upon the importance of the *emergence of originals*. The highest reach of intellectual achievement is found in this attribute. In the common failure to emphasize this quality, both mental tester and teacher are vulnerable. It is not a matter of a treasure hunt for genius, desirable as such a step would be. More simply, it is to extend to each child, at every mental age, real opportunities to do things in his own way. Except to plague the teacher, the pupil will not choose to say "two plus two equals five." Such a statement is wrong, but not original. Similarly, it would be hard to devise new ways of misspelling words in the English language—only a machine could exhaust the permutations for a given word. At the same time, the child may want to describe *his* solutions, findings, and feelings and may choose original word combinations in order to do so. This approach is, at root, artistic. Teachers and parents, above all others, themselves need a mental set that applauds departures from the run-of-mine. There is no need to worry about intellectual anarchy; the discipline of subject matter and structure will take care of that. Often variations are permissible only in the approach; the "solution" is contained in the problem, and the problem itself is formulated in terms of logical modes. The crust that hardens over habitual responses will not be broken in any area where it is useful: all the more reason to offer allurements to originality where the mark of quality is a compound of what the child wants to do and what society permits him to do. If intelligence is to flower at any level, all subject matter should be developed with a full play to "originals."

I trust we shall retain the concept of a *concentration of energy* as a mark of intelligent behavior, even though mental tests are notably deficient in this respect. Most test items are passed or failed in a few minutes, perhaps seconds. A professor's "essay" examination, if it calls for analysis, synthesis, and some ability to write, is, to this extent, superior to intelligence testing. The test item may substitute a reliable scoring system for significance of content. The ability to select "freely," to put things together that belong together, to project logical thought upon a complex problem, is foreign to the objective test item. In teaching we help the pupil to concentrate and persevere; we are not, every minute, appraising his status. There is patience in the total teaching situation that overrides any snapshot picture of where a pupil is at a given time.

A resistance to emotional forces should be placed on the same high plane as the *emergence of originals*. (It, too, is absent from standard mental tests.) It could be generalized to read: *a resistance to all forces that are inimical to straight thinking.* This is where the school often is supreme; it is not its business to prove an irrational point, to sell something, to support dogma in politics or religion, to "brainwash." The school's function extends beyond information, skill, and knowledge to the paramount task of keeping the mind open, elastic, and invested with the desire to take on new learning. In so doing, the school improves human relations in the only way that stands up under test. Any society based on ignorance, fear, or intellectual dishonesty is deadly to the aspirations of a free mind. *To get understanding* is still the supreme act.

The verbal factor in tests of intelligence is so strong that if teachers will encourage, analyze, and test *reading ability* in every pupil, they will reach a close approximation of mental age. A battery that includes a reliable test of general information and reading ability, together with aptitude tests in science, art, and music, will leave little mental territory unexplored, as far as the classroom teacher is concerned. The teacher will, of course, also be helped by parent contacts, sociological ratings, and occasional measures of pupil achievement.

The older the child gets, the more crucial are measures of originality, special ability, and a generalized ability to work with abstract structures of thought that are different from the little games found in tests. Failure at the low level of abstraction demanded by most test items is hardly conducive to high-level success, but low-level success tells little about the intellectual or creative potential. Persons who habitually do not choose to think develop a form of mental defectiveness; as a numerous company, they join the ranks of those with hereditary, congenital, or acquired defects in cerebral structure. In my experience, these rusted-out mentalities lack the charm of the true defective who, early sheltered against life's problems, rarely indulges in malice, greed, or aggression.

Thus we discern the limits, as it were, of the school's pressure for intellectual performance on the part of all pupils, consistently with their general and special ability. A roughshod mass compulsion will not do; differences in ability are substantial and elusive. Moreover, motivation finally is *in* the child. In education we are not persuading the child to believe something only because he is told to do so. We are asking the child to examine, to compare, to understand, to achieve—to make some good decisions now, and others later by the same process.

MOTIVATION AND PERSONALITY

So, we try to guide the child expertly and lovingly, but what we hold out to him is the satisfaction of learning and achieving. Even for the very dull, the rewards are not wanting. A *rational* level of expectation is ascertained for each pupil, and it is a stage that can be lowered or raised. In a first-rate school, the pupil is calmly expected to do his best; he is not expected, by omitting the factors of work and concentration, to lay claim to mental incompetence. But nothing he does, or fails to do, is weighed in the supreme balance of his status as a person. Admiration may be a function of effort or achievement, but love should run its own sovereign course.

The phenomenon of "E" (excellent) for effort is all about us, at levels from the vulgar to the divine. The wrestler grunts, the boxer winces, the acrobat looks to the crowd to see if his remarkable *efforts* are appreciated. Many people dislike to hear a speech read, forgetting that a manuscript at least indicates prior effort; they place a premium on the sheer power to memorize or to extemporize. Pianists and violinists are truly handicapped because an audience may resent any reference to a score; thus as soloists they confine themselves to what they have memorized. Perhaps this audience reaction is a transfer from the art of the theater. Since an actor pretends to be somebody else, obviously he can only read what the character himself would have read, if the illusion is to hold; all vocalists share this transposition to some extent. Is it possible the audience dreamily identifies the performer of Bach or Beethoven or Chopin with the composer himself? Certainly it likes to see as well as hear, and the seeing may be in part this identification and in part the appearance of effort alluded to above.

The teacher who knows something about psychotherapy cannot, without complete training, become a therapist or a clinical psychologist. Mental hygiene (a branch of psychology) is a resource for the teacher as is a knowledge of English, biology, history, or sociology. Some knowledge of Freudian theories will be helpful, but a deep involvement in analysis, either personally or vicariously, more often than not is harmful. Since experience in the shifting of dynamic patterns is a strong determiner of the child's reactions, the rich material in the Gestalt School, and especially in the works of Kurt Lewin, should appeal to the teacher.

Many a teacher is impressed by the rationality and balanced nature of young children under decent home and school conditions. It is not a question of children being little angels; inevitably they will fend for themselves in their little world. Altruism is for survivors. On the other hand, children are not little devils who need to be cowed or whipped in order to behave properly. A good example, friendly interest, and the inpouring of affection from children of like age will accomplish wonders for the incipiently intractable. The urge to belong can be channeled peacefully. A child, like an adult, may behave badly for reasons that are not inherently bad—in fact, under other circumstances, they might be called good. In any case, "bad" and "good" are improper terms to apply to a child who responds to confusing demands; if linked to genetic necessity, they fail to make sense. Admittedly, defensive child behavior designed to protect a distorted self-image is annoying, and the word "bad" springs all too easily to the lips, but with some awareness of the inner mental stresses, the teacher can help the child. This type of teacher helpfulness often eludes the grasp of literary critics, for whom "life adjustment" is a trigger word. For the most part, the social anthropologists and sociologists concur in favoring a positive culture that contains both sheltering and freedom-giving propensities. It is not anything unique to Western society.

If we are given teacher specialization superimposed upon a sound basis of the liberal arts and child development, and hold to clear but not fixed ideas as to what is imperative and what is elective in our society, it seems to me we are well prepared to design the school of the future.

INDEX